IMAGES
of America

GORGAS HOUSE AT THE UNIVERSITY OF ALABAMA

On the Cover: This c. 1890 photograph of the Gorgas House was taken by Eugene A. Smith. (Courtesy of the University Libraries Division of Special Collections, the University of Alabama, Tuscaloosa.)

IMAGES
of America

Gorgas House at the University of Alabama

Erin E. Harney and Jun A. Ebersole
Foreword by Sarah Woolfolk Wiggins

ARCADIA
PUBLISHING

ISBN 978-1-4671-2384-6

Published by Arcadia Publishing
Charleston, South Carolina

Printed in the United States of America

Library of Congress Control Number: 2016934560

For all general information, please contact Arcadia Publishing:
Telephone 843-853-2070
Fax 843-853-0044
E-mail sales@arcadiapublishing.com
For customer service and orders:
Toll-Free 1-888-313-2665

Visit us on the Internet at www.arcadiapublishing.com

For those who have helped preserve the Gorgas House
and to those who will continue to do so.

Contents

Foreword

Few buildings on any college campus have been used for as many different purposes as the Gorgas House at the University of Alabama. Most campus structures serve a specific purpose or a specific segment of the campus population, although a variety of departments might take occupancy during a structure's lifetime. However, the oldest surviving building at the University of Alabama, the Gorgas House, has had a remarkable variety of uses: as a dining hall, infirmary, post office, classroom, public hotel, faculty housing, girls' study hall, residence, and museum.

Built in 1829, the Gorgas House initially was intended to be a student dining hall, with the university steward and his family residing on the second floor. Unruly student behavior led university trustees to end such use within a few years of the university's opening. And thus began a parade of different roles for the building that have continued over the last 187 years. The history of the house became a history of life on the Tuscaloosa college campus and a history of the people who made the university. The Gorgas House now is as much a symbol of the University of Alabama as a whole as is the Denny Chimes.

Copying something has been considered the most sincere form of flattery. In the case of the Gorgas House, homeowners and architects alike have been smitten with the simplicity and grace of the house, with its double staircases reaching out like welcoming arms to visitors. And they have built offices and homes across Tuscaloosa and Alabama—even out to California—that are instantly recognizable as influenced by the design of the Gorgas House.

The following photographs illustrate the ever-changing roles for this charming structure that has grown to be the University of Alabama's genuine multipurpose building.

—Sarah Woolfolk Wiggins

Acknowledgments

We thank Sarah Woolfolk Wiggins, Robert Mellown, and Leah Rawls Atkins for their expertise, guidance, and gracious support during this project. We also want to recognize the research and publications of James B. Sellers and Suzanne Rau Wolfe, who wrote seminal works of university history. In addition, we want to recognize the following individuals who provided great assistance throughout the course of this project: Paul Hardin Kapp, Sarah Brown, Megan Spainhour, Phyllis Vermillion, Bill Allen, Matt Gage, Gene Ford, Matthew Reynolds, Gene Ball, Brittany Ray, Meredith McDonough, Nancy Dupree, Haley Aaron, Jennifer Ford, Bruce Bizzoco, Marcus Strudwicke, Jason Thompson, Camilla Canty, and Marina Klaric and the other staff at the W.S. Hoole Special Collections Library.

For their unwavering support of the Gorgas House, we would like to recognize Gene Ellis, Gigi McCutcheon, Ned Uehling, Ron and Elizabeth Howard, Marion Pearson, Joyce Lamont, Georgia Wise, Jerry Oldshue, and the University of Alabama administration, facilities and grounds, and building operations. We also thank Caitrin Cunningham, Alex Sharp, Lydia Rollins, Peter Spearman, and the rest of the editorial and production team at Arcadia Publishing for all their assistance throughout the production of this volume. A special thank-you is extended to Shannon Harney, Kevin Ray, William Bomar, and Lydia Ellington Joffray, who were instrumental in helping this book to publication.

Unless otherwise noted, all images appear courtesy of the University Libraries Division of Special Collections (W.S. Hoole Special Collections Library), the University of Alabama, Tuscaloosa (ULDSC). Other images are courtesy of the following institutions and are credited with their respective institutional abbreviations: Alabama Department of Archives and History, Montgomery (ADAH); Alabama Power Company Archives and Museum, Birmingham (APC); L.R. Wilson Library Special Collections at the University of North Carolina, Chapel Hill (WLSC); Gorgas House Museum, Tuscaloosa (GHM); Library of Congress, Washington, DC, (LOC); Mississippi Department of Archives and History, Jackson (MDAH); National Library of Medicine, Bethesda (NLM); Office of Archaeological Research, Moundville (OAR); Tennessee State Library and Archives, Nashville (TSLA); University of Alabama Museums, Tuscaloosa (UAM); University of Mississippi Archives and Special Collection, Oxford (UMASC); University of the South Archives and Special Collections, Sewanee (USA). We also thank Jaron Berman, Ashley Hester, Dennis Pappas Sr., and Rod Wirtz for providing items from their private collections. Additional images were provided from the authors' collection.

Introduction

In this book, the history of the Gorgas House is recounted from its establishment as the first building constructed on the University of Alabama campus in 1829 through the years of the Gorgas family, for whom the building was later renamed, and finally its preservation as a museum. Since its establishment, the history of the Gorgas House has been intertwined with many of the significant events and prominent figures associated with the state and University of Alabama. As a result, this book includes elements of the state's founding, the history of the campus, and significant individuals involved with the history of the Gorgas House.

Throughout its long history, the Gorgas House has undergone multiple renovations to meet the ever-changing needs of the university. The building was originally designed as the university hotel, dining hall, and residence for the campus steward. Later, it was renovated into a faculty residence, student infirmary, university post office, family home, and finally, memorial and museum dedicated to its most famous residents, the Gorgas family. Over the years, the following titles have been associated with the building:

The Hotel (1828–1831)
The Steward's Hall (1831–1860s)
The Pratt House (mid-1860s–1879)
The Hospital, Post Office (1879–1907)
The Gorgas House (1907–1953)
The Gorgas House Museum (1954–Present)

In this book, the history of the Gorgas House has been divided into the following three chronological periods:

Chapter 1: The Hotel, Steward's Hall, and Pratt House: 1818–1870
Chapter 2: The Gorgas Family and the University: 1878–1953
Chapter 3: The Legacy of the Gorgas House: 1934–Present

The first chapter begins with the founding of the state and the University of Alabama, highlighting key individuals who laid the groundwork for the university, many of whom also helped achieve Alabama statehood. In addition, this chapter addresses the challenges the new university faced and the devastating impact of the Civil War.

During the early 19th century, as the territory of Alabama was applying for statehood, one of the leading initiatives for territorial citizens and legislators was the establishment of a state university. Many of the early settlers were from the Southeast and sought to define the new territory with the amenities and institutions to which they were accustomed.

With support from the US Congress, the University of Alabama was officially established in 1820, and construction began on the Tuscaloosa campus in 1828. The early campus was designed by English architect William Nichols, who emulated elements of the University of Virginia campus. In 1829, the first building, a modest two-story structure, was complete. It served as the university hotel, student dining hall, and quarters for the steward.

The university's inaugural class of 1831 was predominantly comprised of the sons of the local planters and pioneers, while the professors were selected from established universities, such as Harvard, Union College, Princeton, and the University of Virginia. The differences in expectations between the professors and students caused immediate rifts. The significant and ongoing issues with student discipline eventually caused the closure of the student dining hall and the conversion of the building into a faculty residence. To further contain the rebellious behavior, the campus administration instituted a military form of governance. The university's success as a military academy ultimately led to the destruction of the campus by the Union army during the Civil War. This chapter concludes with the reopening of the university in 1870.

The second chapter chronicles the lives of the Gorgas family and the 75 years they served the university community. Josiah Gorgas, a native of Pennsylvania, met and married Amelia Gayle, daughter of Alabama governor John Gayle, while serving at a US Army post in Mount Vernon, Alabama. Their life together was difficult, heavily defined by military appointments, the Civil War, and financial difficulty. Despite the adversity, they raised a close-knit family and served as an anchor for many of their friends and extended family during times of hardship and loss.

In 1878, the couple returned to Amelia's home state when Josiah was offered the presidency at the University of Alabama. This "good fortune," as Josiah described it, provided a stable home and income for him, Amelia, and their children. Following Josiah's term as president, the family remained on campus in the former Steward's Hall. Josiah and Amelia jointly served as the university librarian, and Amelia also was appointed as the university nurse matron and postmistress. During this time, the Steward's Hall became known as the Gorgas House.

This chapter highlights the lives and contributions of both the Gorgas and Gayle families. Members of these two prominent families include the following:

Gorgas Family
Joseph and Sophia (Atkinson) Gorgas
Children: Jacob, William, Thomas, Sarah, Charles, Mary, Eliza, Christiana, Solomon, and Josiah

Gayle Family
John and Sarah Ann (Haynsworth) Gayle
Children: Matthew, Sarah, Amelia, Mary, Richard, and Anna Maria

Josiah and Amelia (Gayle) Gorgas
Children: William Crawford, Jessie, Mary "Mamie," Christine "Minnie,", Maria "Ria," and Richard

The third chapter records the passage of the Gorgas House from a family residence into a historic site and museum. While the Gorgas name is well known in the fields of medicine and warfare strategy, the importance of the building extends beyond the Gorgas family. The building's architect, historical uses and longevity, and other former residents add to the rich history of the building. Today, the Gorgas House Museum preserves and shares the Gorgas family legacy of dedication and service and stands as a reminder of the university's antebellum past.

Gorgas House at the University of Alabama seeks to capture the many people, stories, and details associated with the oldest building on campus. The history of the Gorgas House was a challenge to document visually, as photography was not widely available in the early 19th century. However, this collection of visual resources from archives, private collections, and the Gorgas House Museum documents the individuals and historic events that helped to shape the history of the campus and the Gorgas House Museum. The authors' proceeds from the sale of this book are donated directly to the Gorgas House Museum to support ongoing preservation.

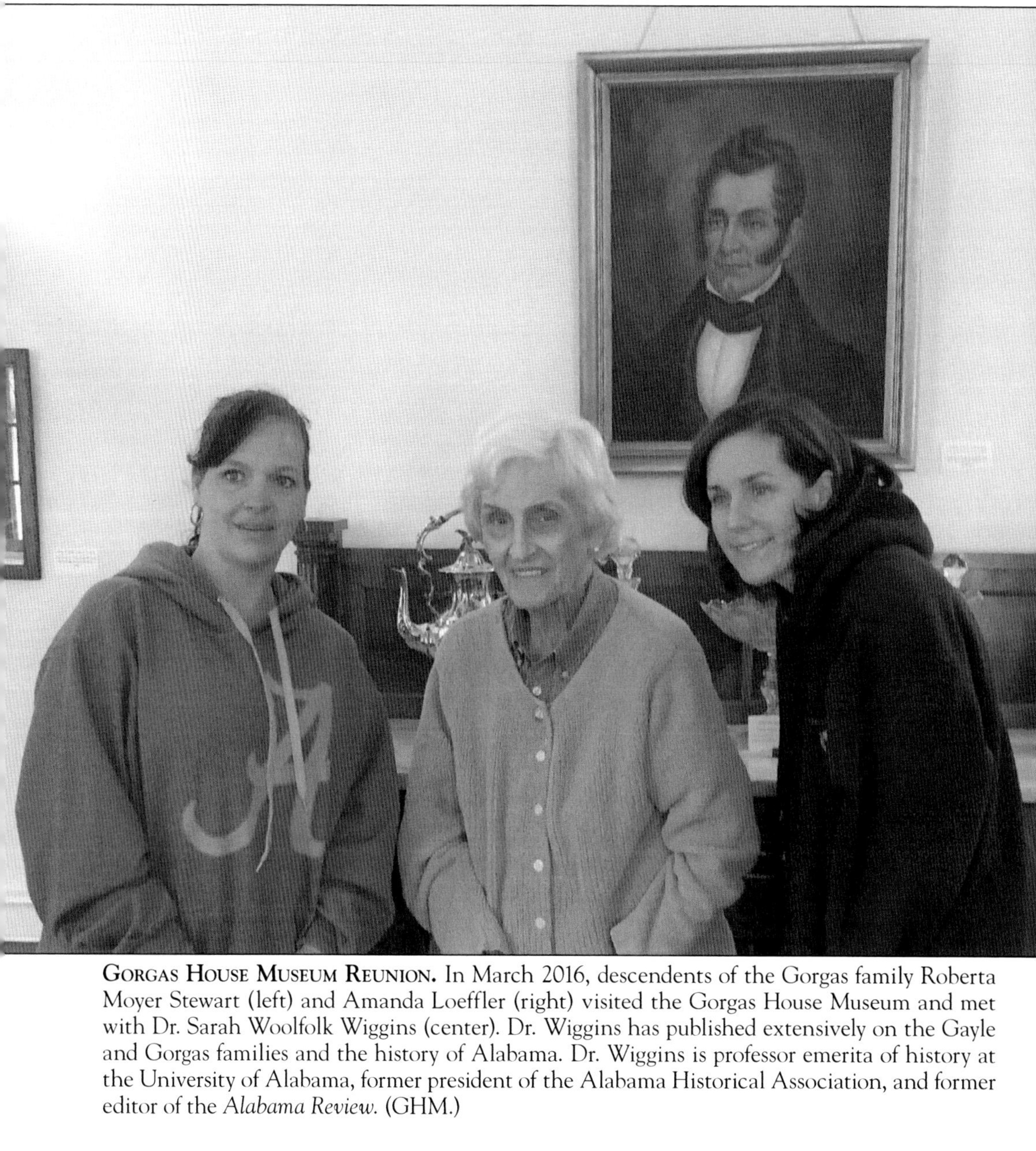

Gorgas House Museum Reunion. In March 2016, descendents of the Gorgas family Roberta Moyer Stewart (left) and Amanda Loeffler (right) visited the Gorgas House Museum and met with Dr. Sarah Woolfolk Wiggins (center). Dr. Wiggins has published extensively on the Gayle and Gorgas families and the history of Alabama. Dr. Wiggins is professor emerita of history at the University of Alabama, former president of the Alabama Historical Association, and former editor of the *Alabama Review.* (GHM.)

One

The Hotel, Steward's Hall, and Pratt House

1818–1870

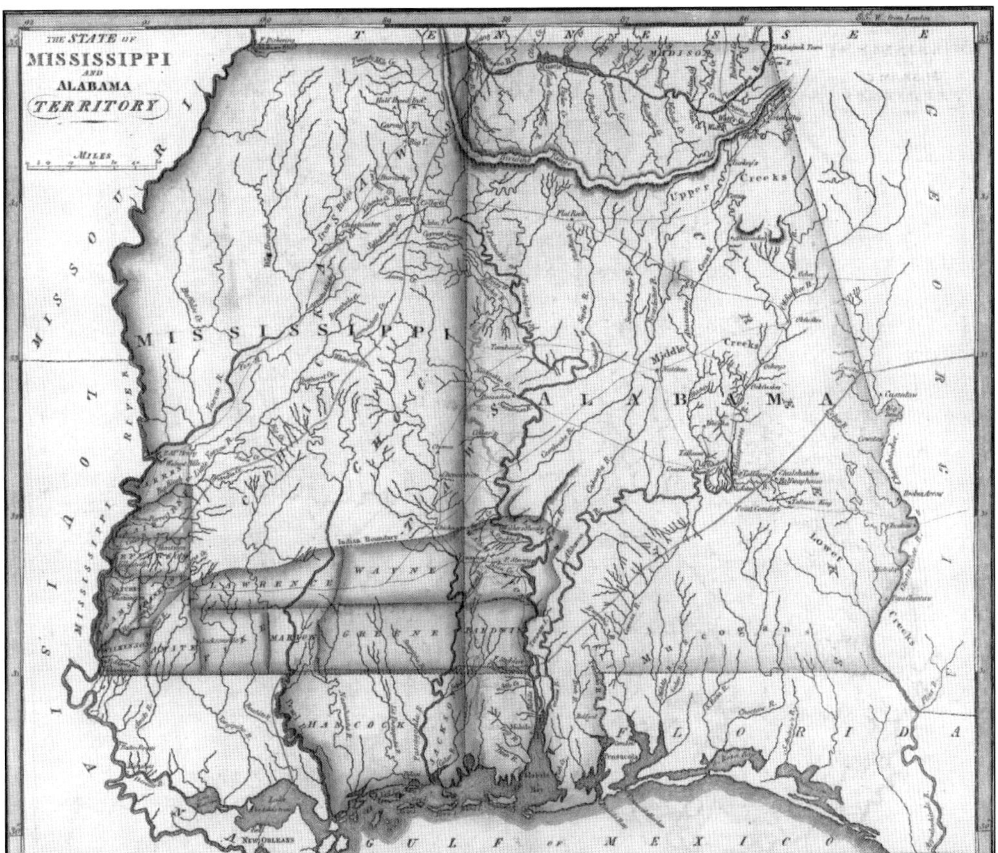

Alabama Territory. By 1818, the population in the Alabama Territory had exceeded the federal government's requirement of 60,000 residents to be eligible for statehood, prompting the US Congress to approve the establishment of the state of Alabama. (LOC.)

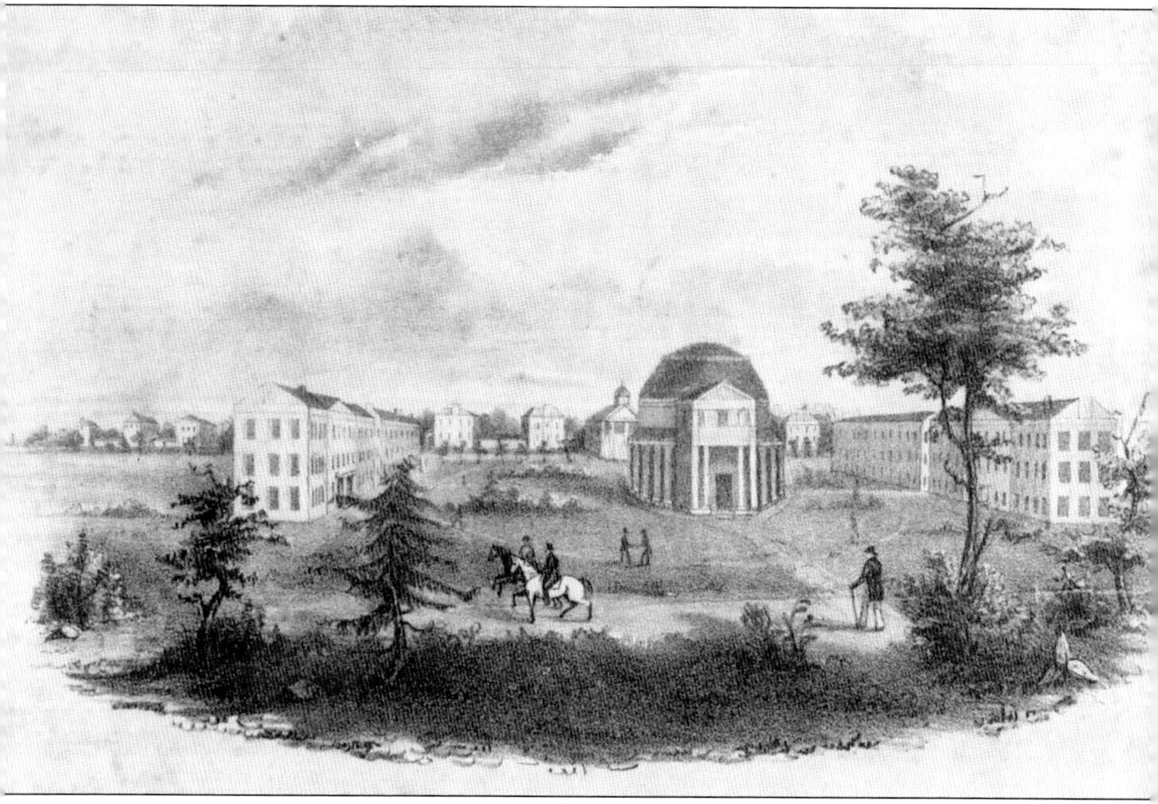

UNIVERSITY OF ALABAMA, C. 1839. Very few educational opportunities were available to the people of the new state. Recognizing the need for an educational institution, the US Congress allocated two townships of land, at a total of 46,080 acres, to fund the new "seminary of learning." Adopted on August 2, 1819, the state constitution states, "Schools, and the means of education, shall forever be encouraged in this state."

CAHAWBA, ALABAMA. In preparation for statehood in 1819, a commission was formed to select the site for the capital. Many territorial legislators were in favor of Tuscaloosa; however, territorial governor William Bibb lobbied for Cahawba in Dallas County and ultimately won. The map at right, drawn by Governor Bibb, depicts his plan for the new capital. The sketch below shows the capitol building constructed in Cahawba for the Alabama Legislature. The building also served as a meeting place for the initial members of the university board of trustees as they laid the groundwork for the university. (Both, ADAH.)

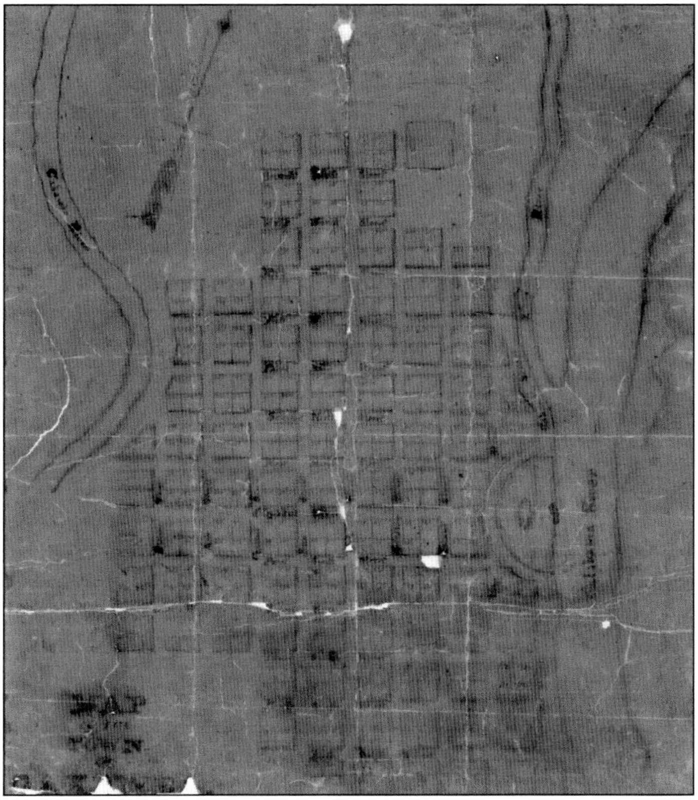

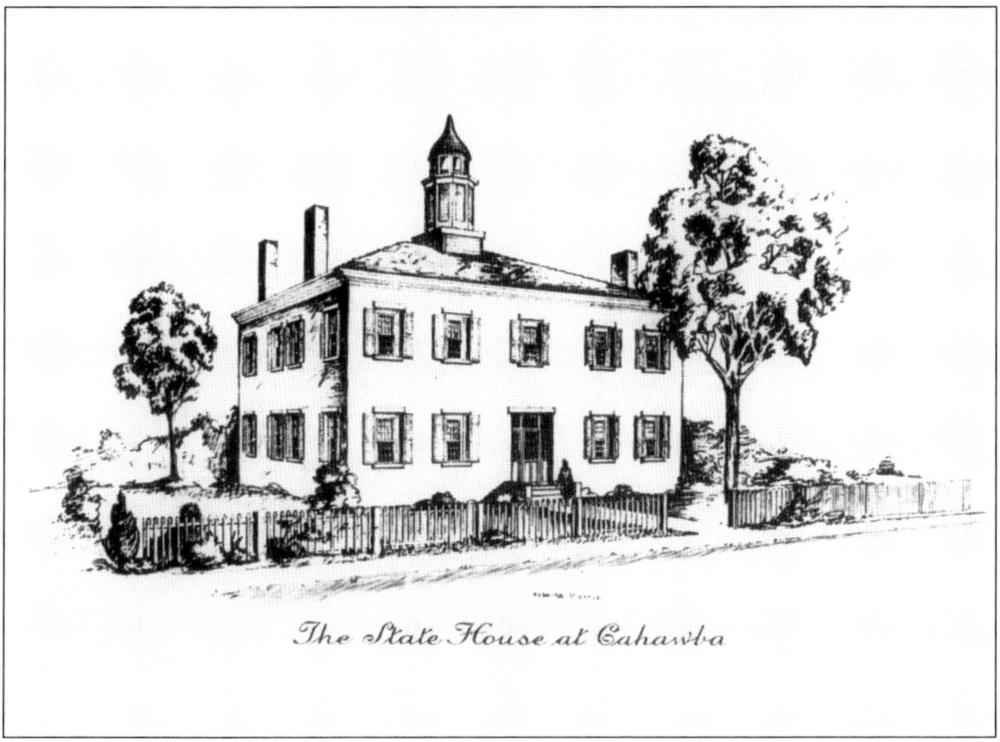

The State House at Cahawba

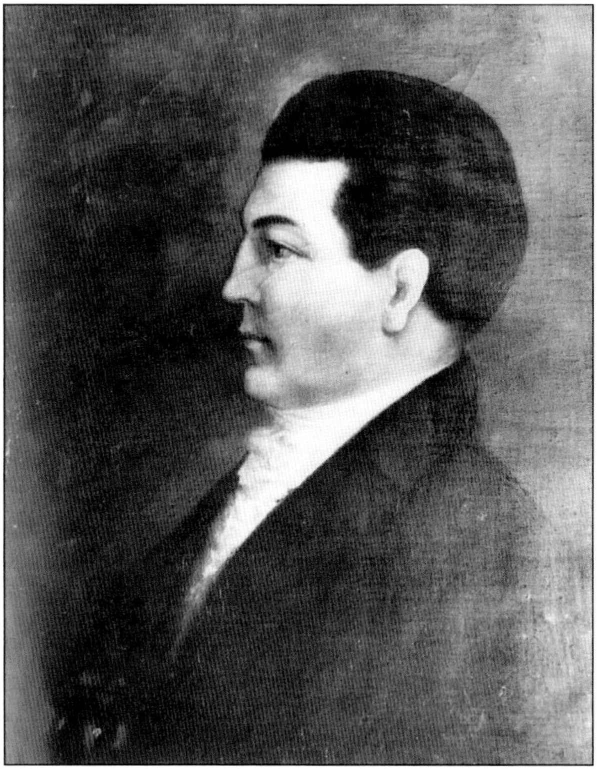

Governors William and Thomas Bibb. The inaugural meeting of the Alabama general assembly took place in 1819, during which the initial members of the university board of trustees were elected. In addition, the assembly required Gov. William Bibb (left) to appoint commissioners to help sell or lease the land gifted by the US Congress to help fund Alabama's first university. Governor Bibb died the following year, and the governorship was passed to his brother and president of the senate Thomas Bibb (below). (Both, ADAH.)

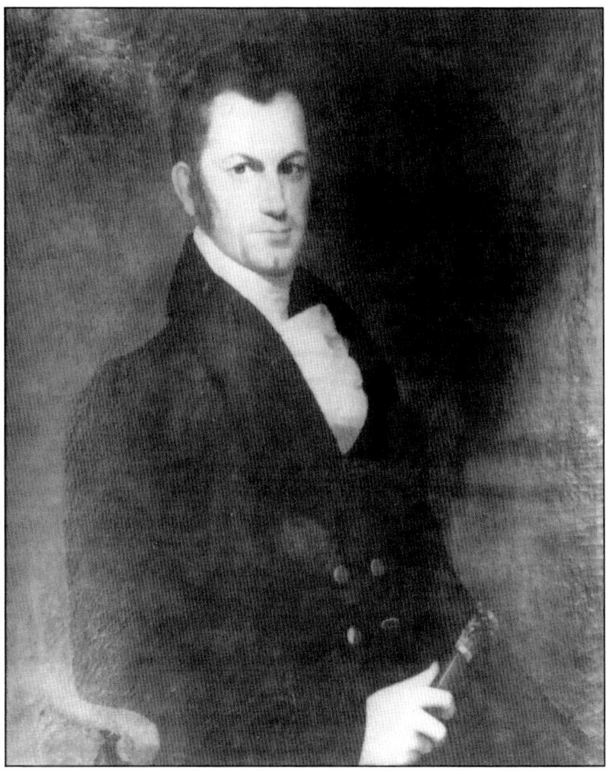

ompensa-
on of ju-
ors.

Sec. 12. *And be it further enacted*, That hereafter, each and every grand juror, and juror of the original pannel, shall be entitled to receive one dollar for each and every day he may serve as such, and mileage as heretofore allowed; which shall be paid out of any monies in the county Treasury on the certificate of the clerk, of his having served as such; and in case there should not be funds in the county treasury for the payment of such demands, the certificate of such juror shall be receivable by the collector of taxes for county purposes, in their respective counties. [*Approved Dec. 21st*, 1820.]

An Act to establish a State University.

niversity
be esta-
shed.

Section 1. *BE it enacted by the Senate and House of Representatives of the State of Alabama in General Assembly convened*, That a Seminary of Learning be and the same is hereby established, to be denominated "The University of the State of Alabama."

om'rs. ap
inted.

Sec. 2. *And be it further enacted*, That three commissioners shall be appointed by the Governor, within each county wherein any of the lands reserved by the United States for a Seminary of Learn-

Act to Establish the University of Alabama. On December 18, 1820, a little over a year after achieving statehood, the second general assembly of Alabama voted to officially establish "The University of the State of Alabama."

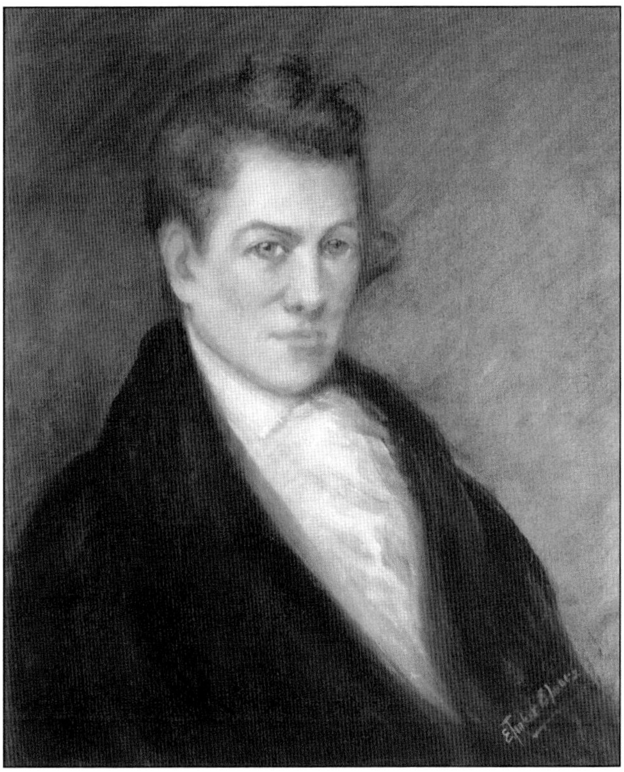

Israel Pickens. In 1821, Israel Pickens was elected as Alabama's third governor. As governor, Pickens served as the ex officio chairman of the university board of trustees and recommended the gifted government land be sold on an installment basis. The general assembly agreed, and the land was sold at a fixed rate of $17 per acre. (ADAH.)

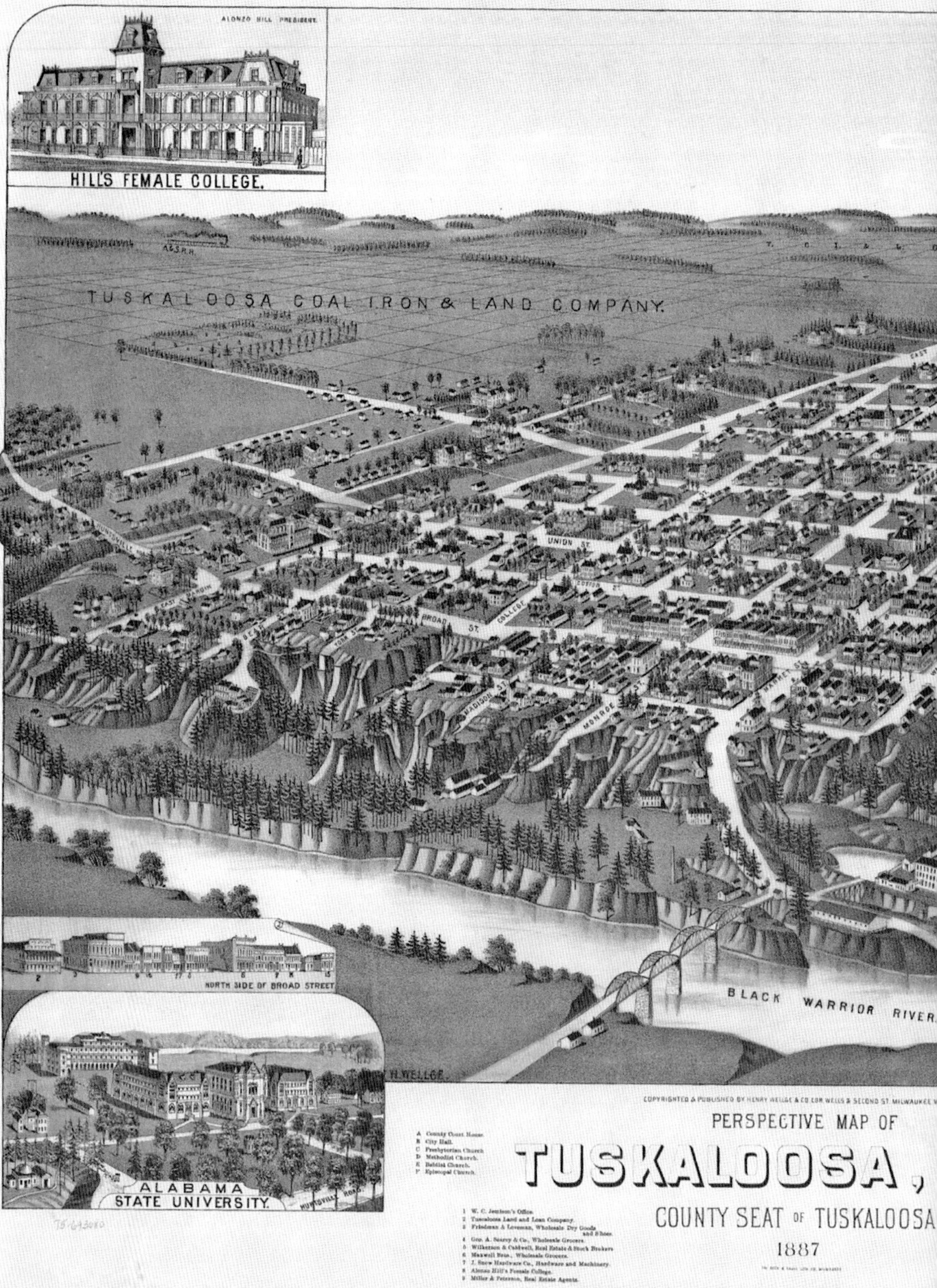
ALONZO HILL PRESIDENT.
HILL'S FEMALE COLLEGE.
TUSKALOOSA COAL IRON & LAND COMPANY.
UNION ST.
BROAD
ST.
COLLEGE
MADISON ST.
MONROE
BLACK WARRIOR RIVER.
NORTH SIDE OF BROAD STREET
ALABAMA
STATE UNIVERSITY.
H. WELLGE.
COPYRIGHTED & PUBLISHED BY HENRY WELLGE & CO COR WELLS & SECOND ST. MILWAUKEE W
PERSPECTIVE MAP OF
TUSKALOOSA,
COUNTY SEAT OF TUSKALOOSA
1887
A County Court House.
B City Hall
C Presbyterian Church
D Methodist Church.
E Baldist Church.
F Episcopal Church.
1 W. C. Jemison's Office.
2 Tuscaloosa Land and Loan Company.
3 Friedman & Loveman, Wholesale Dry Goods and Shoes.
4 Geo. A. Searcy & Co., Wholesale Grocers.
5 Wilkerson & Caldwell, Real Estate & Stock Brokers
6 Maxwell Bros., Wholesale Grocers.
7 J. Snow Hardware Co., Hardware and Machinery.
8 Alonzo Hill's Female College.
9 Miller & Peterson, Real Estate Agents.

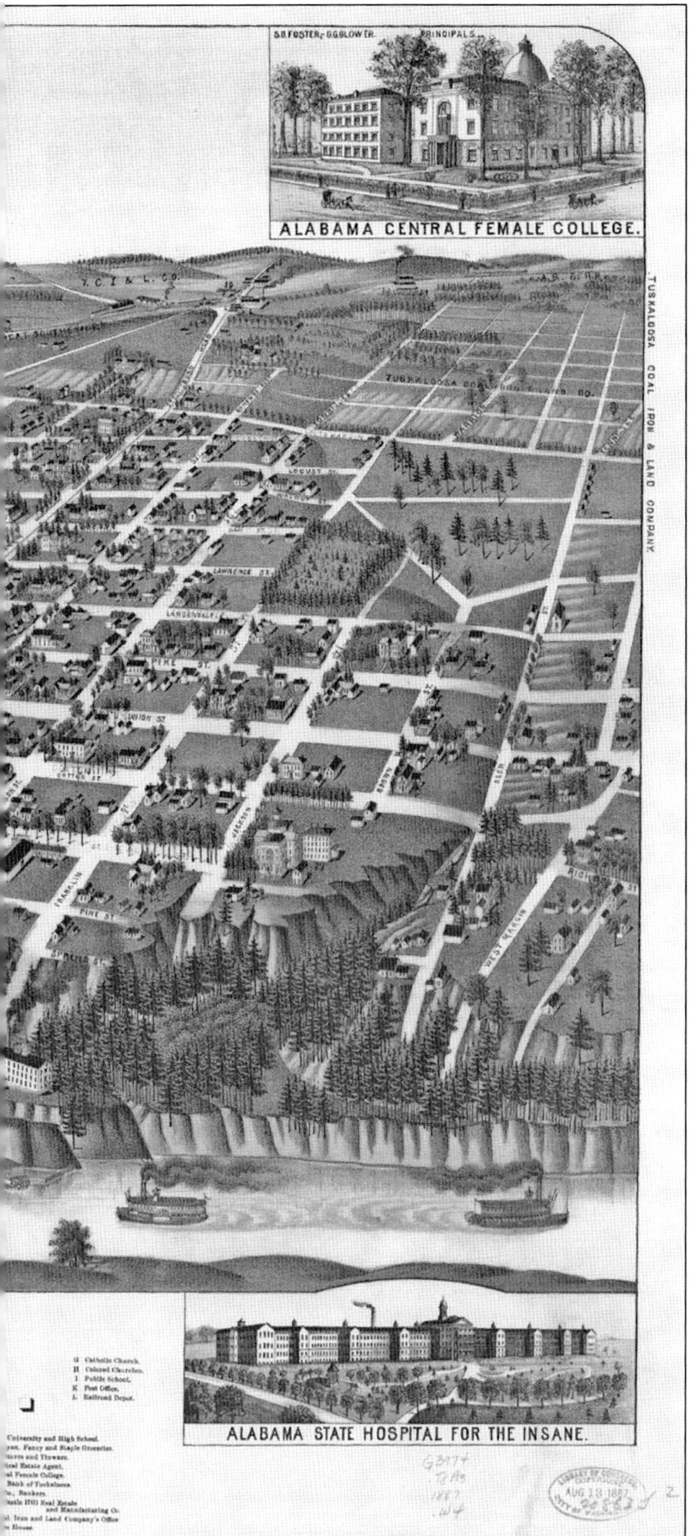

Tuscaloosa as Capital. In 1825, amid ongoing issues with flooding in Cahawba, state officials voted to move the capital to a more suitable location. After considering 13 sites, state legislators selected the town of Tuscaloosa (previously spelled Tuskaloosa) as the site for the new capital city of Alabama. At that time, Tuscaloosa was located in the center of the most densely populated region of the state, with approximately 9,000 inhabitants. Tuscaloosa was situated along the Black Warrrior River, a major waterway for freight and passenger transportation and was at a higher elevation and therefore less prone to flooding. This perspective map was published by Henry Wellge & Co. in 1887. (LOC.)

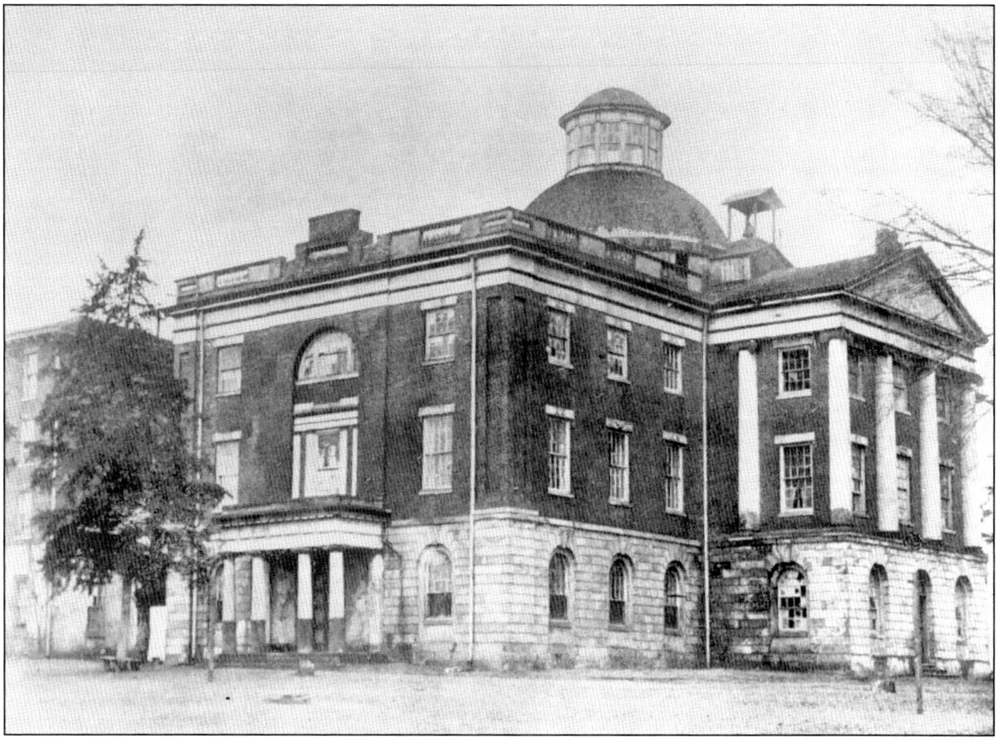

Alabama State Capitol Building. The general assembly met in Tuscaloosa for the first time on November 20, 1826. In 1827, the Alabama Legislature hired William Nichols as the state architect to oversee the construction of the Tuscaloosa capitol building (above). Originally from Bath, England, Nichols started his architectural career in North Carolina as the state architect and architect for the University of North Carolina at Chapel Hill. There are no known photographs or portraits of William Nichols; however, a few documents exist that contain his signature (below). (Above, LOC; below, MDAH.)

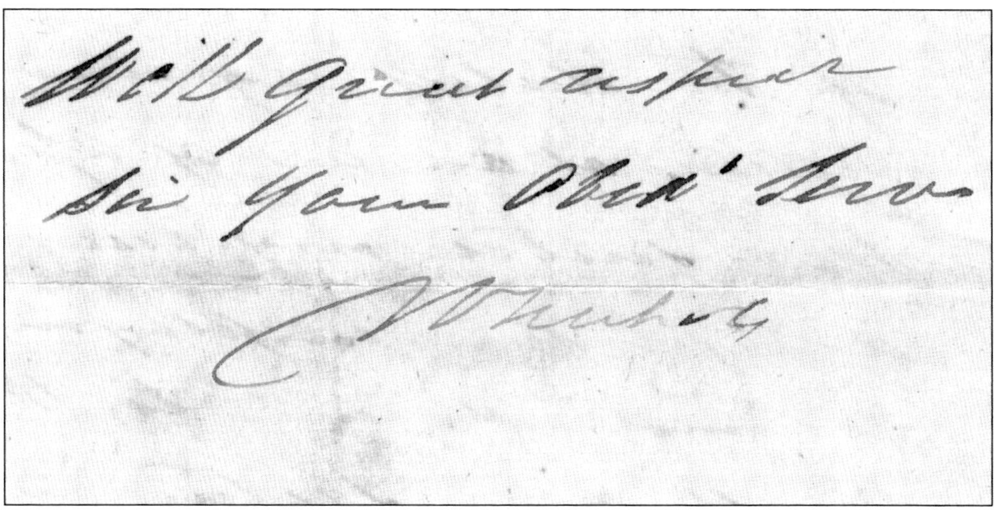

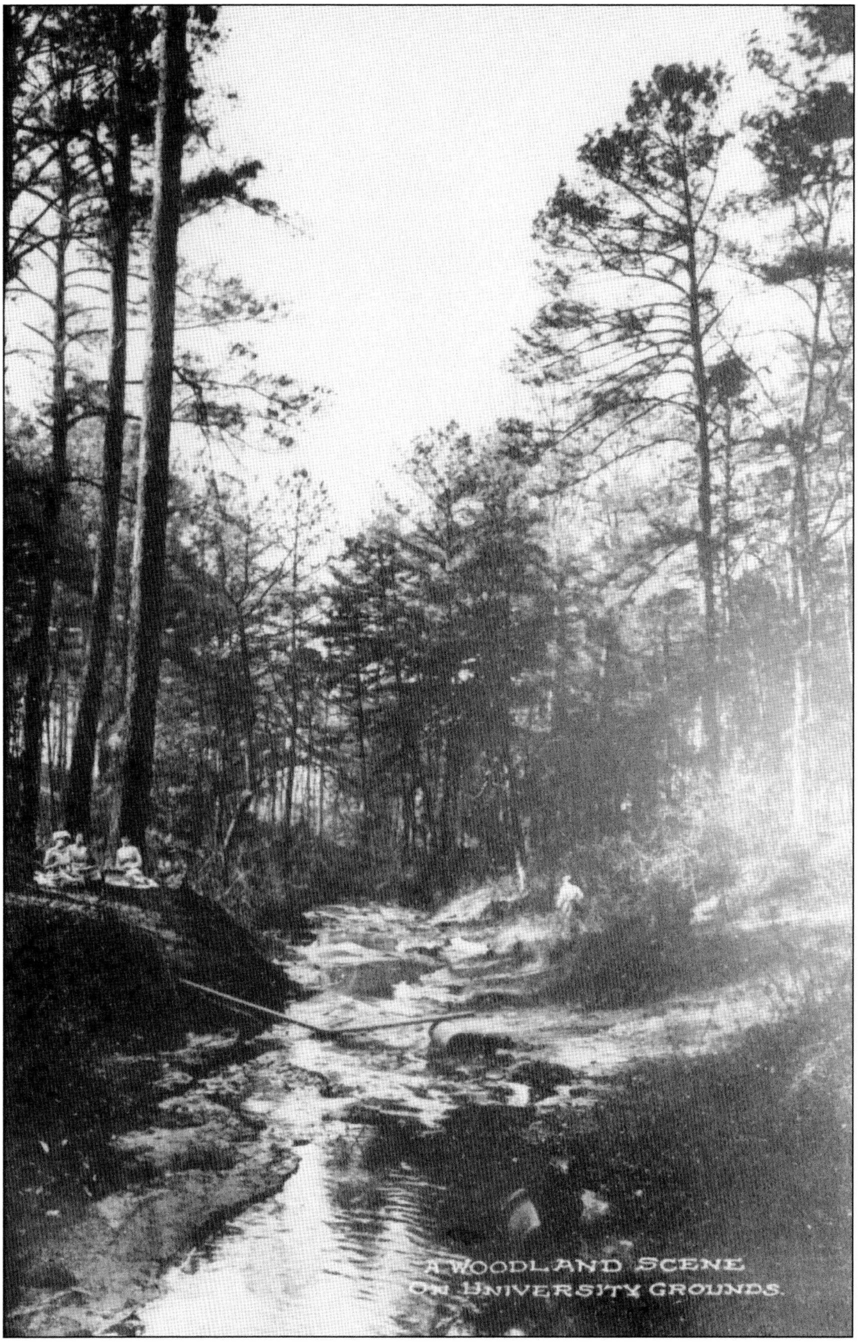

UNIVERSITY OF ALABAMA SITE. The Alabama Legislature tasked the university board of trustees with finding a suitable location for the university that was within 15 miles of the capital. On March 22, 1828, the university trustees selected a site located just one and a half miles from town. The location was considered ideal, as it was in proximity to woodland, coal, clay deposits, stone quarries, and, most importantly, a freshwater spring known as Marr's Spring. The spring was named for William Miller Marr, a plantation owner who leased the land. Marr's Spring provided freshwater for the university until the mid-20th century.

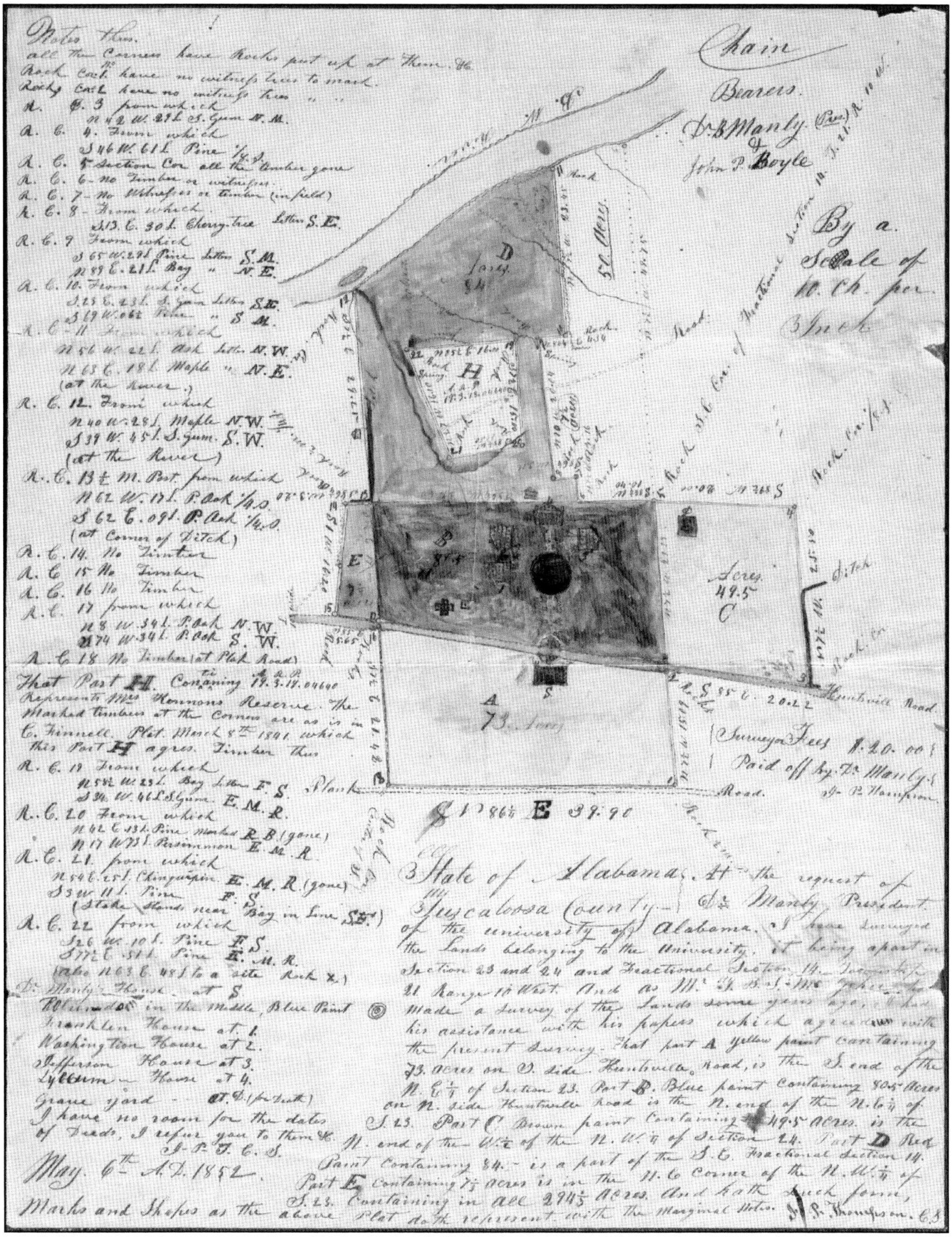

Campus Map. The trustees hired William Nichols as the university architect, with an annual salary of $750. On March 24, 1828, two days after the selection of the campus site, Nichols presented the trustees a plan for the university. His initial plan consisted of fourteen campus buildings, seven of which were constructed by the time the university opened in 1831. Although Nichols's drawings were lost, this 1852 map and land survey by the university's second president, Basil Manly, shows the location of the original campus buildings.

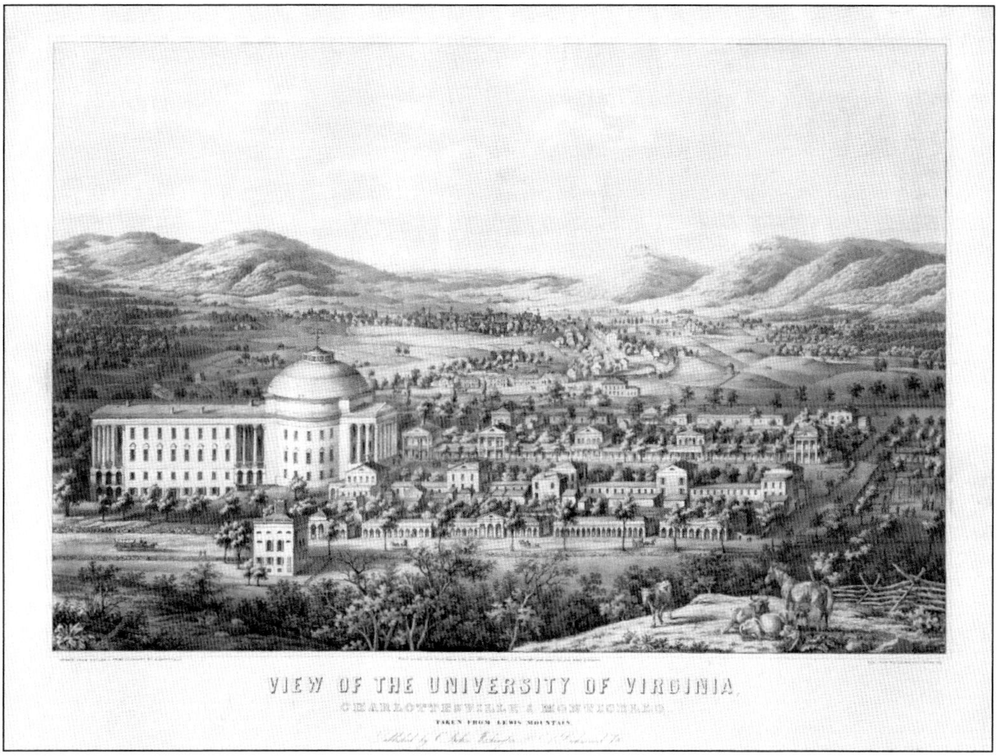

UNIVERSITY OF VIRGINIA. William Nichols's plans for the University of Alabama emulate portions of the University of Virginia campus, designed by Thomas Jefferson. Rather than centering the campus around a church, as was common at that time, Jefferson chose a rotunda with a library (below). Jefferson believed in "illimitable freedom of the human mind" and that students had the right to study and specialize in subjects outside of law, medicine, and religion. (Both, LOC.)

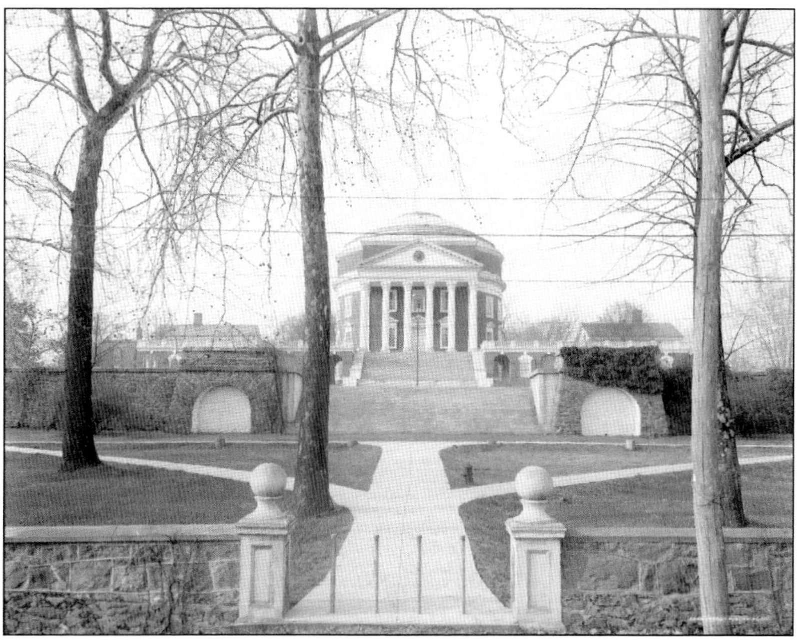

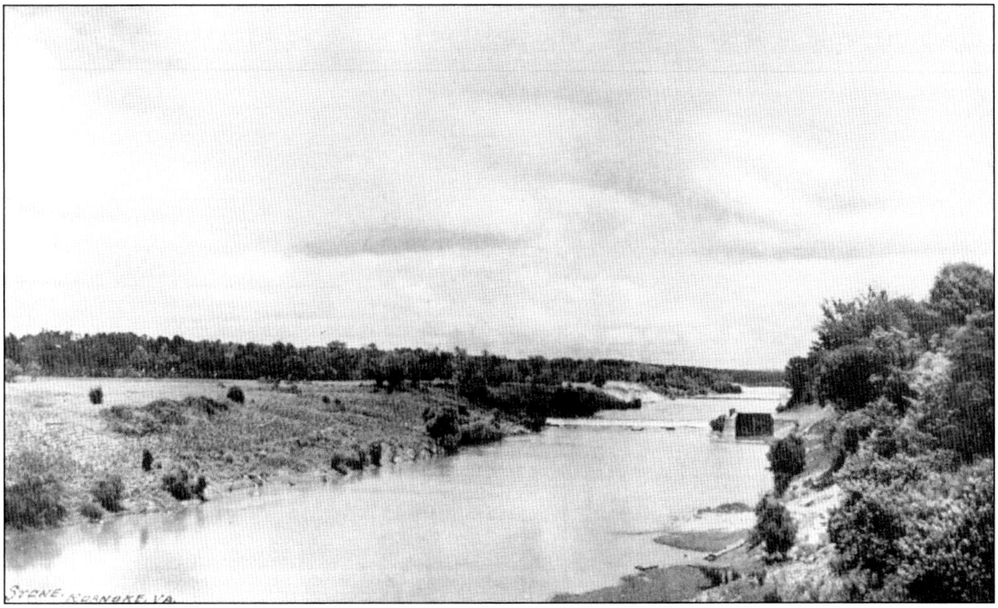

LOCALLY PROCURED BUILDING MATERIALS. Local materials were used for the initial university buildings. Lumber was cut from the university's local timber tracts, and sandstone was quarried from the banks of the nearby Black Warrior River (above). In addition, bricks were produced in the university's brickyard, which was located where the Biology Building (below) stands today.

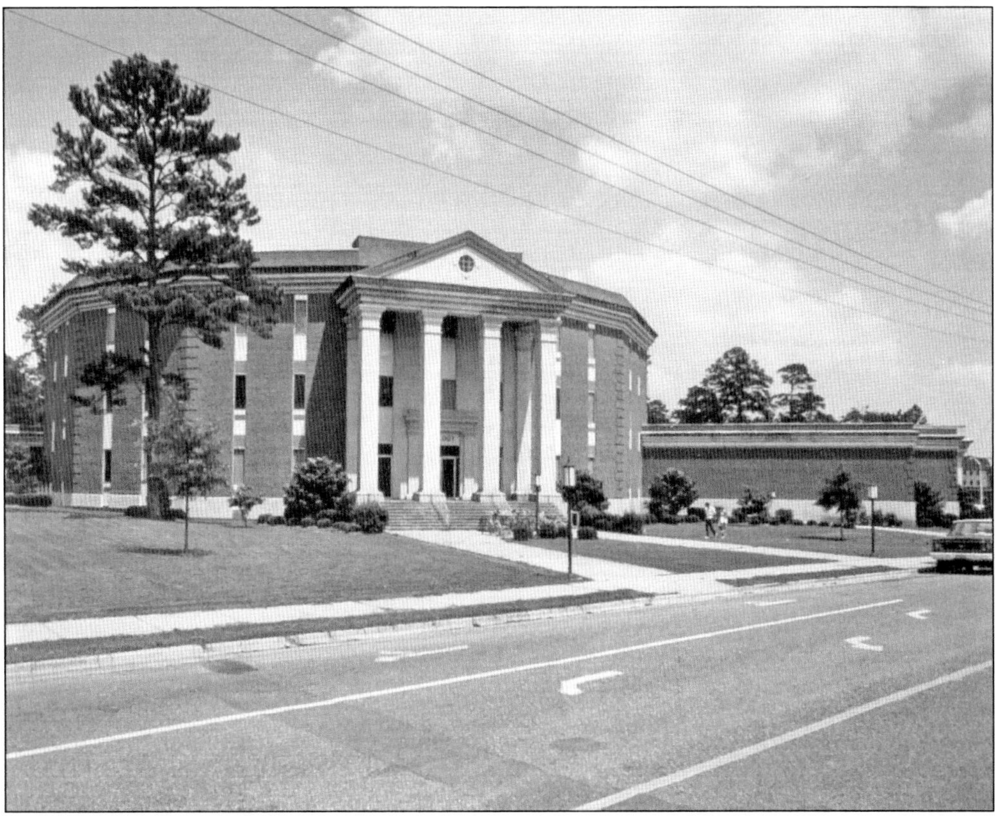

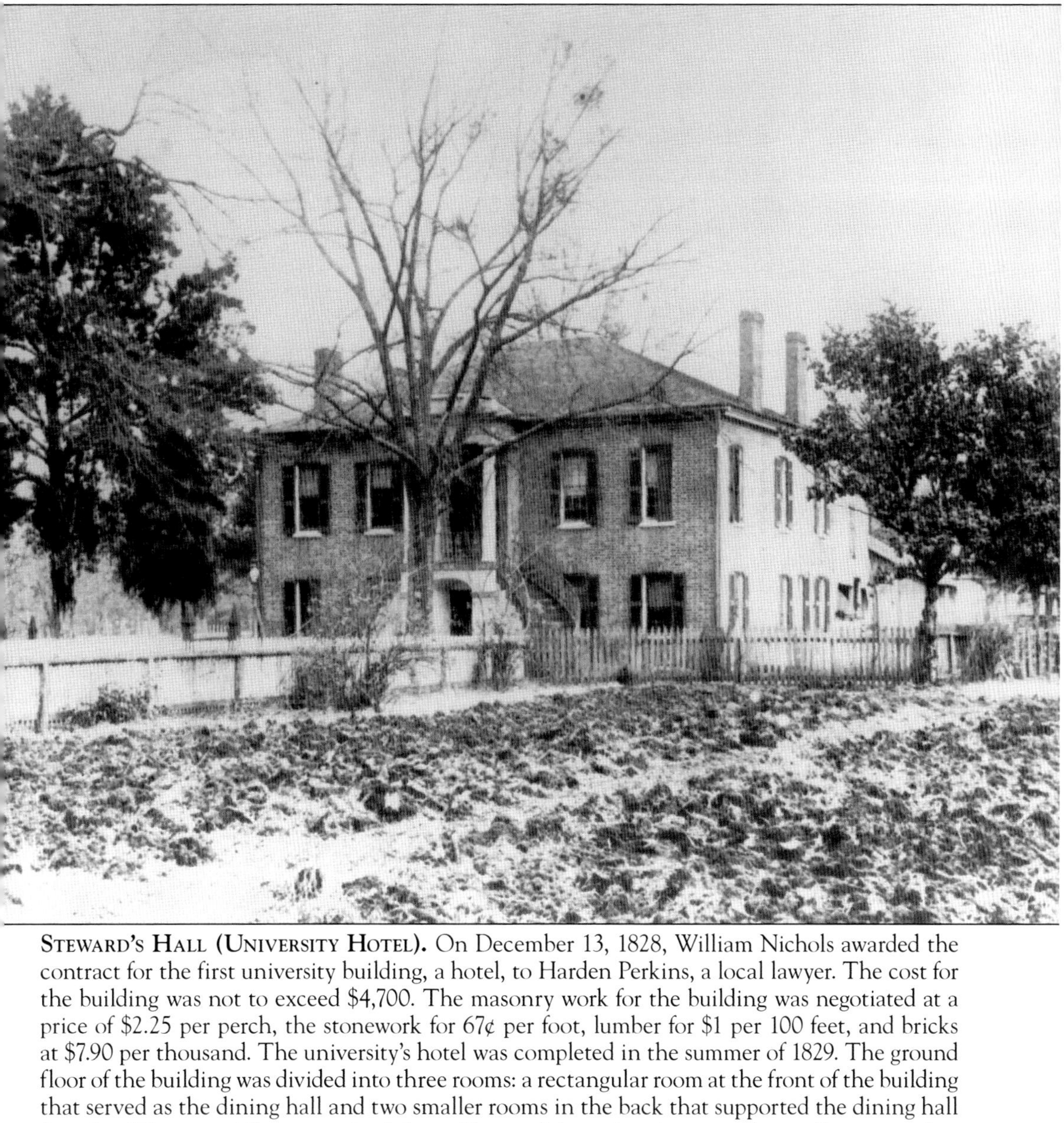

Steward's Hall (University Hotel). On December 13, 1828, William Nichols awarded the contract for the first university building, a hotel, to Harden Perkins, a local lawyer. The cost for the building was not to exceed $4,700. The masonry work for the building was negotiated at a price of $2.25 per perch, the stonework for 67¢ per foot, lumber for $1 per 100 feet, and bricks at $7.90 per thousand. The university's hotel was completed in the summer of 1829. The ground floor of the building was divided into three rooms: a rectangular room at the front of the building that served as the dining hall and two smaller rooms in the back that supported the dining hall function. The second floor contained the residence of the university steward, as well as rooms that served as the hotel for university visitors. Nichols's original plan called for two identical hotels to be constructed at the east and west sides of the campus; however, the trustees determined only one was necessary. This photograph was taken in the 1890s.

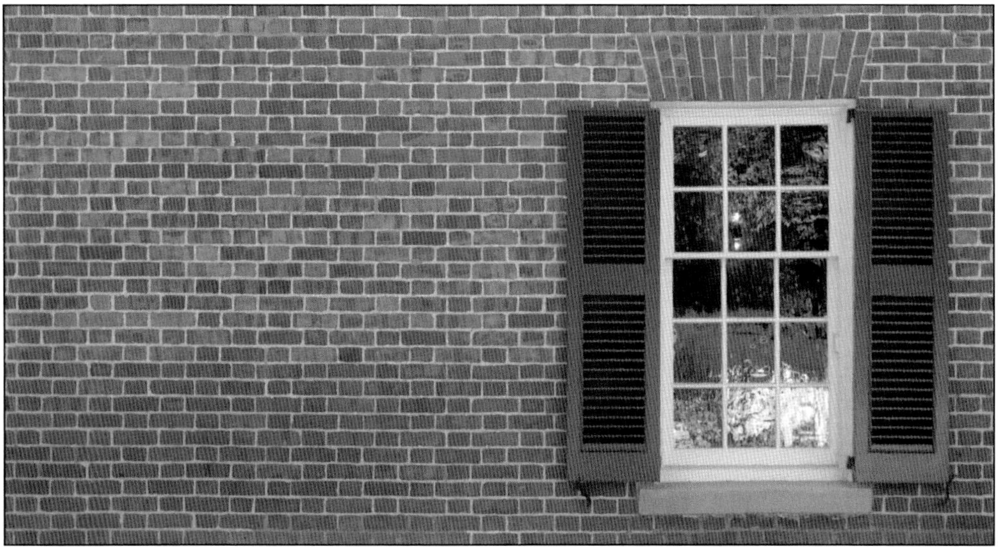

ARCHITECTURAL ELEMENTS OF THE STEWARD'S HALL. Compared to the other campus buildings, the Steward's Hall was simple in design, suited to its function as a dining hall and hotel. The brickmason employed a Flemish bond style (above), a complex method of laying bricks that results in a pattern displaying headers (short ends) and stretchers (long sides) alternating in each course, with the center of each header over the center of the stretcher directly below. As seen in this 1934 Historic American Buildings Survey (HABS) drawing (below), the mason further enhanced the exterior of the building by creating brick jack arches over the window and door openings. This brick masonry technique served a structural purpose and also provided an attractive architectural element that, like the bond pattern, complemented the building. Nichols also employed jack arches in his design of the campus dormitories. (Above, authors' collection; below, LOC.)

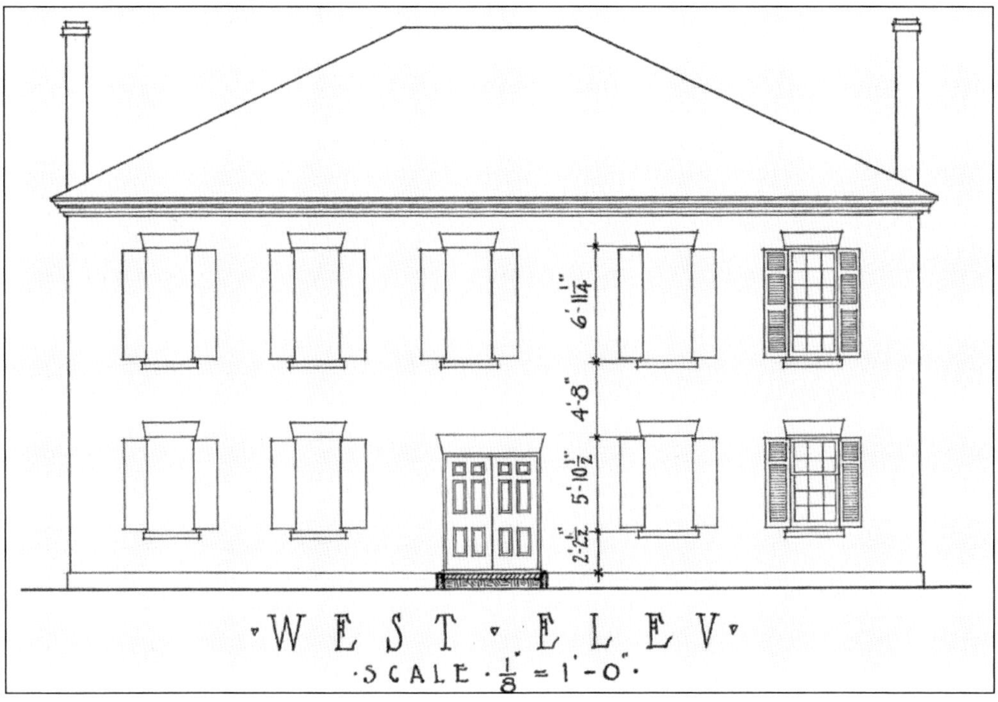

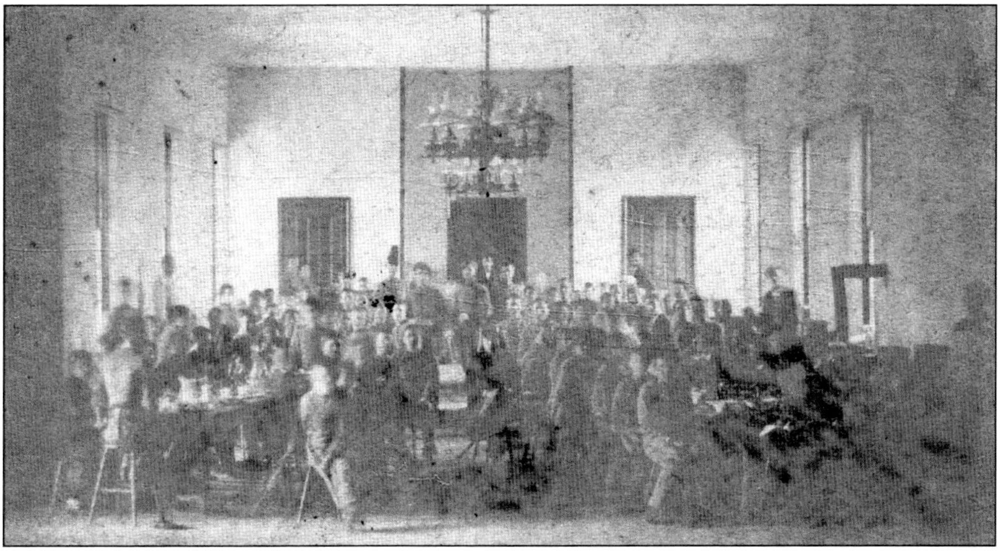

Woods Hall Dining Room. There are no known images of the original dining room at the Steward's Hall, but in 1830, a Huntsville newspaper provided the following description: "[The room was a] hall 36 feet in length by 22 feet in breadth, paved with brick . . . intended as a dining room for students, of whom it can entertain upwards of 100. The other two rooms, behind this one, are places of deposite for deserts, culinary utensils, and for other conveniences." This photograph, taken in the 1870s, shows the student dining room that was located in Woods Hall. (ADAH.)

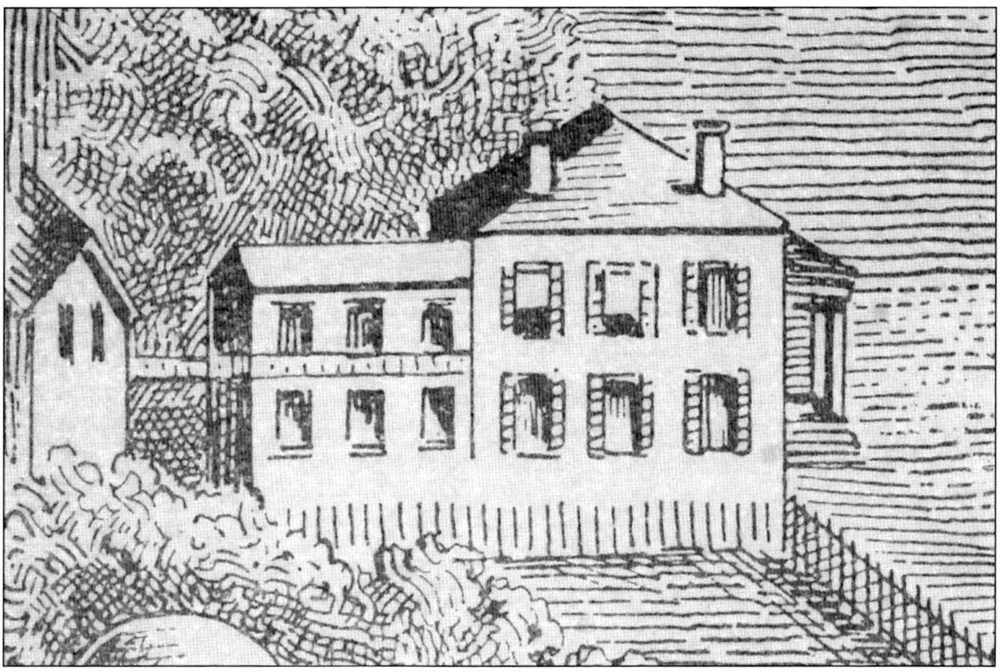

Steward's Hall Kitchen Building. To support the dining hall, a separate kitchen building was constructed at the rear of the Steward's Hall. The building was a two-story brick structure with the kitchen facilities on the first floor and quarters for the Steward's Hall servants on the second floor. A brick path (which is still visible today) and a second-story wooden walkway connected the kitchen to the Steward's Hall. (Authors' collection.)

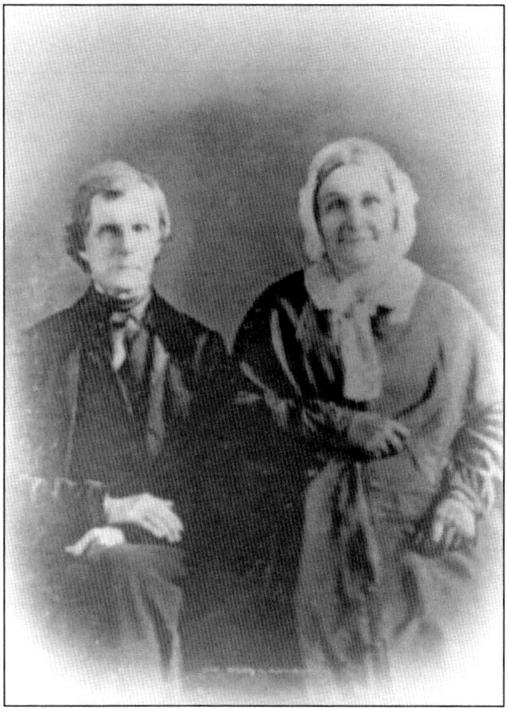

Pasquale Paoli Ashe and Eliza Strudwick Ashe. On December 13, 1829, the trustees appointed Pasquale Paoli Ashe as the first university steward. A month later, the trustees voted to allow Pasquale, his wife, Eliza, and their children to take residence on the second floor of the Steward's Hall. Pasquale served as the campus steward until 1833. Pasquale and subsequent stewards provided a number of services to the university, including monitoring of the dining hall, hiring and oversight of the servants in the hall, and tending to hotel guests. (Courtesy of Rod Wirtz.)

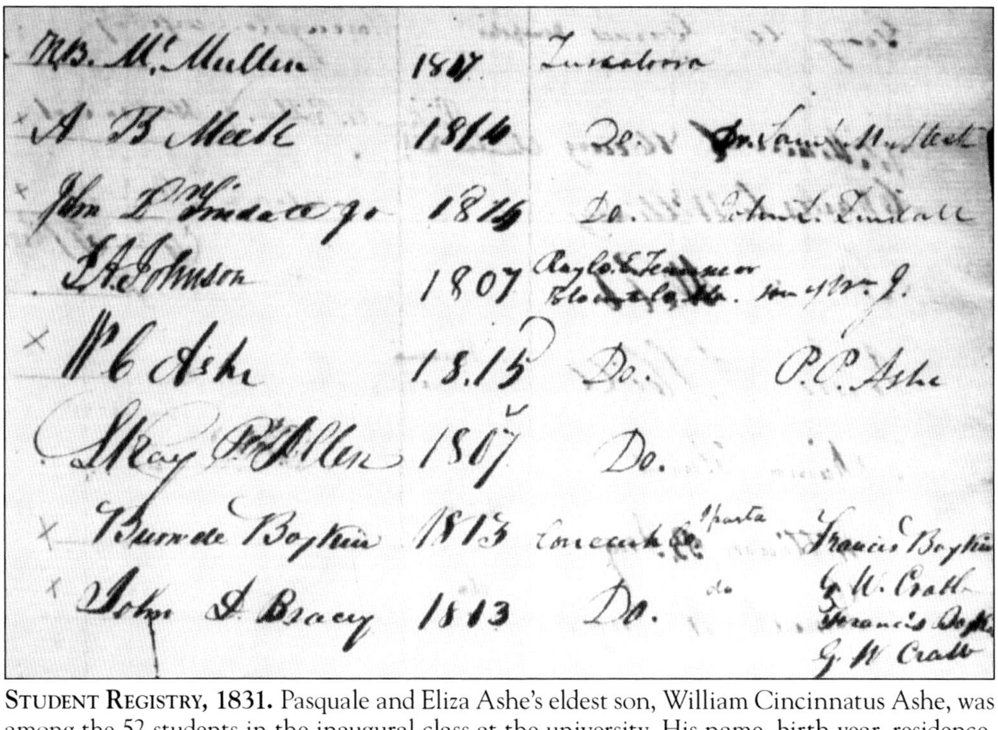

Student Registry, 1831. Pasquale and Eliza Ashe's eldest son, William Cincinnatus Ashe, was among the 52 students in the inaugural class at the university. His name, birth year, residence, and father's name, P.P. Ashe, are recorded in the 1831 student registry (fourth entry from the bottom). Ashe went on to receive a medical degree from the University of Pennsylvania and served as a surgeon with the 11th Alabama Infantry during the Civil War.

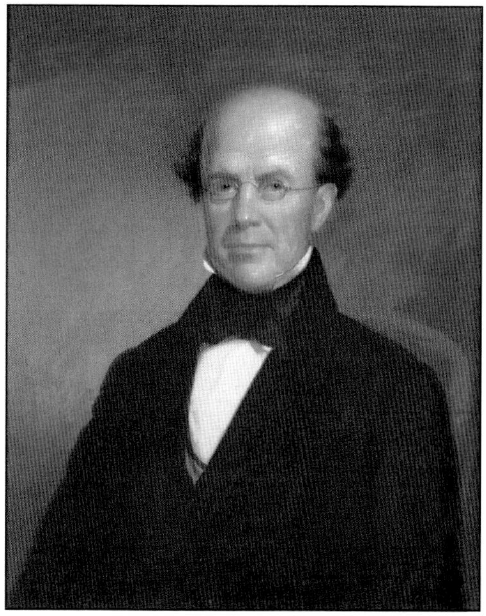

Alva Woods. Alva Woods (right) was inaugurated as the first president of the University of Alabama on April 12, 1831. The inauguration was held at the Christ Episcopal Church in Tuscaloosa (below), a church designed by architect William Nichols. In addition to his role as president, Woods was appointed professor of moral and mental philosophy. During his tenure, Woods imposed strict rules, including banning card playing, excessive noise, drinking, profanity, and unauthorized visits into town. For students unaccustomed to discipline and consequences, issues arose almost immediately and persisted throughout Woods's presidency.

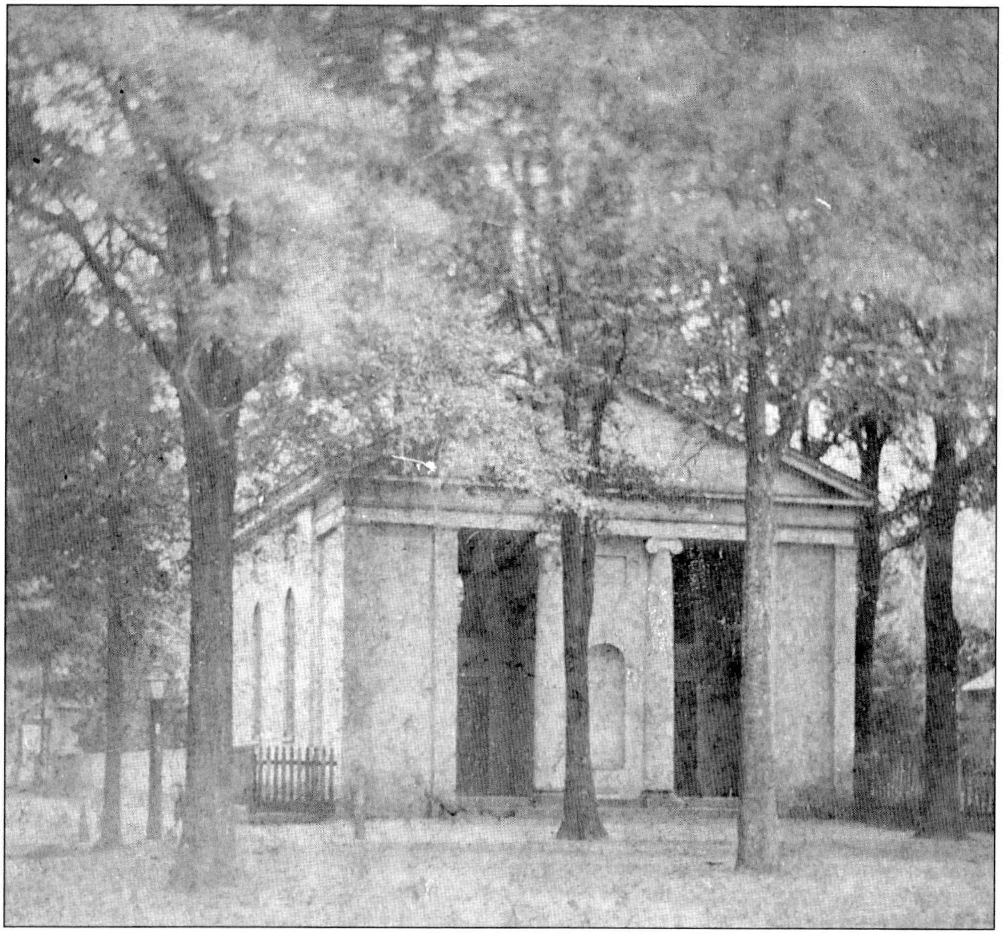

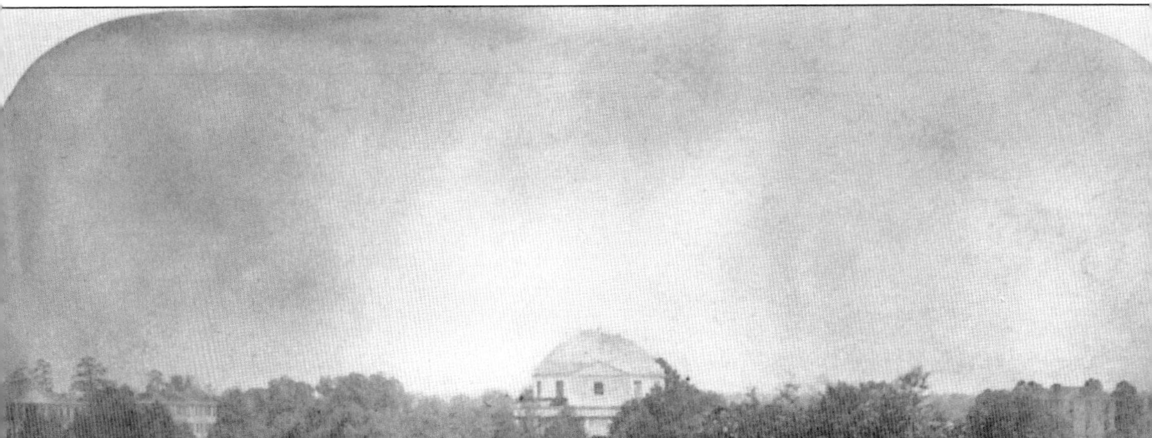

UNIVERSITY OF ALABAMA. On April 18, 1831, the University of Alabama opened with seven buildings, which included the rotunda, lyceum, Steward's Hall, two faculty duplexes, and two dormitories. The estimated cost for the initial buildings was $56,000. This 1859 photograph is the oldest known photograph of the antebellum campus and shows the rotunda at the campus center, with the dormitories visible on either side: (from left to right) Franklin (1832), Washington (1831), Jefferson (1831), and Madison (1859). The Steward's Hall was located behind Washington Hall and is not visible in this photograph. According to the *Alabama State Intelligencer* newspaper from April 20, 1831, "The college year will begin and end with the civil year . . . In order to extend the advantages of education as widely as possible, the charge for tuition, lodging, and study room, use of library and public rooms is only 30 dollars for the collegiate year, payable in advance. The charge for board in the college refectory, payable quarterly in advance, is 80 dollars for the collegiate year. The Student furnishes his own bed, bedding, furniture, fuel and lights."

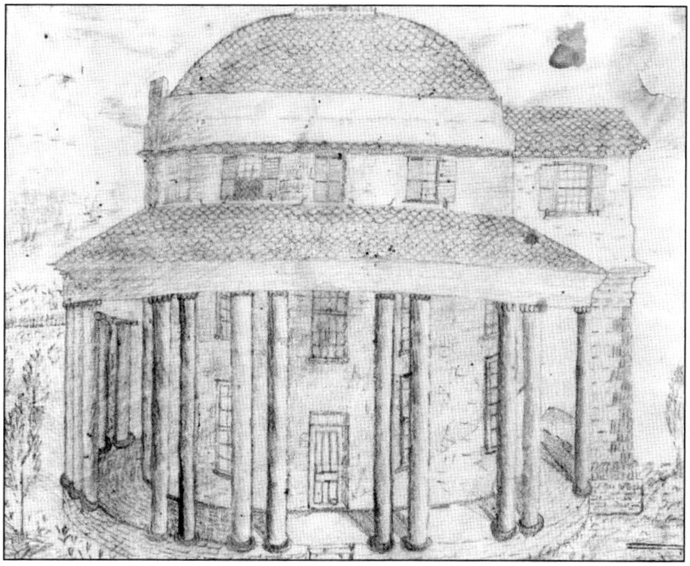

Rotunda Sketch. The rotunda was the focal point of campus. The lower level served as an auditorium for commencement and chapel services, and the upper level contained a natural history collection and library. In the beginning, the faculty and students were delegated responsibilities for the university library. In 1834, Joseph D. Jenkins served as the student librarian, receiving free meals at the Steward's Hall in exchange for his services.

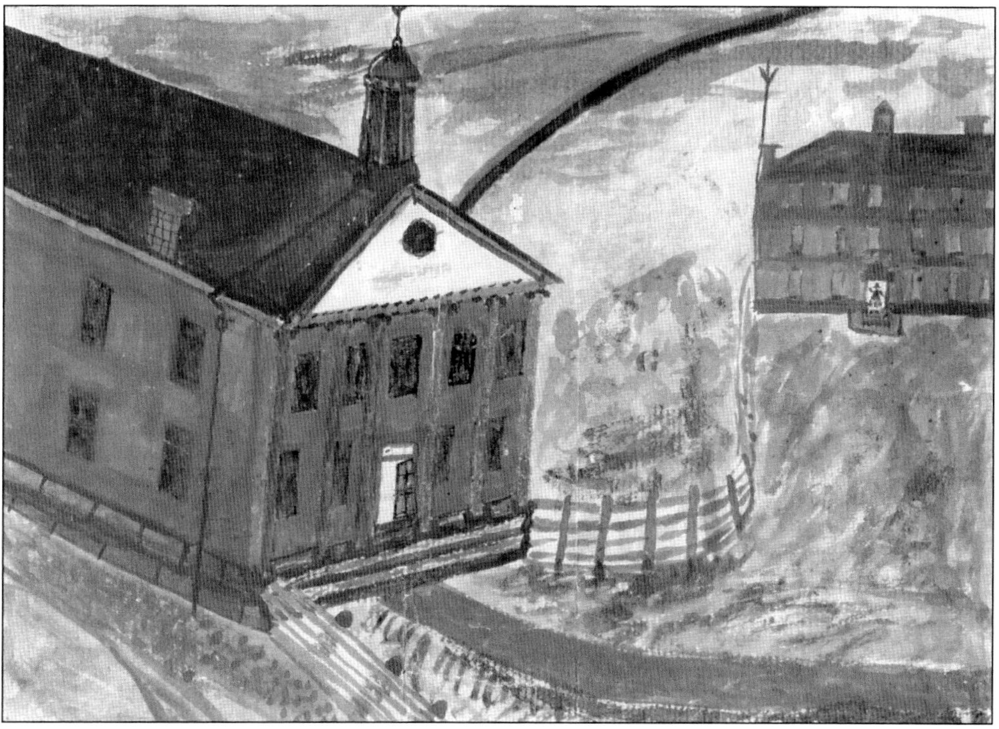

Lyceum and Jefferson Hall. The ornate two-story lyceum (left) housed the main campus lecture rooms and laboratories. Jefferson Hall (right) and Washington Hall (not pictured) were designed to each accommodate up to 48 students. Both dormitories contained 12 apartments, each with two bedrooms and a sitting room. Although Nichols's original plan included four dormitories, their construction was staggered to match enrollment.

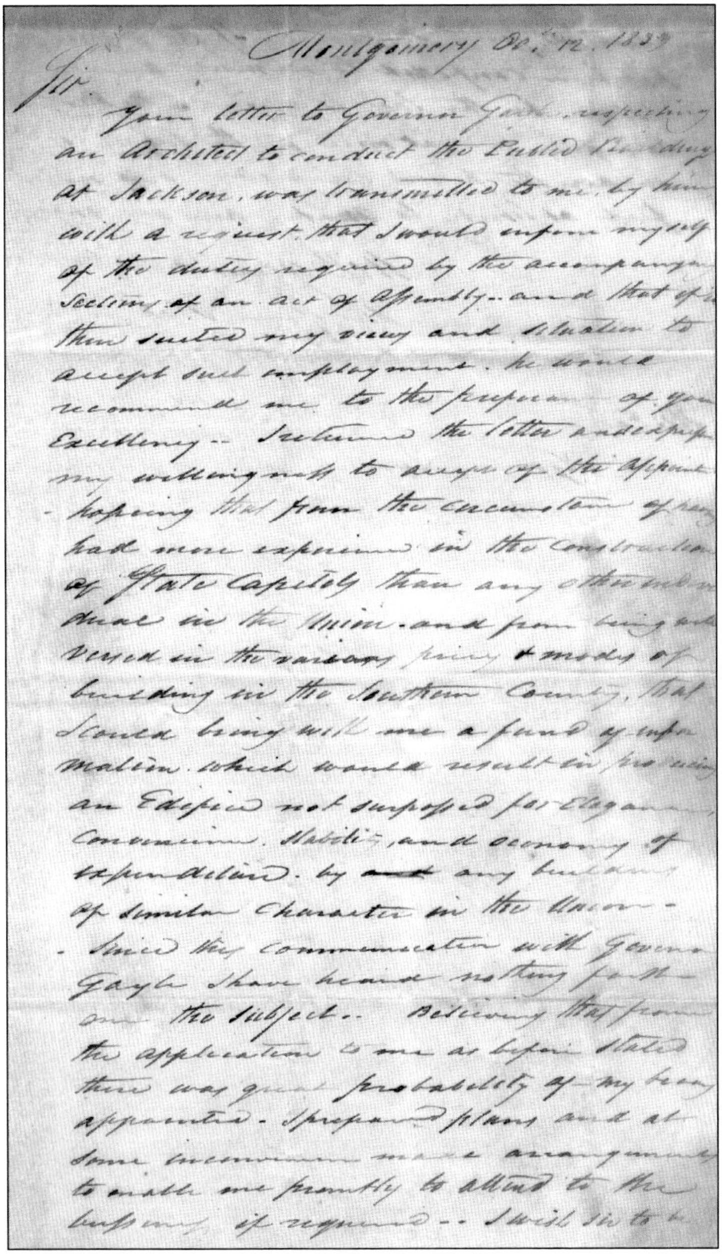
Montgomery Oct. 12. 1833

Sir.

Your letter to Governor Gayle respecting an Architect to conduct the Public Building at Jackson, was transmitted to me, by him with a request that I would inform myself of the duties required by the accompanying Sections of an act of Assembly.. and that if them suited my views and situation to accept such employment. he would recommend me to the purpose of your Excellency.. I return the letter and express my willingness to accept of the appointment. - hoping that from the circumstance of having had more experience in the construction of State Capitols than any other individual in the Union. and from being well versed in the various prices & modes of building in the Southern Country, that I could bring with me a fund of information which would result in producing an Edifice not surpassed for Elegance, Convenience, Stability, and economy of expenditure. by any building of similar character in the Union - - Since this communication with Governor Gayle I have heard nothing further on the subject.. Believing that from the application to me as before stated there was great probability of my being appointed - I prepared plans and at some inconvenience made arrangements to enable me promptly to attend to the business, if required - - I wish Sir to be

William Nichols's Letter to Gov. Charles Lynch. By 1833, William Nichols had completed his initial contracts with the State of Alabama and the university and needed additional work. With a recommendation from Alabama governor John Gayle, Nichols sent this letter to the governor of Mississippi, Charles Lynch, to inquire about the vacant state architect position in Mississippi. Nichols was not selected for the position, which prompted him to accept the position of assistant state engineer in Louisiana in 1833. There, he oversaw the construction of the state penitentiary in Baton Rouge and renovated the old Charity Hospital in New Orleans into the Louisiana statehouse. In 1836, the Mississippi state architect position reopened; Nichols again expressed an interest and was hired. Nichols worked in Mississippi until his death in 1853. (MDAH.)

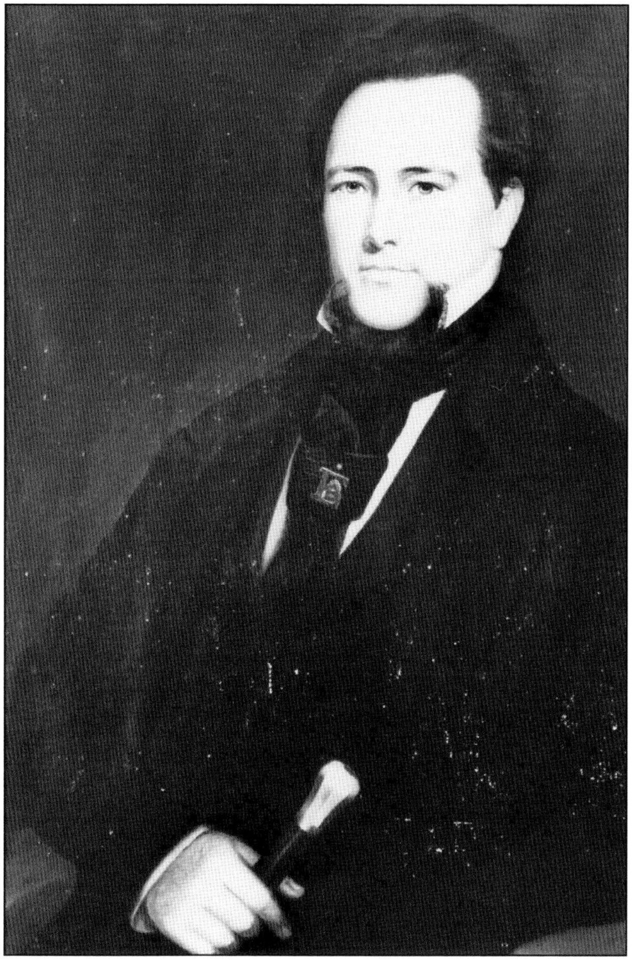

William Inge. For many students, the experience of living on campus, with strict rules and expectations, was new and challenging. Discipline issues arose shortly after the campus opened. Records from the early years are littered with reports of student fights and poor conduct toward faculty and staff. One example from 1833 involves brothers William and Samuel Inge and fellow student Boling Smith. While the start of the confrontation is unclear, it proceeded with William throwing a rock at Smith and Samuel stabbing Smith near his heart. Samuel was suspended, and the other two were reprimanded. Within a few months, Smith was suspended for attacking William in retribution.

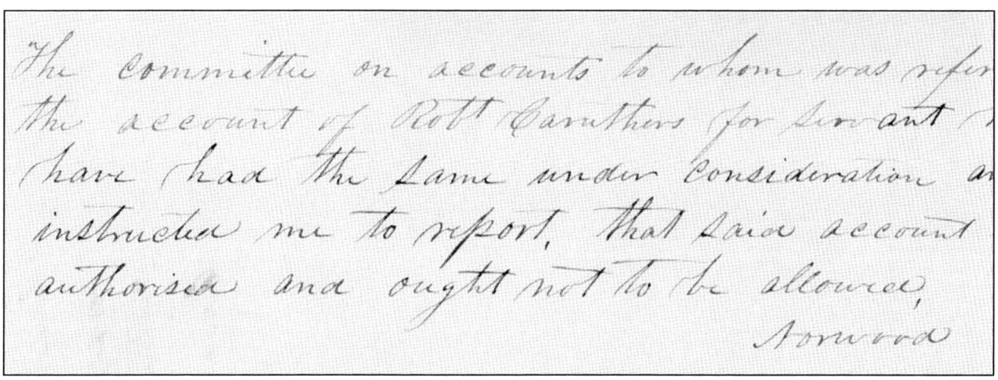
The Committee on accounts to whom was refer
the account of Robt Caruthers for Servant
have had the same under consideration an
instructed me to report, that said account
authorised and ought not to be allowed,
Norwood

Record Denying Steward's Hall Assistance, c. 1842. The dining hall at Steward's Hall was the most frequent site of student misconduct, resulting from the limited staffing resources and autonomy for decision-making afforded to the university steward. This lack of support from the university leadership is exemplified in this record in which university trustee Daniel Norwood denies Steward Robert Caruthers's request for a dining hall servant. During the first 16 years the university was in operation, the trustees had to fill the steward position at least five times. Caruthers was followed as steward by Thomas Gaines Richardson and, later, William P. Barnett.

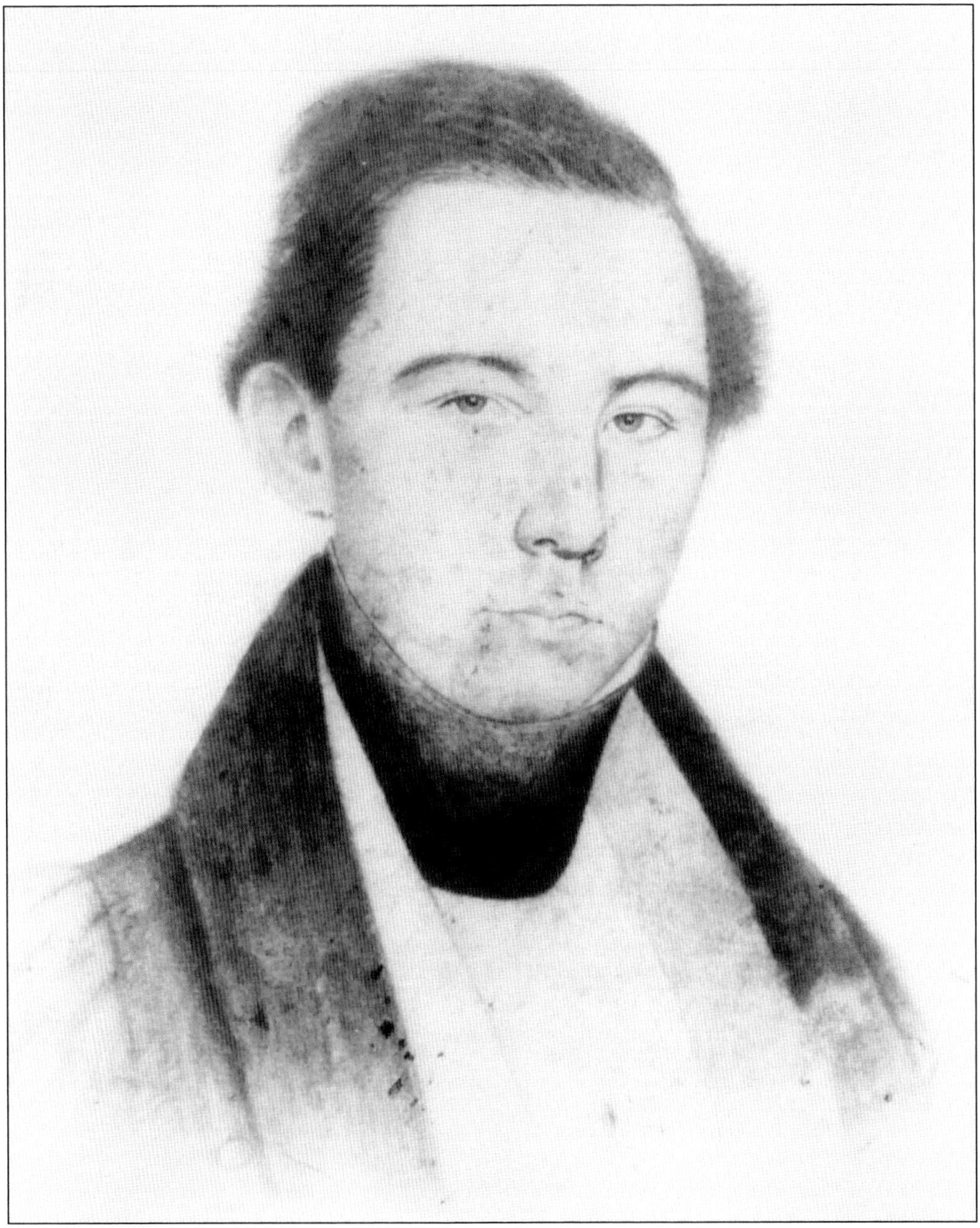

ORAN MILO ROBERTS, C. 1835. In 1892, university graduate Oran Roberts reminisced about his 1836 experiences on the university campus. In this account, Roberts recalls students "throwing biscuits" at the Steward's Hall servants and the frequent reprimands they received by the steward, John "Red" Brown. Prior to his appointment as campus steward in 1834, Brown had served as a judge in Jefferson County and in both houses of the Alabama Legislature, where he cast the deciding vote in favor of relocating the capital from Cahawba to Tuscaloosa. Brown left the university to continue his political career in Texas. After graduating from the university, Roberts served one term in the Alabama Legislature before relocating to Texas, where he served in the state legislature with Brown. Roberts's political career culminated in his election as governor of Texas in 1878.

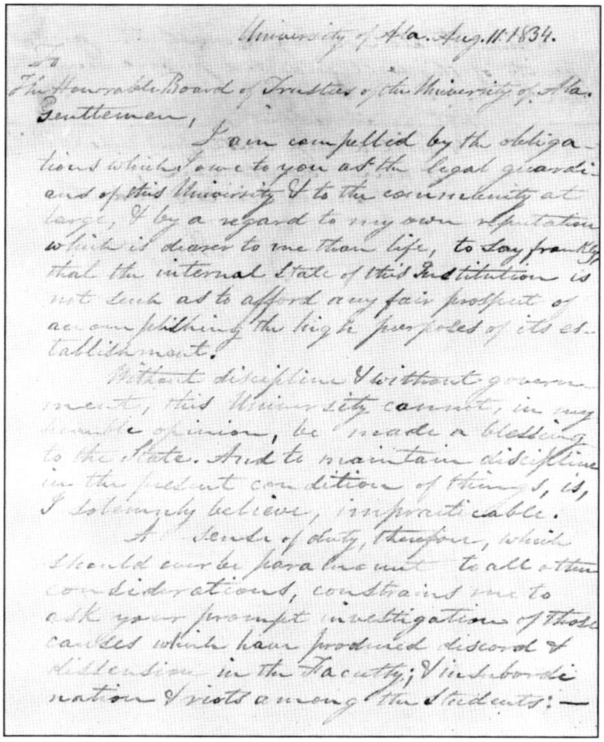

University of Ala. Aug. 11. 1834.

To
The Honorable Board of Trustees of the University of Ala.

Gentlemen,

I am compelled by the obligations which I owe to you as the legal guardians of this University & to the community at large, & by a regard to my own reputation which is dearer to me than life, to say frankly that the internal state of this Institution is not such as to afford any fair prospect of accomplishing the high purposes of its establishment.

Without discipline & without government, this University cannot, in my humble opinion, be made a blessing to the State. And to maintain discipline in the present condition of things, is, I solemnly believe, impracticable.

A sense of duty, therefore, which should ever be paramount to all other considerations, constrains me to ask your prompt investigation of those causes which have produced discord & dissension in the Faculty; & insubordination & riots among the Students:—

LETTER TO THE BOARD OF TRUSTEES. In this letter (right) dated August 11, 1834, university president Alva Woods states, "Without discipline and without government, this University cannot, in my humble opinion, be made a blessing to the State. And to maintain discipline in the present condition of things, is, I solemnly believe, impracticable." Woods was unable to resolve the disciplinary issues and resigned in 1837. Basil Manly (below) was appointed as the second university president, a position he held until 1855.

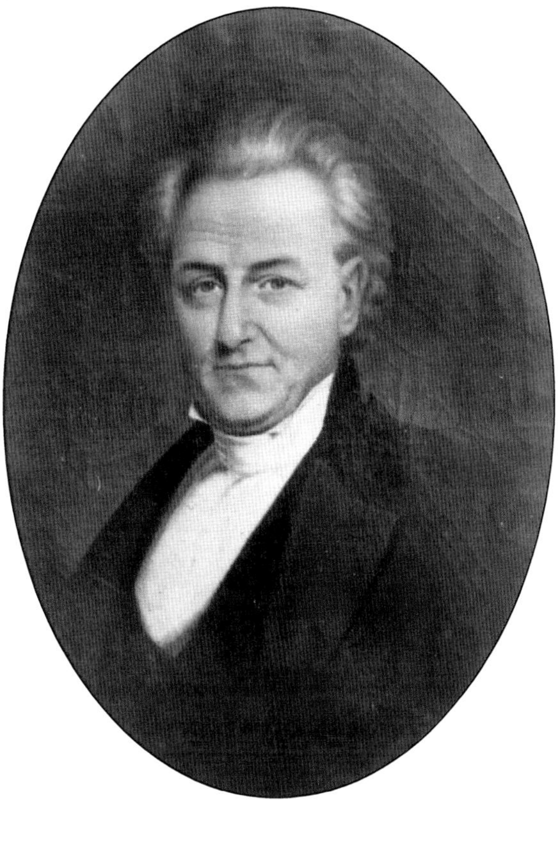

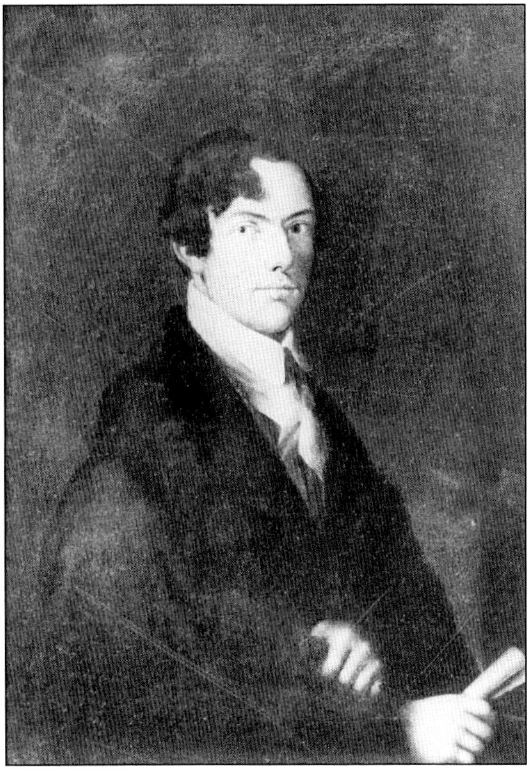

Frederick A.P. Barnard. To remedy the shortage of faculty housing, which had been a provision of employment, the university trustees had two rooms at the Steward's Hall remodeled as a faculty residence for Frederick A.P. Barnard in 1844. Hired in 1837, Barnard taught for 17 years at the university in the subjects of mathematics, natural philosophy, and chemistry.

Observatory. Frederick A.P. Barnard was instrumental in establishing the study of astronomy at the university. In 1838, he presented plans for a state-of-the-art observatory to be built on campus. Barnard designed both the building and equipment, the latter of which was handmade in London and Paris per his specifications. The observatory was completed in 1844 and was the first building of its kind in the southeastern United States.

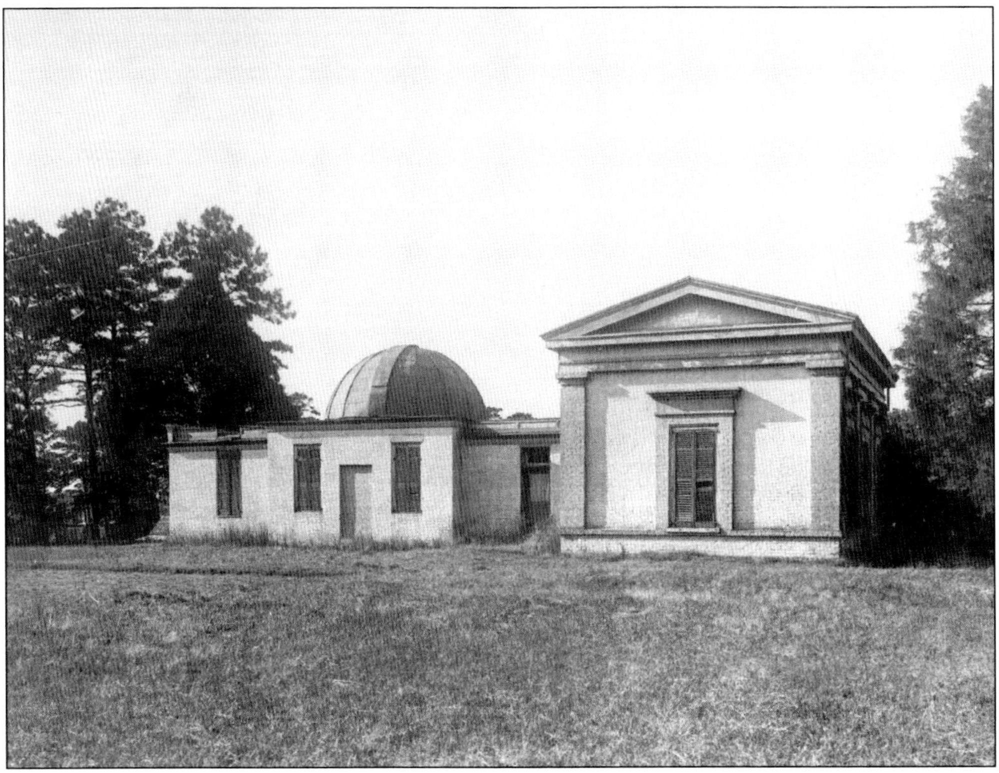

MICHAEL TUOMEY. In 1847, in an effort to resolve issues with student discipline, the dining hall at the Steward's Hall was closed. The entire upper level was officially designated as a faculty residence, and the lower level was retained for educational use. Frederick A.P. Barnard was soon to be married, so the university trustees provided him a $250 allowance to rent a home elsewhere and offered the residence at the Steward's Hall to newly hired professor Michael Tuomey.

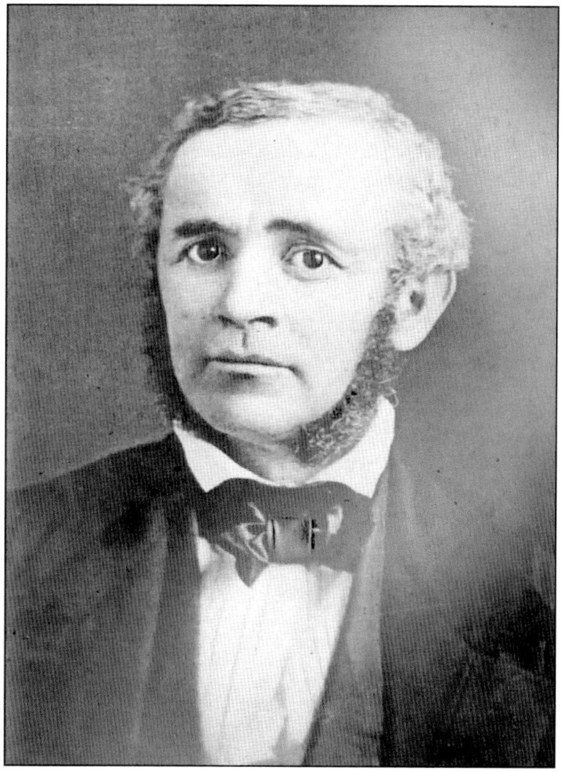

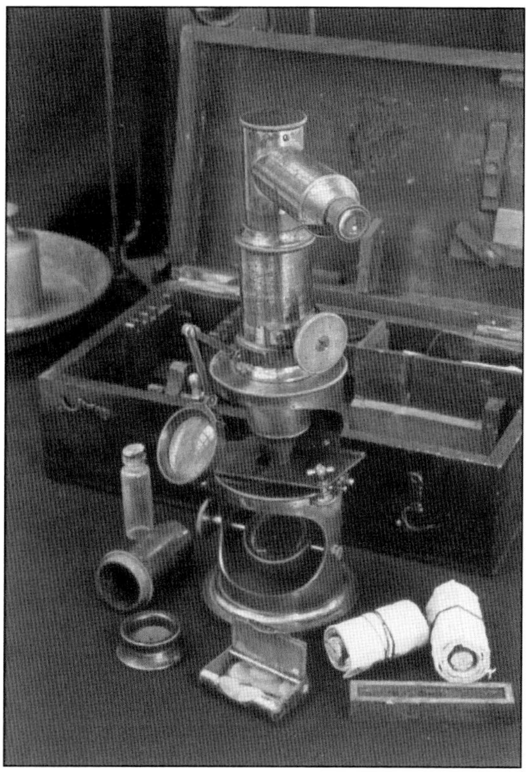

MICHAEL TUOMEY'S MICROSCOPE. Michael Tuomey joined the university as a professor of geology in 1847. In 1850, part of the lower level of the Steward's Hall was converted into a well-equipped chemistry laboratory to accommodate Tuomey's classes. In addition, Tuomey served as the first Alabama state geologist. At the request of the Alabama Legislature, Tuomey conducted Alabama's first large-scale geological investigation to determine the state's mineral wealth.

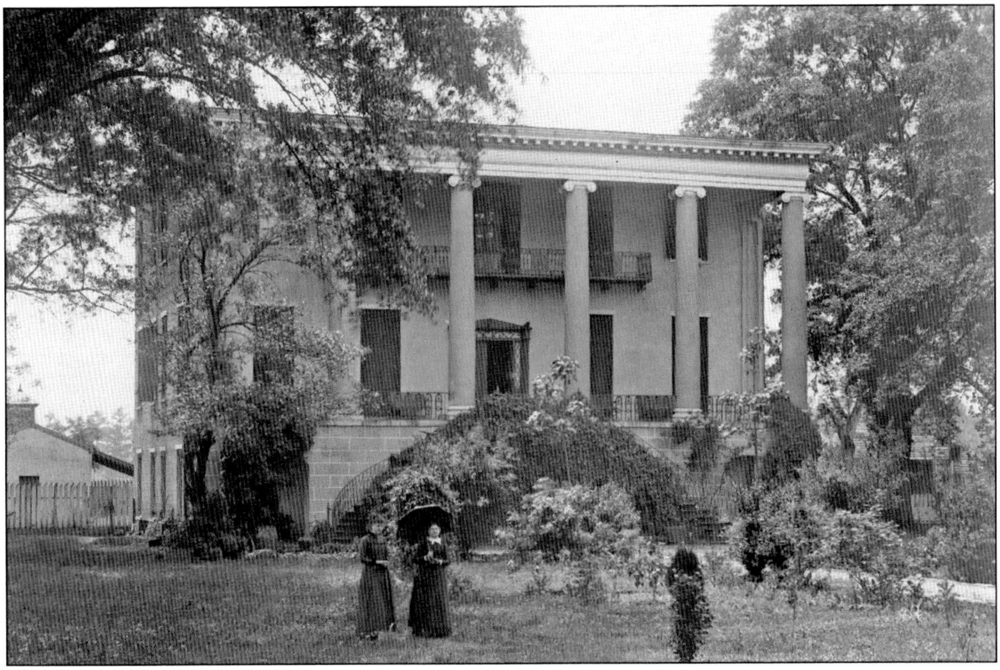

President's Mansion and Greenwood Cemetery. When the dining hall at the Steward's Hall was closed in 1847, the students were instructed to find their meals in town. Many students took their meals at the residence of Alexander Baird. As a local stonemason, Baird assisted with the stonework at the University of Alabama President's Mansion (above), constructed between 1839 and 1841. This c. 1900 photograph was taken by Eugene Allen Smith, professor of geology. Baird also carved much of the stonework at Greenwood Cemetery (below), one of Tuscaloosa County's oldest cemeteries. (Above, ULDSC; below, LOC.)

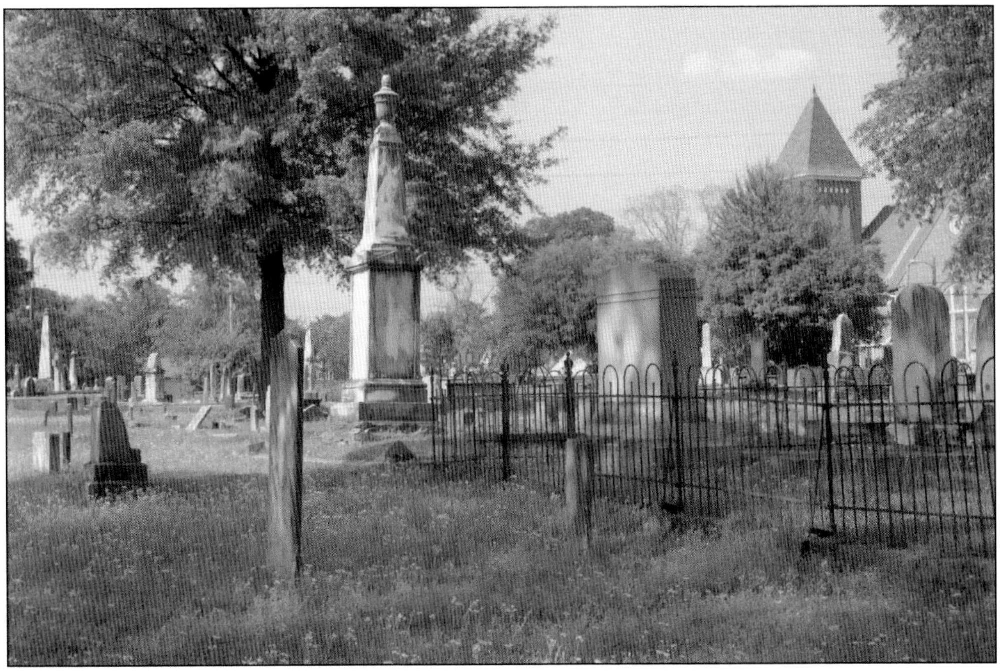

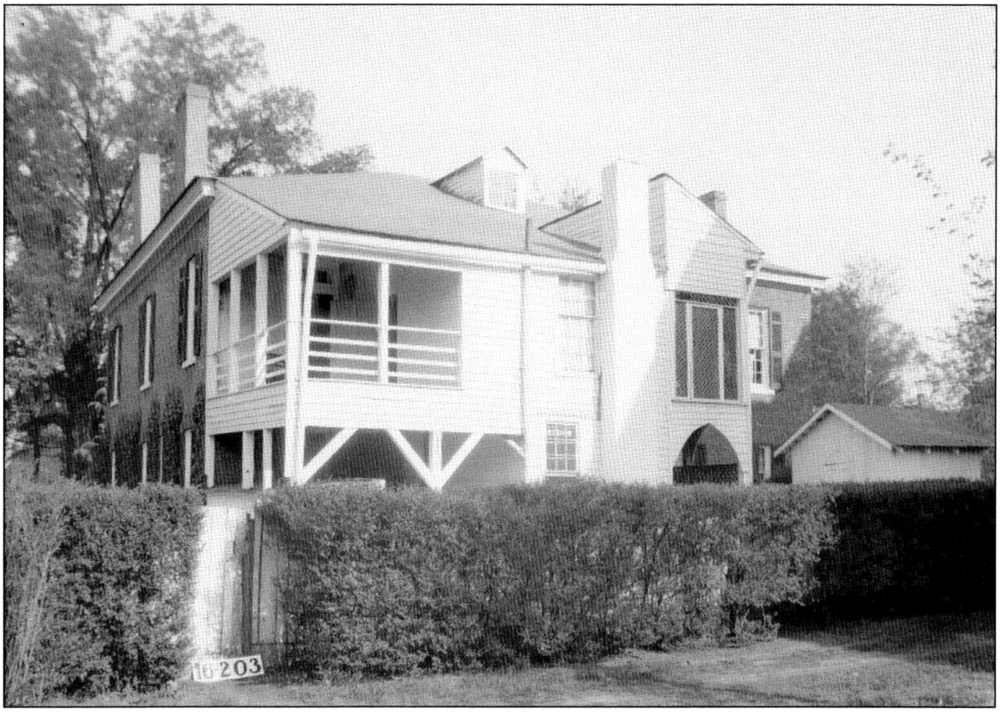

STEWARD'S HALL RENOVATIONS. In the late 1840s, the university commissioned renovations to Steward's Hall to facilitate its use as a faculty residence. Included in the renovation was a wooden addition at the back of the building (above). Museum lore suggests that, at one time, a bathroom was built on the upper level, and later, there was a small kitchen installed on the lower level. In addition, the large dining hall, located along the front of the lower level, was divided into two rooms. These rooms were separated by a hallway that contained a newly constructed main interior staircase (right). The dining hall's original brick flooring was covered with planks of heart pine. Both photographs were taken in 1934. (Both, LOC.)

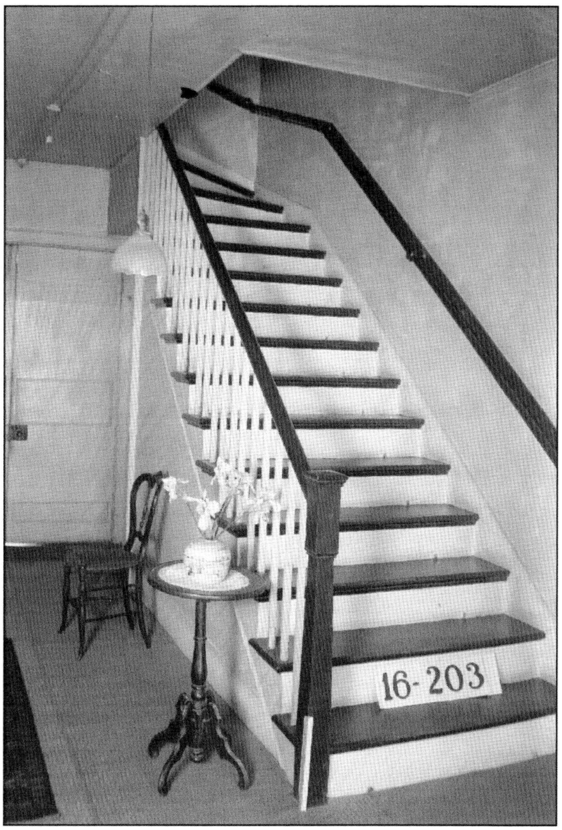

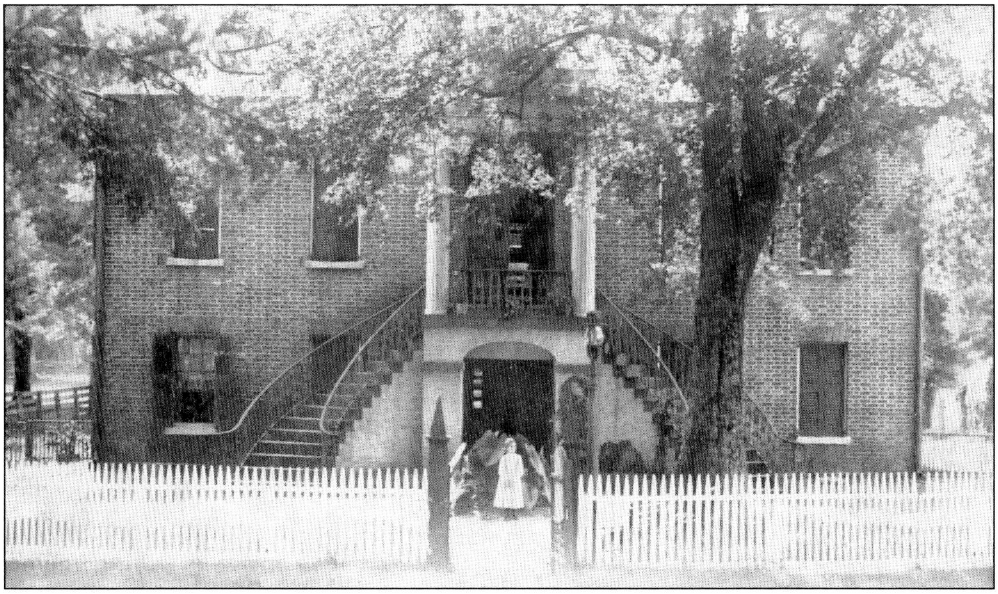

Steward's Hall Exterior Renovations. In the 1850s, the front exterior of the Steward's Hall was renovated, likely to suit its new use as a residence. Two staircases were added to the existing porch, and the decorative cast-iron railings were purchased from the Cornell Company Iron Works in New York.

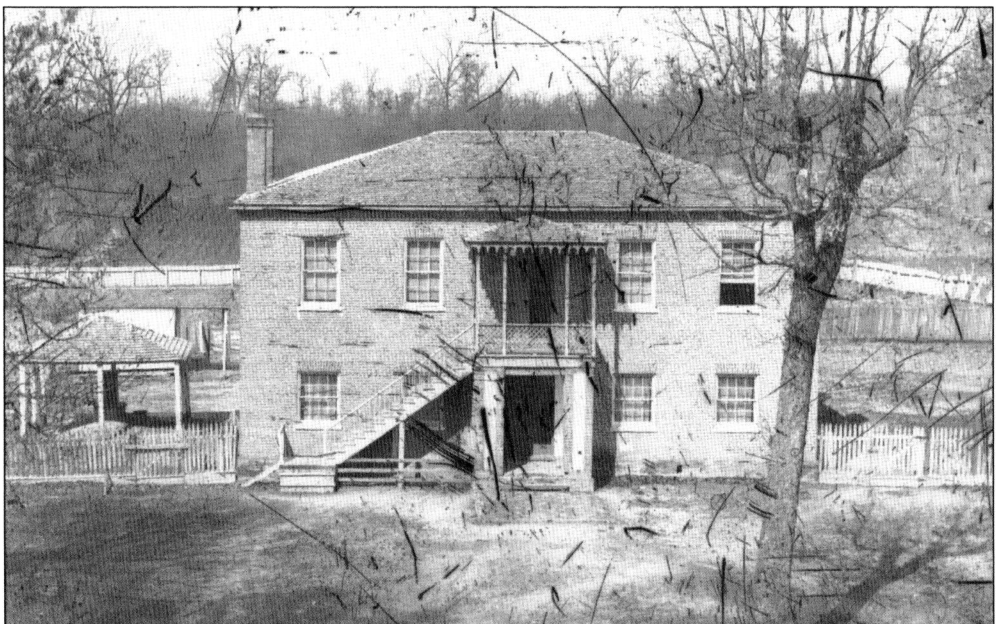

Steward's Hall, University of Mississippi, c. 1856–1861. There are no known photographs of the University of Alabama Steward's Hall taken prior to the 1850s exterior renovations. However, there is a striking resemblance between drawings and descriptions of the University of Alabama Lyceum and Steward's Hall (top of page) and photographs of their counterparts at the University of Mississippi. William Nichols was the architect for both campuses, and it is likely that he reused elements of the Tuscaloosa campus in Oxford, Mississippi. (UMASC.)

Landon Garland, c. 1860. Landon Garland was appointed as the university's third president in 1855. Confronted with ongoing student disciplinary issues, Garland lobbied the trustees to convert the university to a military form of governance. His request was granted in July 1860. The trustees passed an ordinance formalizing the conversion, which also established President Garland as superintendent of the university's Alabama Corps of Cadets.

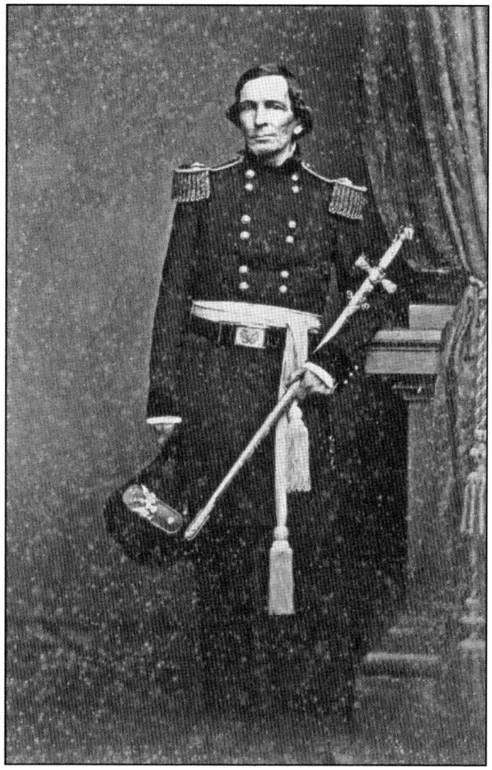

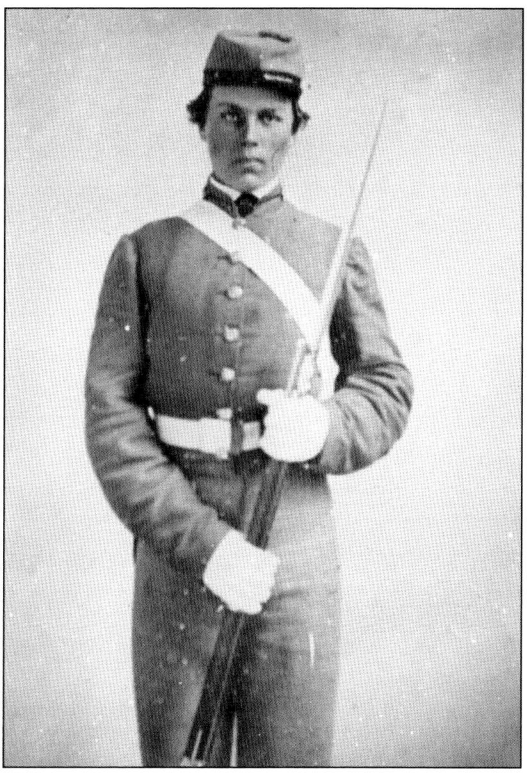

Student Cadet Green Marshall Labuzan. In addition to the standard curriculum, the University of Alabama required students to complete courses in military tactics, wear uniforms, and take part in drills. These changes had immediate positive effects on student discipline, which allowed Superintendent Garland to mend the university's reputation for having students who were "drunkards and ruffians."

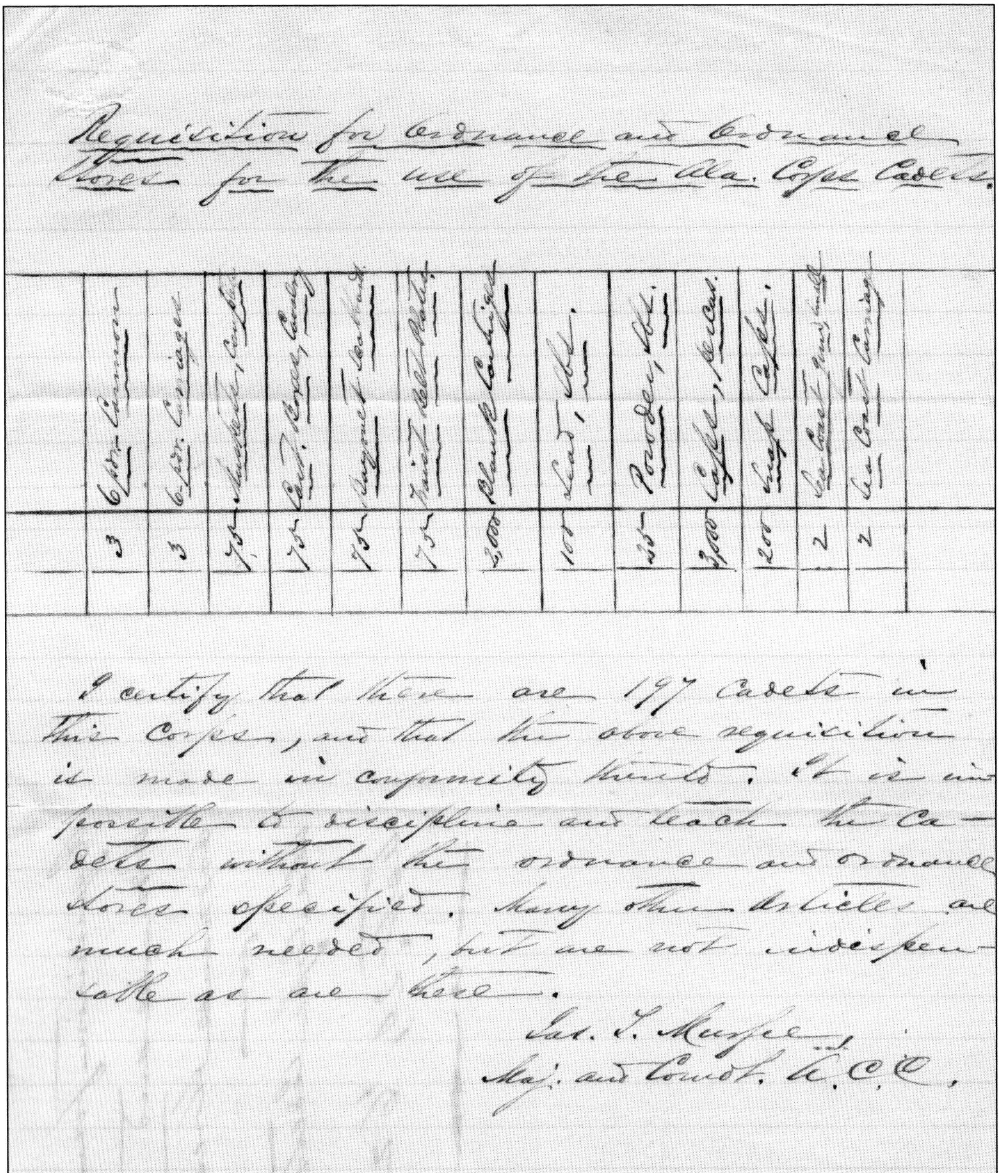

Requisition for ordnance and ordnance stores for the use of the Ala. Corps Cadets.

3	6 pdr. Cannon
3	6 pdr. Carriages
75	Muskets, complete
75	Cart. Boxes, Cavalry
75	Bayonet Scabbards
75	Waist belt Plates
2,000	Blank Cartridges
100	Lead, lbs.
25	Powder, lbs.
3000	Caps, percus.
200	Snap Caps.
2	Sea Coast [illegible]
2	[illegible]

I certify that there are 197 Cadets in this Corps, and that the above requisition is made in conformity thereto. It is impossible to discipline and teach the Cadets without the ordnance and ordnance stores specified. Many other articles are much needed, but are not indispensable as are these.

Jas. T. Murfee,
Maj. and Comdt. A.C.C.

Requisition Form, October 20, 1862. The conversion to military governance required the university to make several changes, including the hiring of military instructors and the purchase of equipment and munitions needed for drills. This requisition, made by new faculty member Col. James T. Murfee in 1862, is for cannons, muskets, powder, and other military supplies.

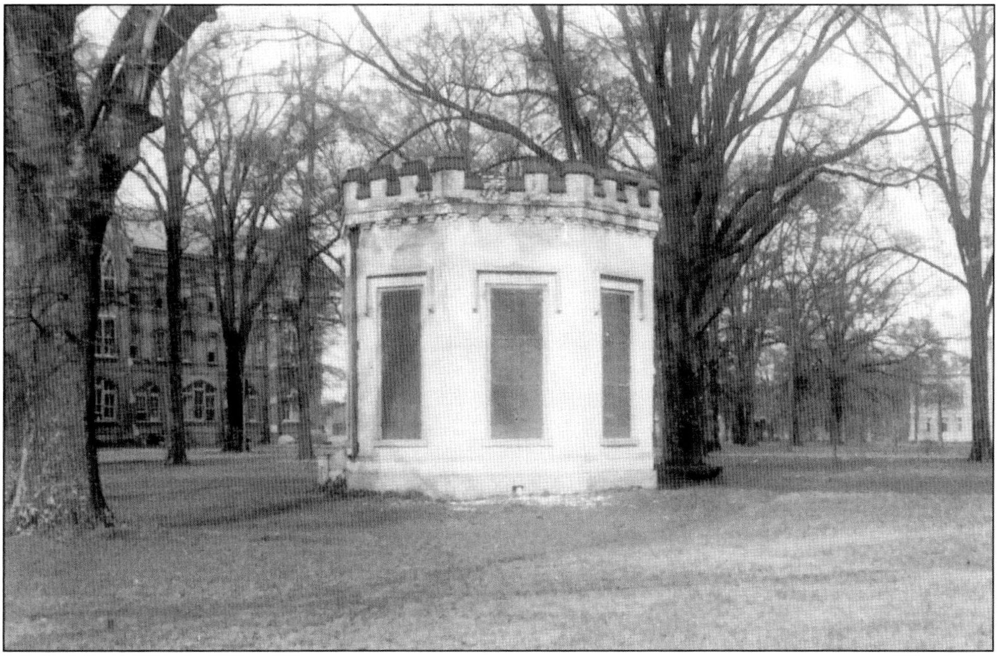

GUARDHOUSE. To support the military function of campus, the university constructed a guardhouse in 1862 and temporary barracks in 1863 and 1864. The guardhouse was built to provide shelter for students on patrol during inclement weather. It was the first building to depart from William Nichols's Classical Revival style and is one of the few buildings still standing from the campus's antebellum period. Today, it is known as the Little Round House.

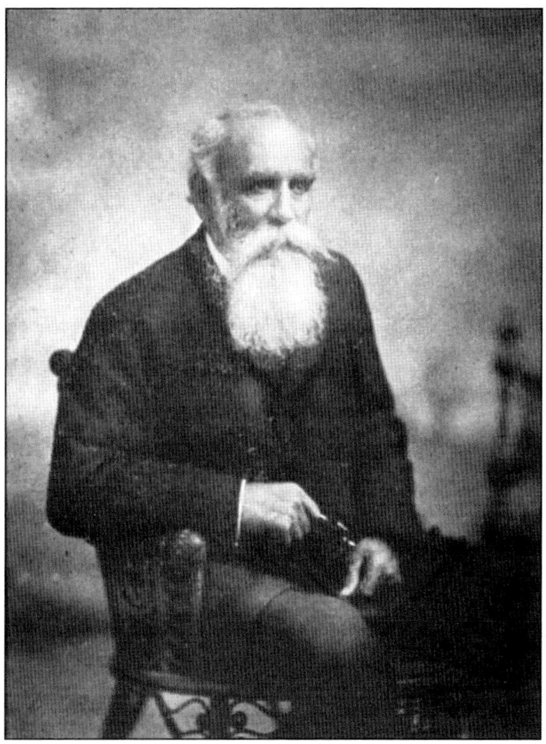

CALEB HUSE. In 1860, Caleb Huse, a West Point graduate and instructor, was appointed as the university's first commandant. Huse was hired to oversee the conversion to military governance, implementing the West Point system. According to a campus historical marker, between 1860 and 1865, the university contributed "seven generals, 25 colonels, 14 lieutenant colonels, 21 majors, 125 captains, 273 staff and other commissioned officers, and 294 soldiers" to the Confederate army.

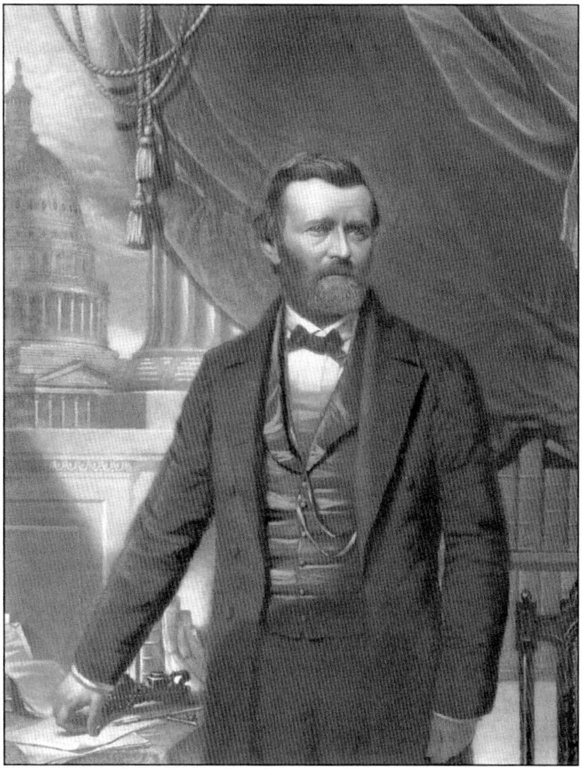

Ulysses S. Grant. Growing tension between the North and South led to the eruption of the Civil War in 1861. The success of the university in developing military personnel for the Confederate army drew the attention of Union lieutenant general Ulysses S. Grant, who designated the campus as a prime military target. On March 29, 1864, Confederate general E.M. McCook ordered Gen. John Croxton to march his 1,500 soldiers to Tuscaloosa to destroy the university. (LOC.)

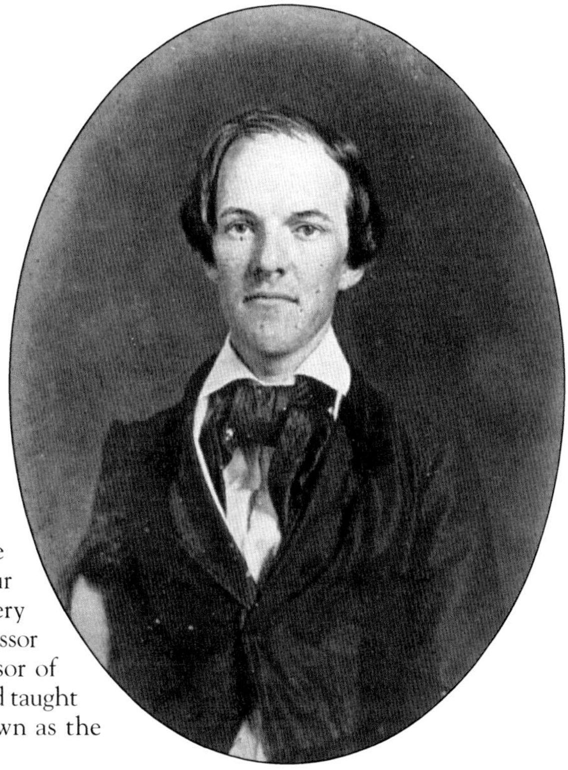

John W. Pratt. On April 3, 1865, rumors of a Union invasion circulated around campus. In a written account, cadet James Cowan recalls his last class in Steward's Hall with Prof. John Pratt prior to the invasion: "As the drum sounded the hour of 3 o'clock, the classes filed out, and very few if any of us ever saw the beloved professor [Pratt] after that hour." Pratt, a professor of logic, rhetoric, and oratory, both lived and taught in the former Steward's Hall, then known as the Pratt House.

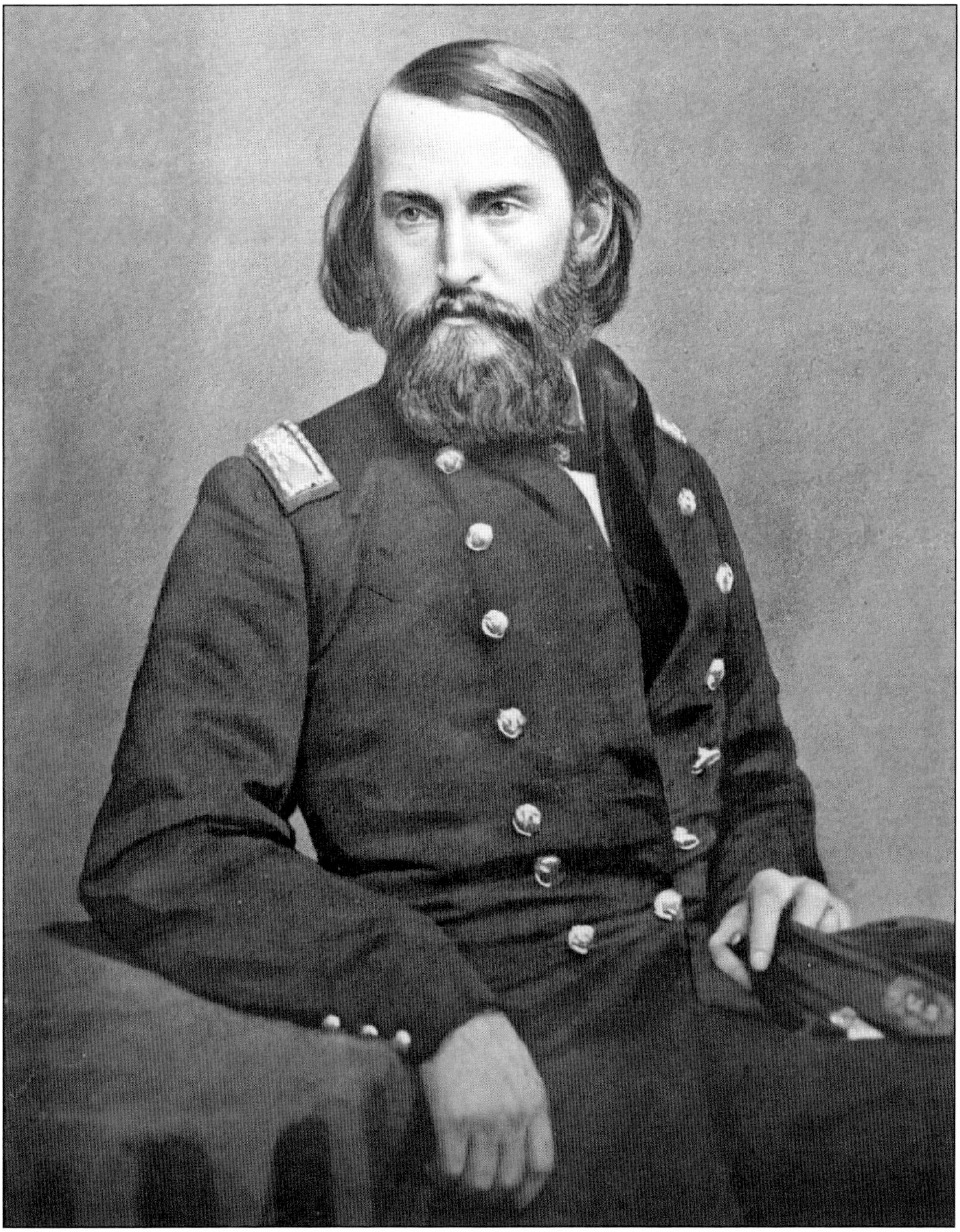

JOHN T. CROXTON. In the early morning of April 4, 1865, Gen. John Croxton marched his troops from the nearby town of Northport toward the university, with the intention of burning every building that served a military function. Meanwhile, Col. James Murfee, who succeeded Caleb Huse as commandant, assembled the 300 students who comprised the Alabama Corps of Cadets in an effort to defend the town and campus. Gen. John Croxton's veteran forces significantly outnumbered the cadets. Unwilling to sacrifice the lives of the cadets for a battle that could not be won, Supt. Landon Garland ordered a retreat and marched the cadets east. The university and surrounding community of Tuscaloosa were left virtually unprotected, and Union soldiers set fire to the campus buildings and nearby factories. (LOC.)

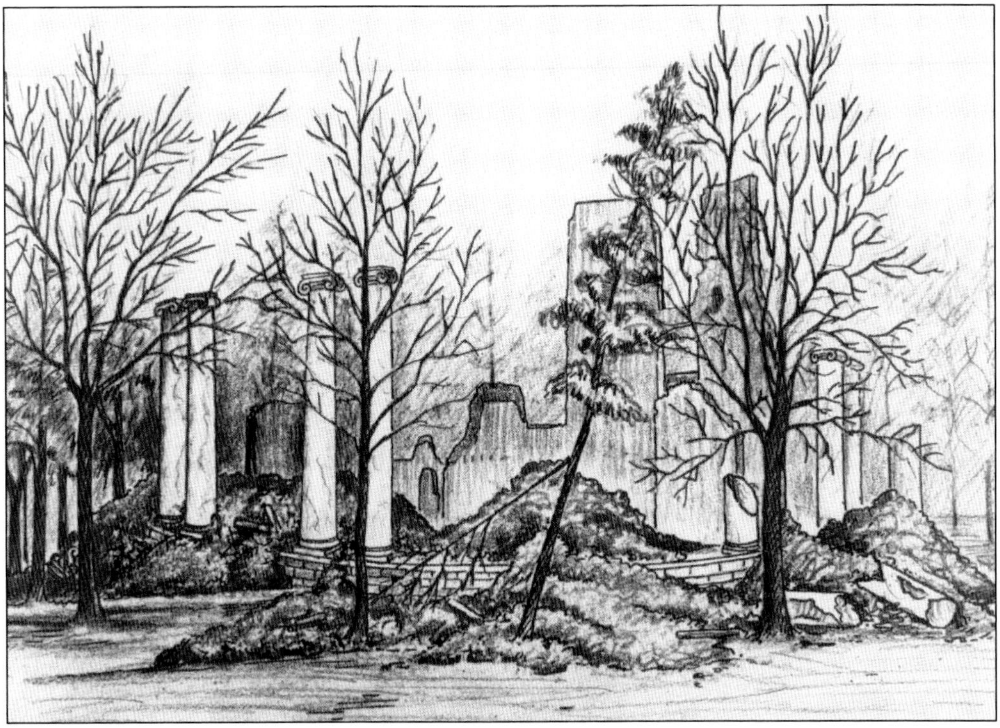

CAMPUS RUINS, C. 1865. By the end of the day on April 4, 1865, nearly all the main campus buildings lay in ruin. William Nichols's four campus dormitories were burned (Jefferson Hall, above), along with the rotunda (below), lyceum, and a faculty duplex. The roof of the guardhouse was also burned, but the walls remained intact. These sketches were made by Eugene Allen Smith. Smith was an 1862 graduate of the university who returned in 1871 as a professor of geology, agricultural chemistry, and mineralogy. Smith succeeded Michael Tuomey as the second state geologist.

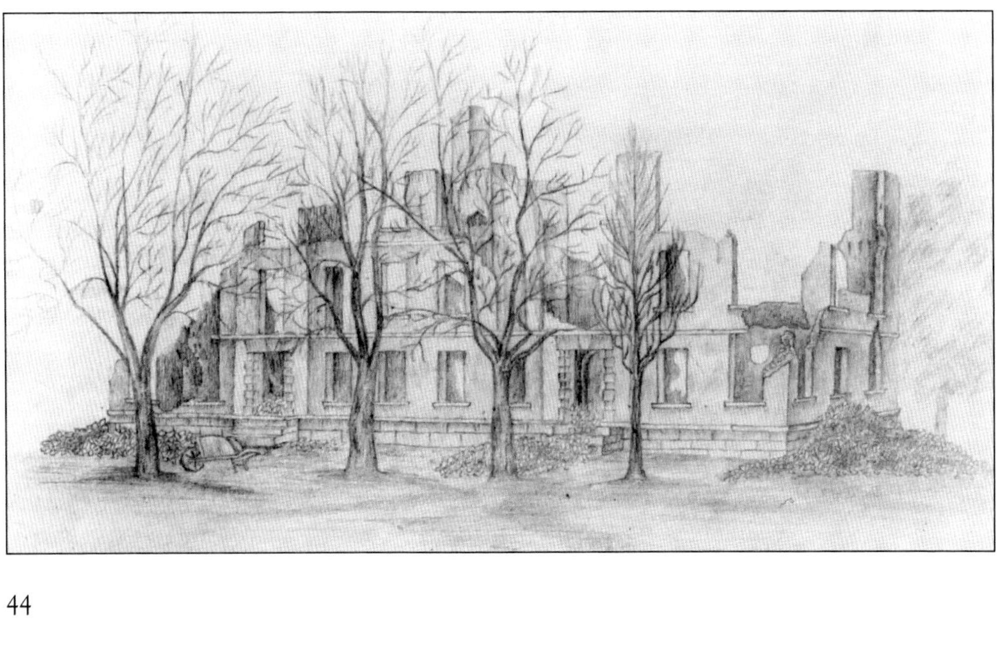

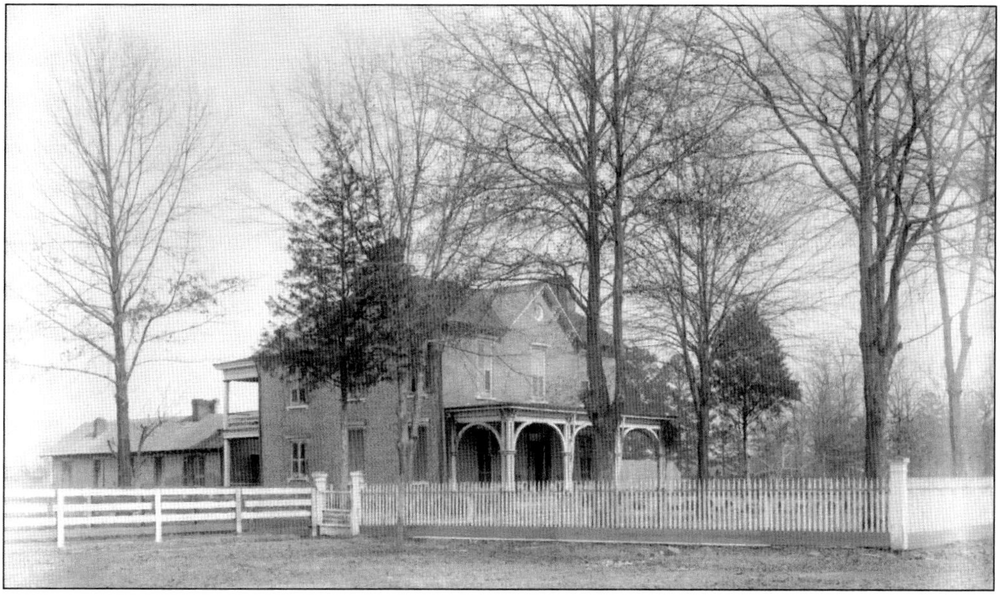

Faculty House. Only seven structures survived the 1865 destruction of the campus, including the President's Mansion, the guardhouse, the Pratt House (former Steward's Hall), three faculty homes, and the observatory. The President's Mansion, the Pratt House, and the faculty houses were probably spared as private residences. The observatory was probably overlooked because of its location away from the center of campus. The faculty house in this photograph was constructed around 1859 and photographed in the late 1880s.

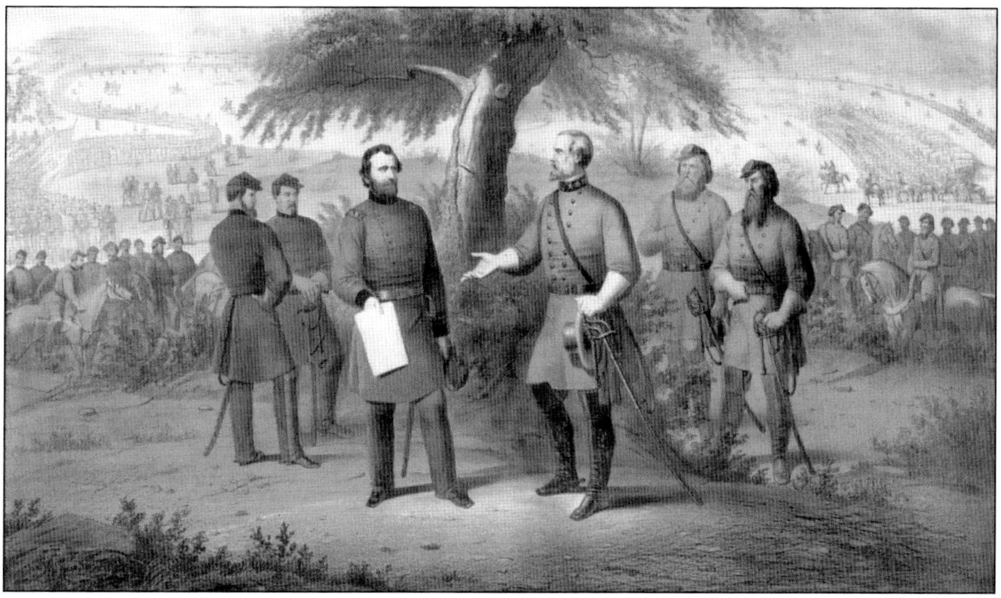

Surrender of General Lee. On April 9, 1865, only days after the destruction of the university, Confederate general Robert E. Lee surrendered to Union general Ulysses S. Grant, marking an official end to the American Civil War. Although the war had ended, the damage to the campus was so extensive that the university was unable to reopen. Landon Garland remained as president and spent the following year raising money to rebuild the university, even going door-to-door seeking book donations to replenish the library. (LOC.)

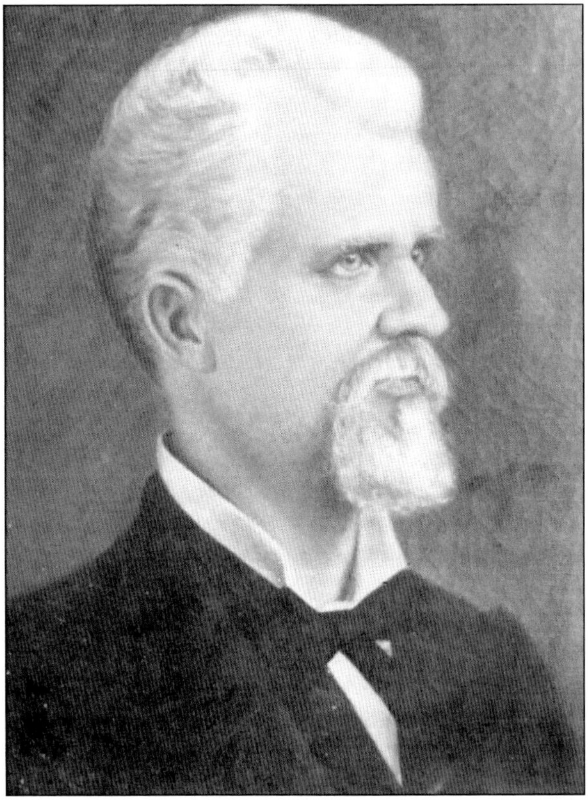

James T. Murfee. Col. James Murfee, former commandant of the Alabama Corp of Cadets, was rehired by the university to oversee the campus reconstruction. Murfee rented a room in the old Pratt House and managed the renovations of the surviving structures and the construction of new buildings.

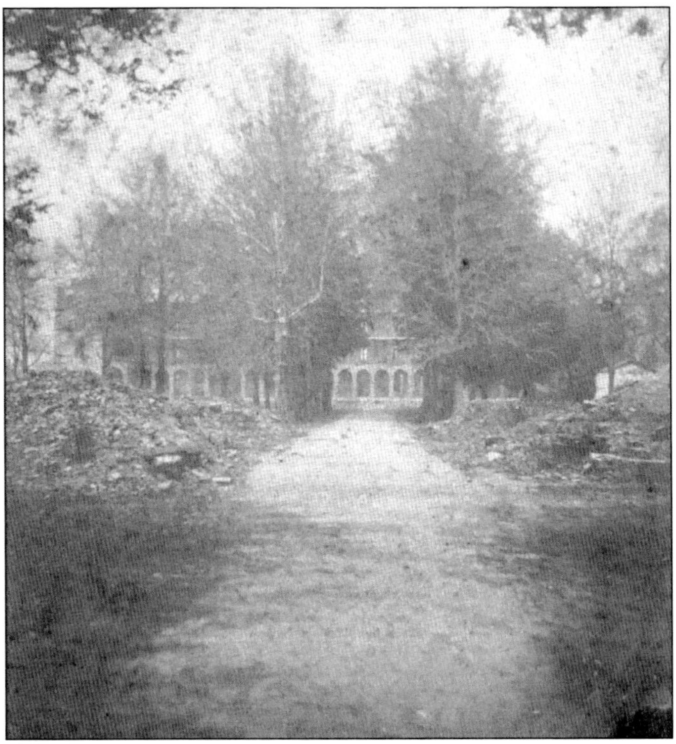

Woods Hall Seen through Campus Ruins. The first post–Civil War structure built on campus was the Barracks. It was primarily constructed of materials salvaged from buildings destroyed during the campus raid. Built between 1867 and 1868, the Barracks was later renamed Woods Hall to honor the university's first president, Alva Woods. The building was designed with dorm rooms, a large dining room, library, and ample laboratory and classroom space. The construction of Woods Hall allowed the university to reopen in 1870.

Two

THE GORGAS FAMILY AND THE UNIVERSITY 1878–1953

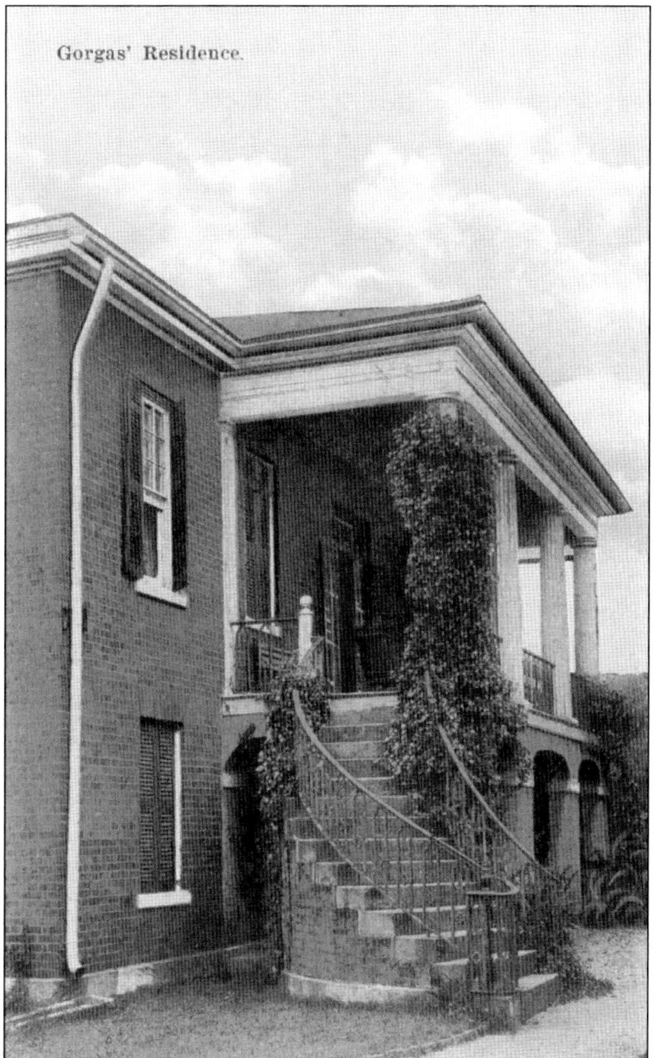

GORGAS HOUSE, c. 1912. In 1878, Josiah Gorgas was appointed as president of the university. Following his term as president, Gorgas and his family remained on campus in the former Steward's Hall. At that time, the building was known as the Pratt House after previous occupant Prof. John Pratt. The Gorgas family resided in the home for 74 years, during which time it became known as the Gorgas House. (Authors' collection.)

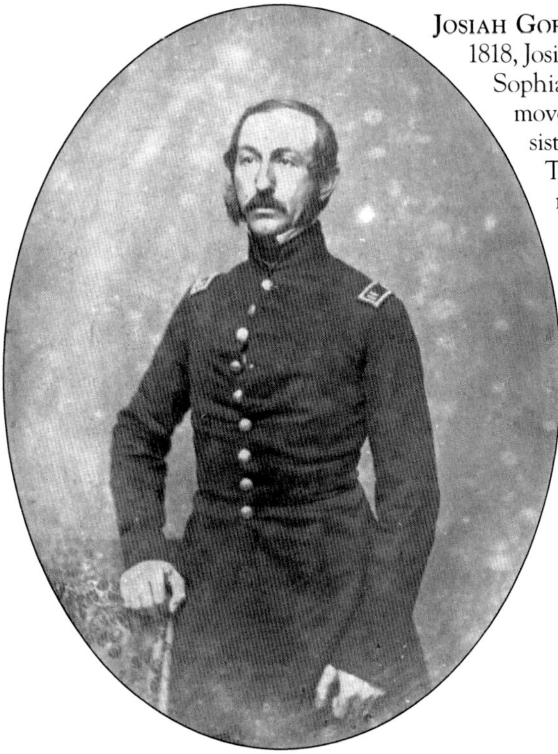

Josiah Gorgas, c. 1841. Born in Pennsylvania in 1818, Josiah Gorgas was the 10th child of Joseph and Sophia (Atkinson) Gorgas. As a teenager, Josiah moved to Lyons, New York, to stay with his older sister, Eliza, and her husband, Daniel Chapman. There, Josiah worked as an apprentice at a newspaper and later read law at the office of Congressman Graham Chapin.

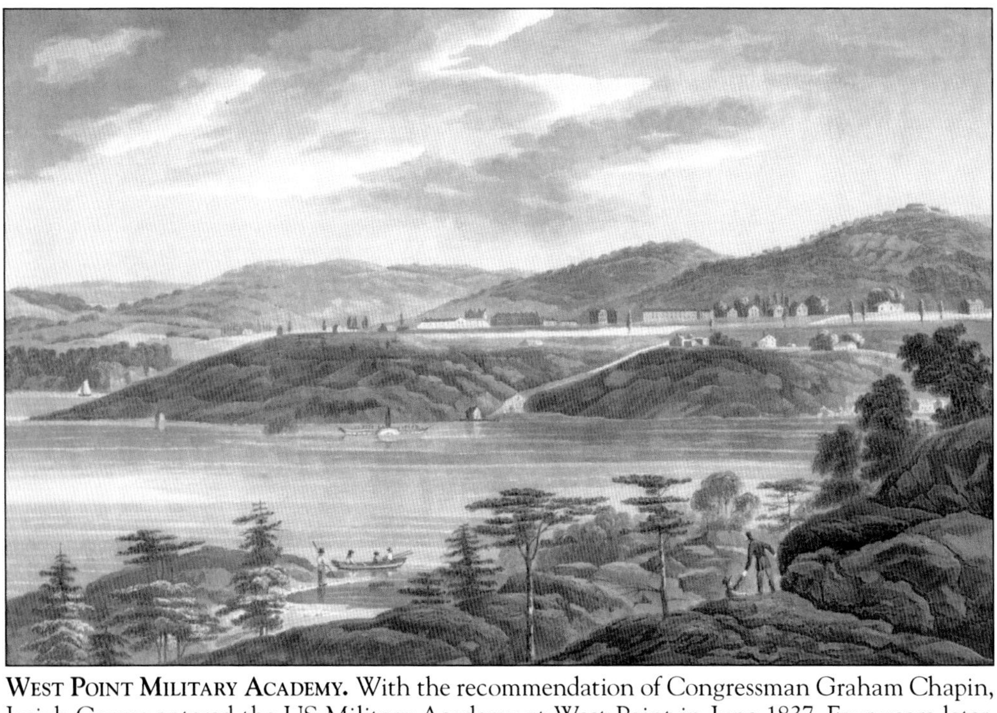

West Point Military Academy. With the recommendation of Congressman Graham Chapin, Josiah Gorgas entered the US Military Academy at West Point in June 1837. Four years later, Gorgas graduated sixth in his class of 52 students and selected the Ordnance Corps for his branch of service. (LOC.)

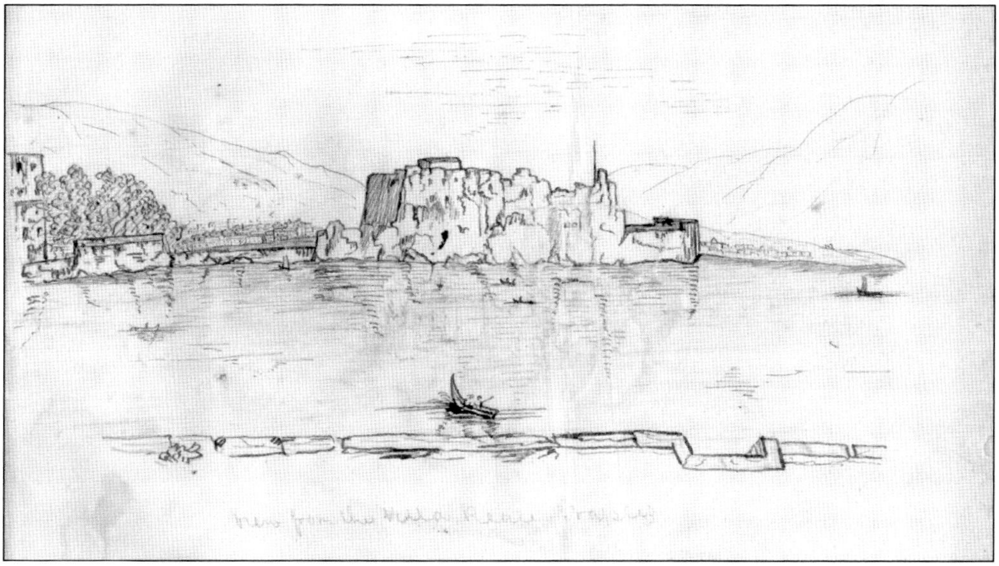

Sketch of Naples, Italy. In 1845, Josiah Gorgas and former West Point classmate John Hillhouse sailed to Europe for a six-month leave. The War Department directed Gorgas to use this time to study foreign ordnance; however, he also indulged his artistic interests by visiting art galleries and cultural heritage sites. Gorgas petitioned for an additional six months' leave, which was granted. He documented his travel and experience in a sketchbook.

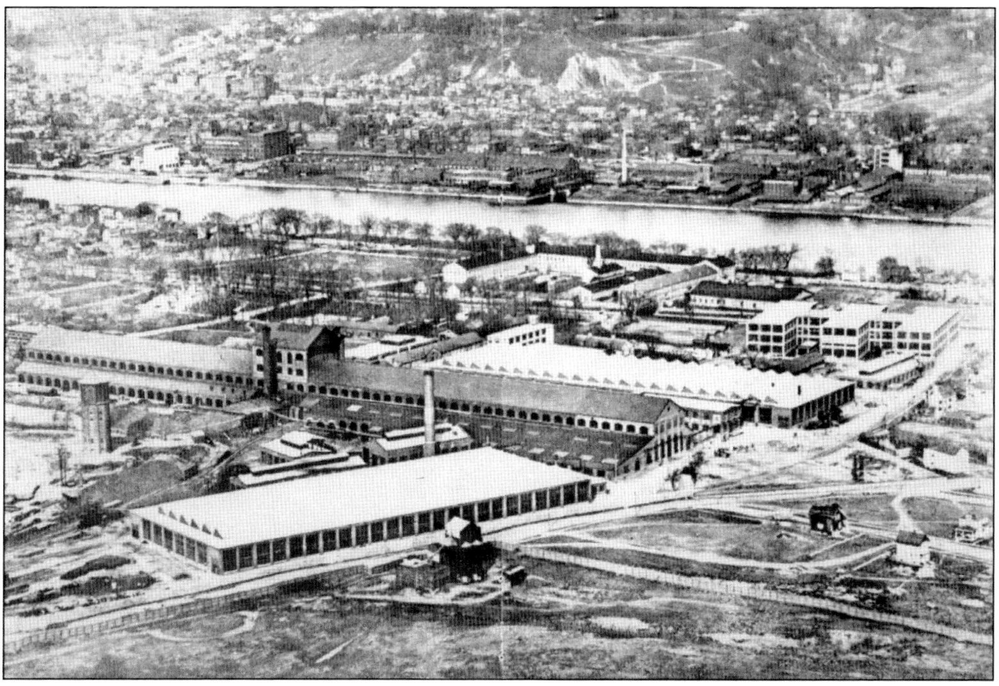

Watervliet Arsenal, New York. Following his European travel, Josiah Gorgas returned to his first post assignment at the Watervliet Arsenal in New York. Thereafter, he requested an assignment with Gen. Winfield Scott's campaign in the Mexican War and departed for Veracruz in 1847. He returned to the United States the following year for a brief post at the Champlain Arsenal in Vermont before returning to the Watervliet Arsenal. (LOC.)

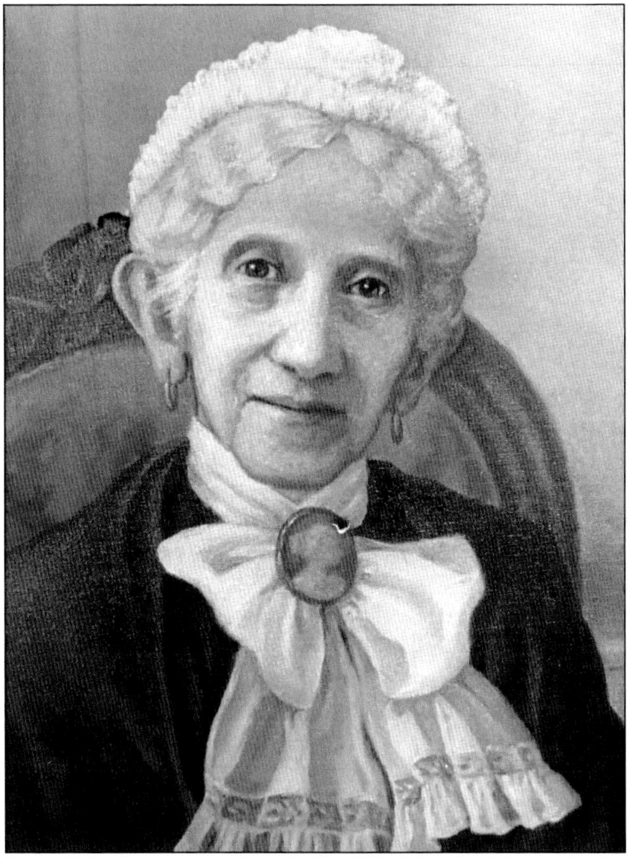

AMELIA ROSS GAYLE. Amelia Gayle, the third child of South Carolina natives John and Sarah Ann (Haynsworth) Gayle, was born in Greensboro, Alabama, shortly after the family relocated there in 1826. John Gayle, a judge for the Third Judicial Circuit, selected Greensboro for its central location within the district and its proximity to the capital in Tuscaloosa. In 1828, John Gayle resigned his judgeship to practice law. During this time, the Gayle family had a residence constructed in Greensboro (below). The following year, Gayle was elected as Speaker of the Alabama House of Representatives (1829–1831). There are no photographs or portraits of Amelia Gayle in her youth. This photograph depicts a portrait painted by Louise Lewis in the 1950s; it hangs in the parlor of the Gorgas House Museum. (Left, ULDSC; below, authors' collection.)

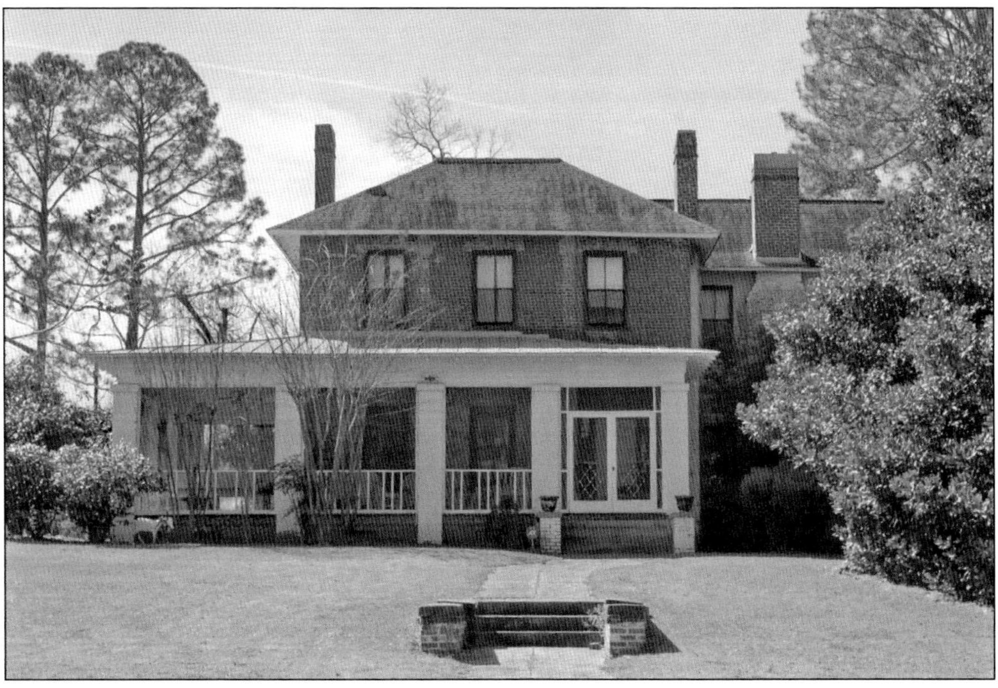

John Gayle, 1830s. John Gayle was elected Alabama's seventh governor in 1831, the same year the University of Alabama opened. Like his predecessors, Gayle also served as president of the university board of trustees. No governor's mansion had been constructed in Tuscaloosa at the time of Gayle's service. Consequently, Gayle and his family—his wife, Sarah, and their children, Matthew, Amelia, Sarah, Anna Maria, Richard, and Mary—boarded at Ewing's Tavern (below) from 1831 to 1833, followed by Medlock's Tavern and later a rental home. In 1835, Sarah Gayle died from tetanus. Governor Gayle's family and friends helped to care for their children until he remarried in 1837. Three of their daughters—Amelia, Sarah, and Mary—lived on the university campus with president Alva Woods and his wife, Almira, one of Sarah Gayle's closest friends. (Right, ADAH; below, LOC.)

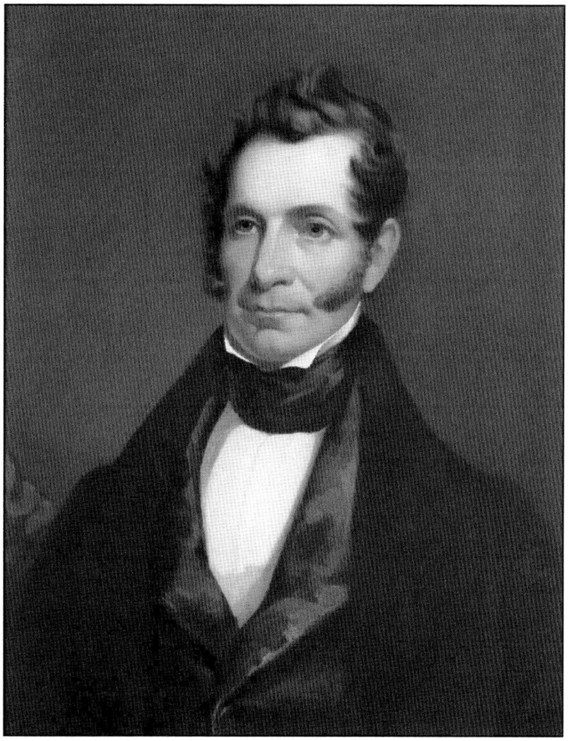

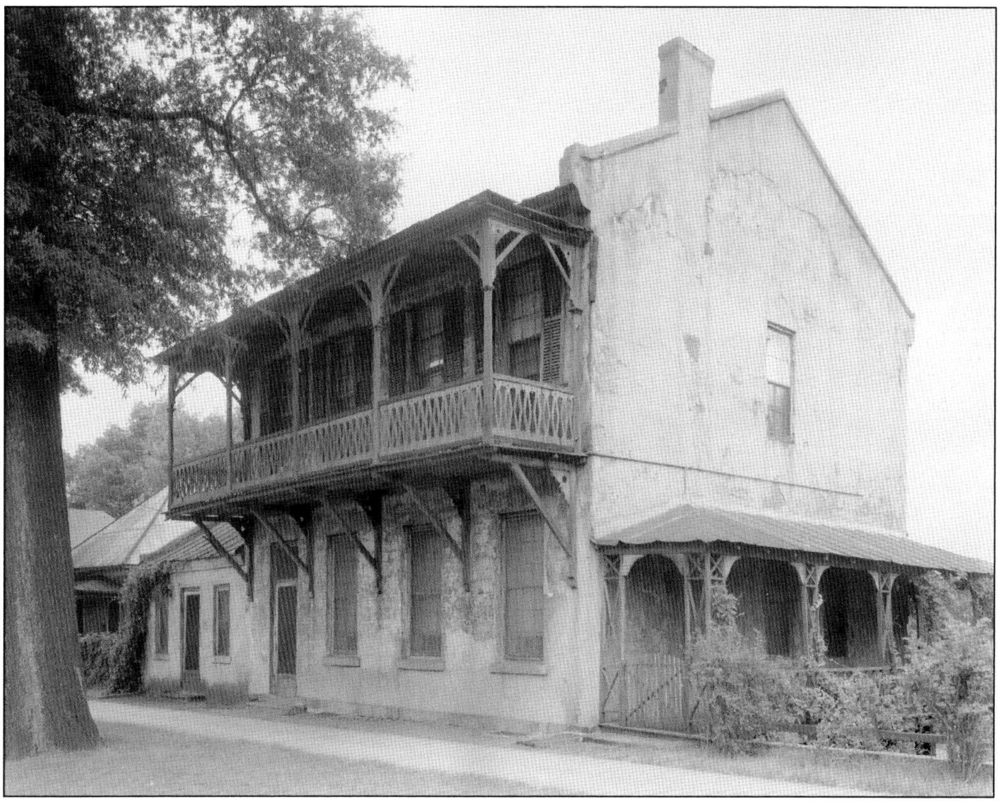

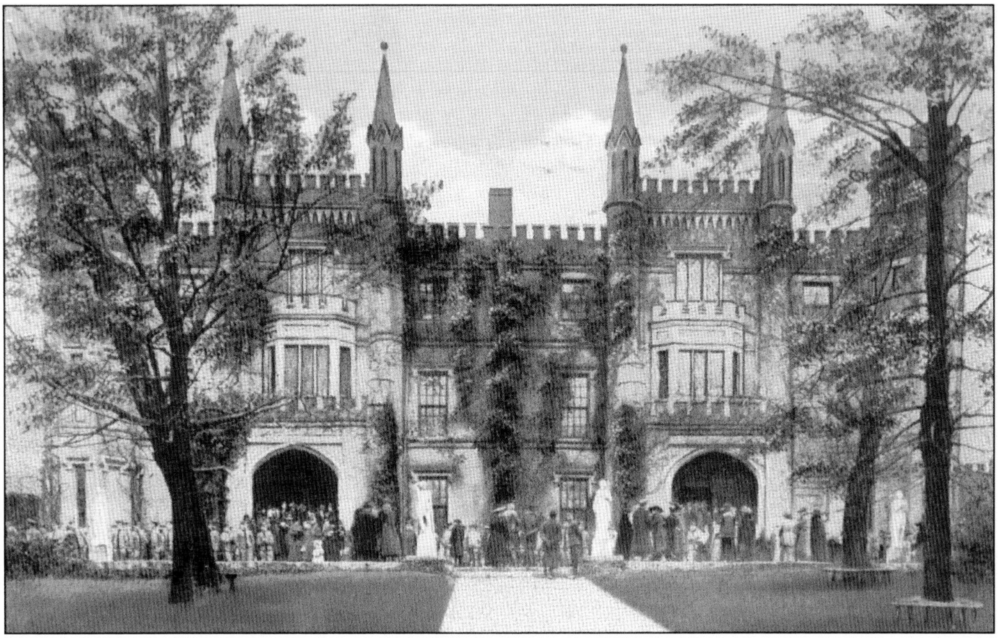

COLUMBIA FEMALE INSTITUTE, TENNESSEE. In 1841, Amelia Gayle was sent to Columbia, Tennessee, to attend the Columbia Female Institute, an Episcopal institution established in 1836. Amelia studied geography, French, arithmetic, music, and reading. After graduating, she returned to her family's home near Mobile. In the 1870s, Amelia's daughters, Jessie and Mamie Gorgas, also attended the Columbia Female Institute. (Authors' collection.)

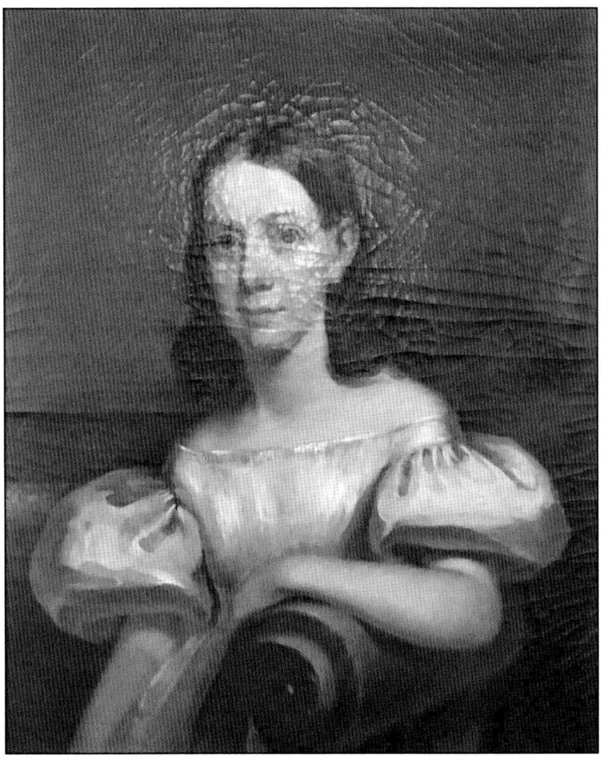

SARAH GAYLE CRAWFORD. Born on March 24, 1824, Sarah Gayle was Amelia's older sister. In 1842, Sarah married William Bones Crawford, a prominent physician from South Carolina. Together, they had four children: Clara, Amelia, William, and Sarah. When Dr. Crawford became ill with consumption (now known as tuberculosis), he and his wife traveled to Spain to seek improvement for his health. During their absence, their children were cared for by Sarah's extended family in Mobile. (GHM.)

Statuary Hall, US Capitol Building. In 1847, John Gayle was elected to the US House of Representatives. Because his second wife, Clarissa Peck, had recently given birth, she remained in Mobile, and Amelia was chosen to assist him in Washington, DC. The Old Hall of the House of Representatives, where Gayle served, was transformed into Statuary Hall in 1857. (LOC.)

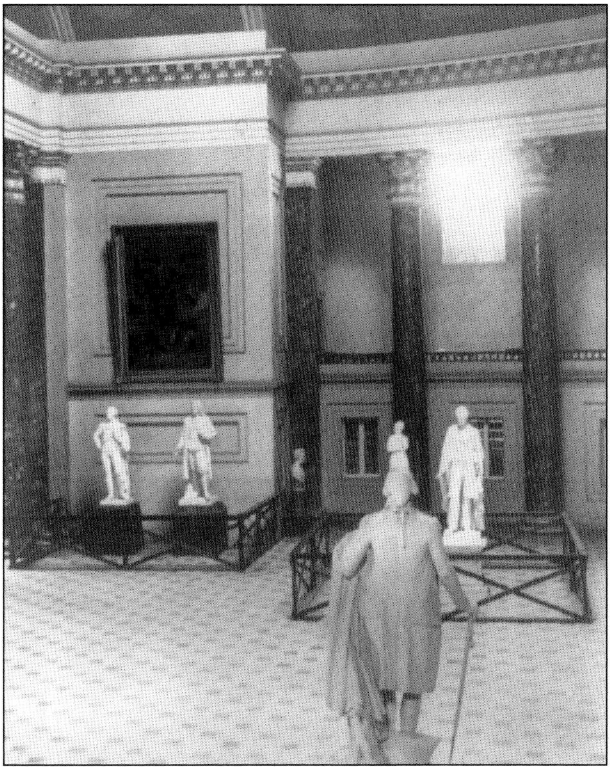

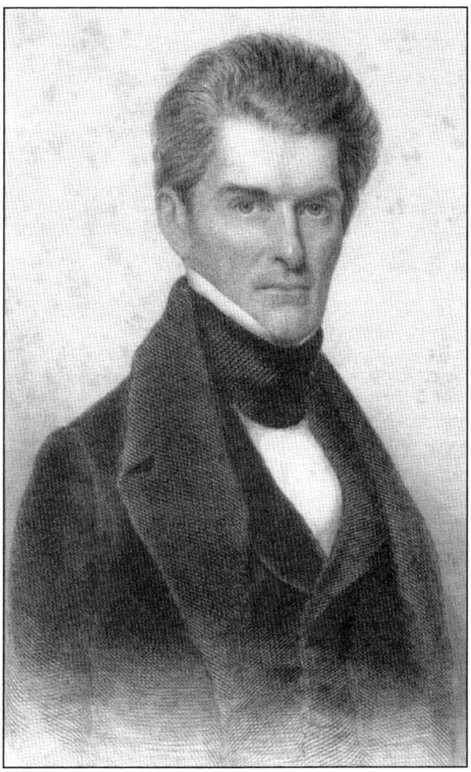

John C. Calhoun. When John and Amelia Gayle arrived in Washington, DC, they boarded in the same house as Sen. John Calhoun of South Carolina. During this time, Senator Calhoun became one of Amelia's close friends, and the two often discussed news and politics on morning walks together. According to archives records, this print of Calhoun was one of Amelia's favorite keepsakes.

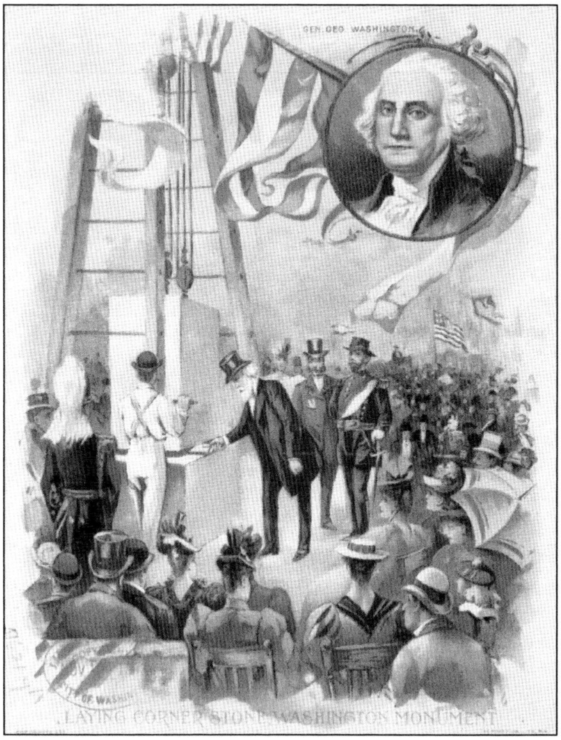

CORNERSTONE CEREMONY, WASHINGTON MONUMENT. On July 4, 1848, at the invitation of John Calhoun, Amelia Gayle was seated on the platform during the laying of the cornerstone of the Washington Monument. Because of financial constraints, John Gayle could not afford for Amelia to remain in Washington, DC, and she returned to Mobile at the end of the summer. (LOC.)

GAYLE HOUSE, TOULMINVILLE, ALABAMA. John Gayle served as a member of the US House of Representatives from 1847 to 1849. He did not seek reelection and returned to Toulminville in Mobile County, where he served as a US district judge until his death in 1859.

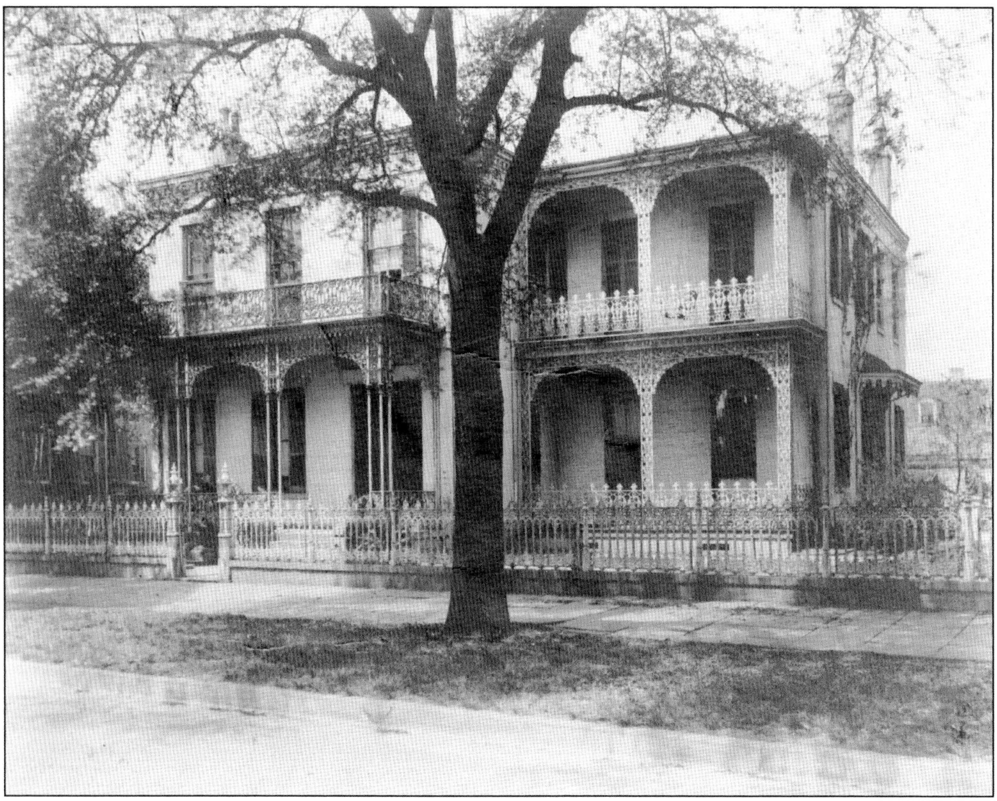

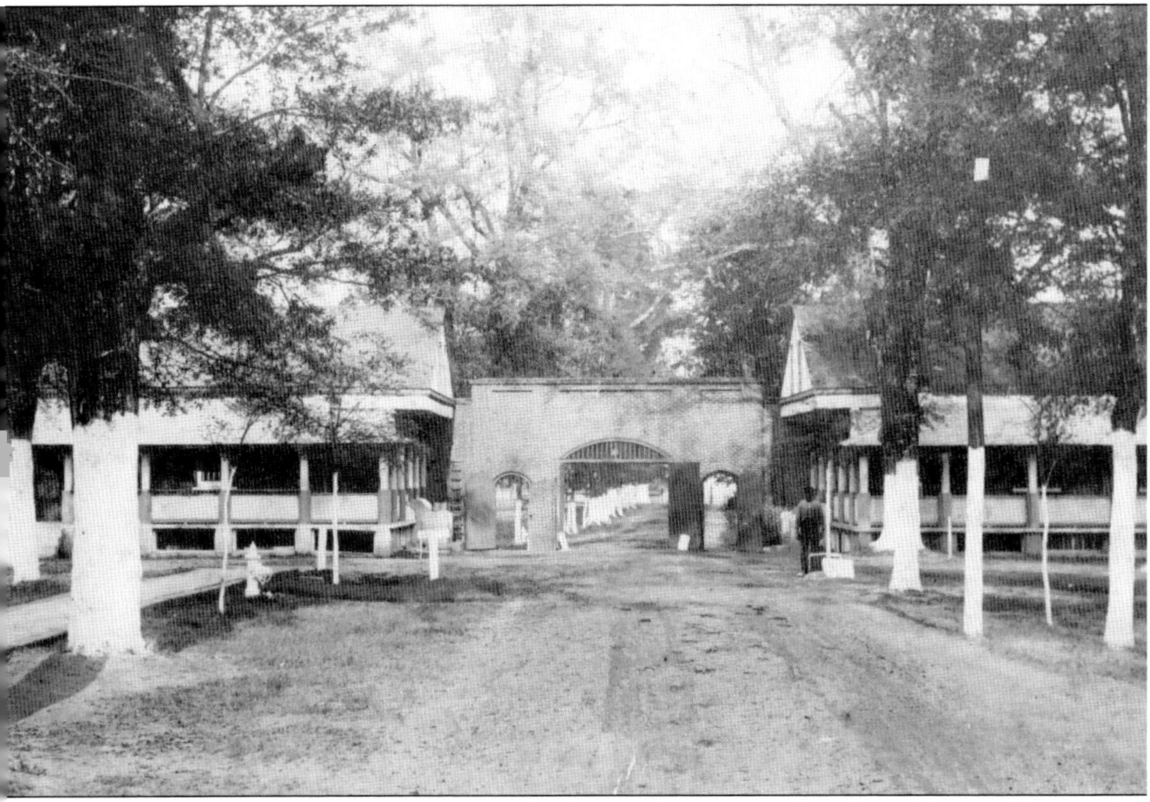

Mount Vernon Arsenal, Alabama. A yellow fever epidemic swept through Mobile in 1853, prompting Amelia Gayle to take her sister's children to an arsenal in Mount Vernon, Alabama, in northern Mobile County. At that time, her brother Matthew Gayle was serving as the arsenal's physician. Josiah Gorgas had been assigned to the arsenal earlier that year. According to museum lore, the proximity of the Gayle family's quarters to those of Josiah Gorgas allowed him to overhear Amelia reading to the children. Josiah supposedly fell in love with Amelia through her voice before ever meeting her. (LOC.)

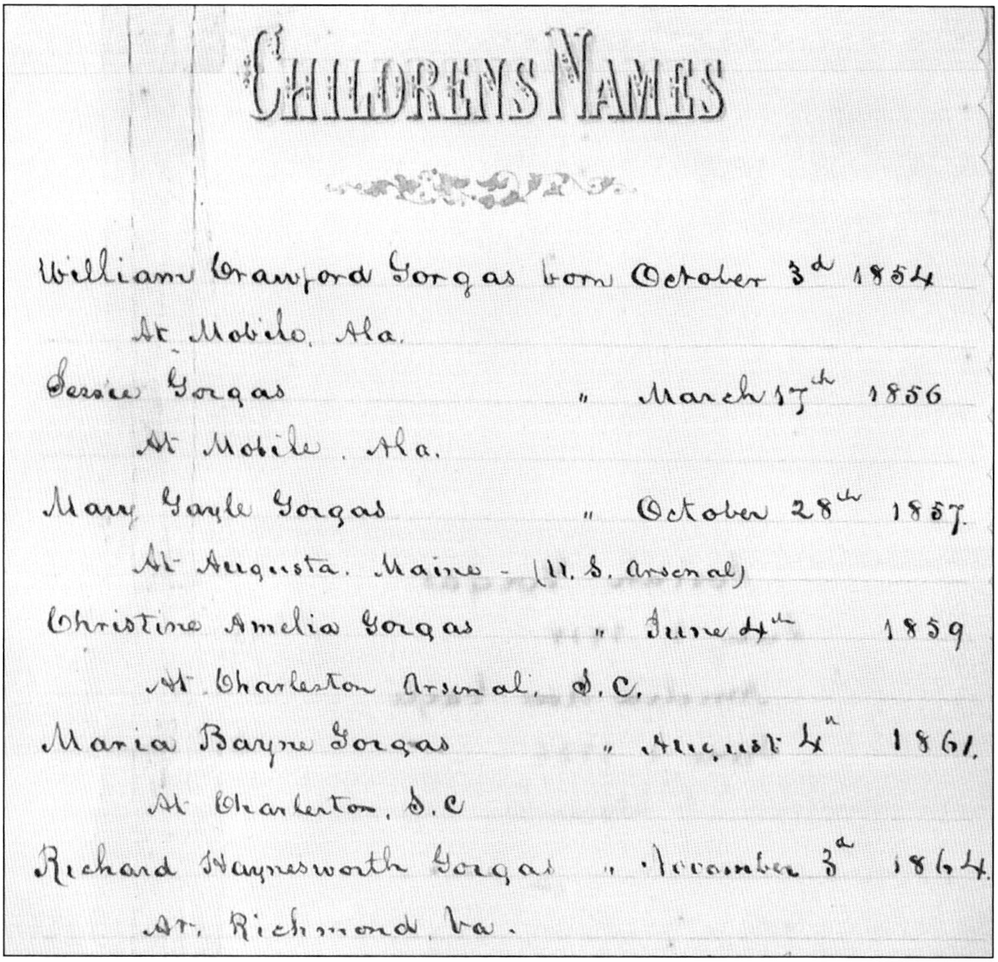

CHILDRENS NAMES

William Crawford Gorgas born October 3d 1854
At Mobile, Ala.
Jessie Gorgas " March 17th 1856
At Mobile, Ala.
Mary Gayle Gorgas " October 28th 1857.
At Augusta, Maine - (U. S. arsenal)
Christine Amelia Gorgas " June 4th 1859
At Charleston Arsenal, S.C.
Maria Bayne Gorgas " August 4th 1861.
At Charleston, S.C
Richard Haynesworth Gorgas " November 3d 1864.
At Richmond, Va.

Gorgas Family Bible. After a brief courtship, Josiah Gorgas and Amelia Gayle married on December 29, 1853. During the first decade of their marriage, they were stationed in various parts of the country, following US Army arsenal assignments in Maine, South Carolina, and Pennsylvania. They had six children: William Crawford, Jessie, Mary "Mamie," Christine "Minnie," Maria "Ria," and Richard. The children's names, places of birth, and birth dates were recorded in the Gorgas family Bible. (GHM.)

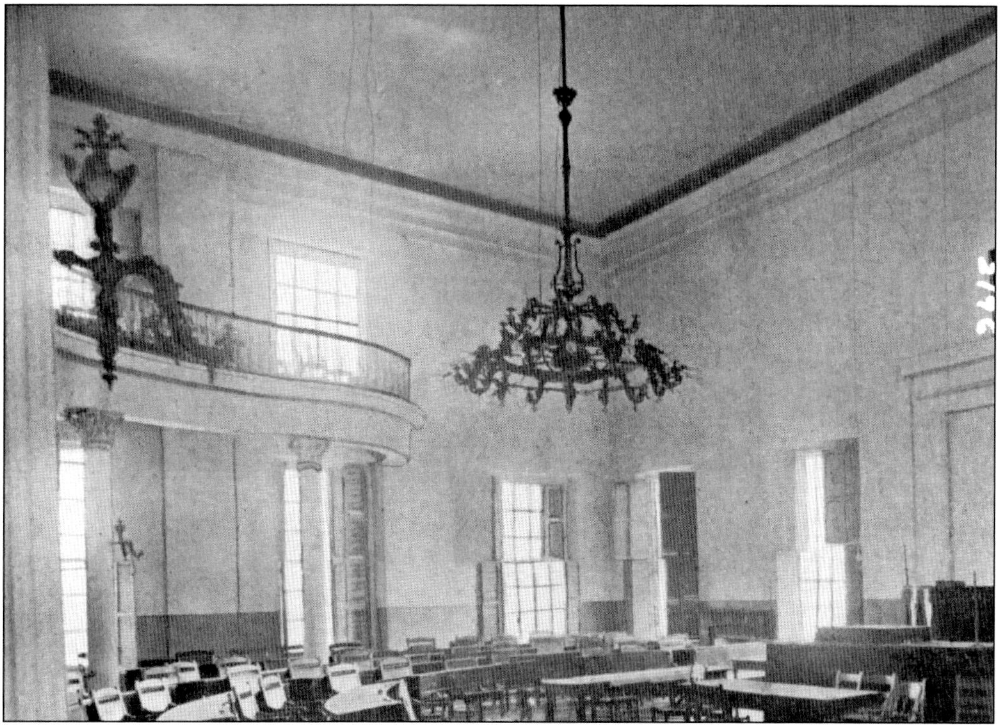

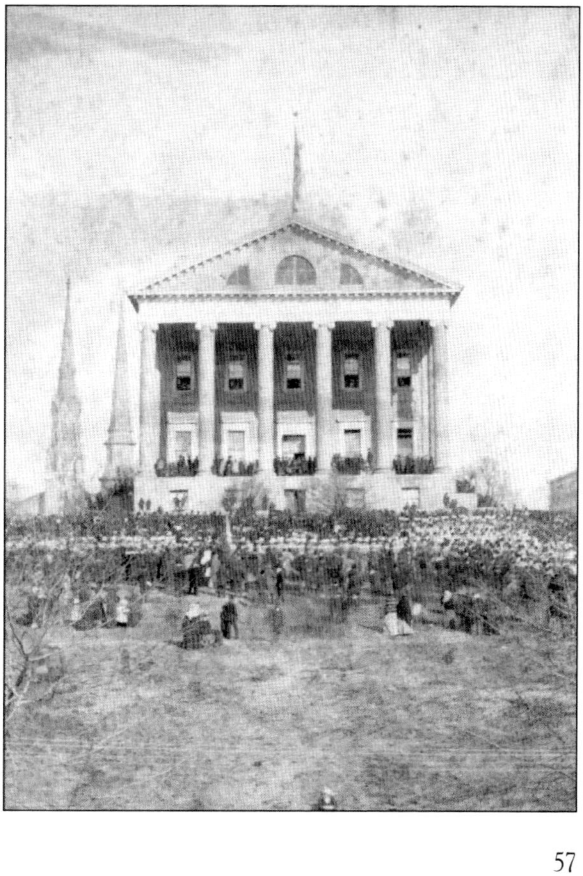

Alabama State House of Representatives. Josiah Gorgas was offered a commission with the Confederate army shortly after it was formed, but he did not accept until March 1861. In his journal dated March 31, Josiah wrote, "We leave here on 3d of April for Charleston where I shall leave all the family, and proceed myself to Montgomery, to report to the Secy of War (L.P. Walker [of Alabama])." On January 11, 1861, Alabama was the fourth state to secede from the Union. The following month, on February 4, the Provisional Confederate Congress convened in Montgomery, Alabama, in the state House of Representatives building (above). During this convention, the Confederate Constitution was drafted, and Jefferson Davis was elected as the provisional Confederate president. The Confederate Congress convened a second time in Montgomery before relocating to the capitol building (right) in Richmond, Virginia. (Both, LOC.)

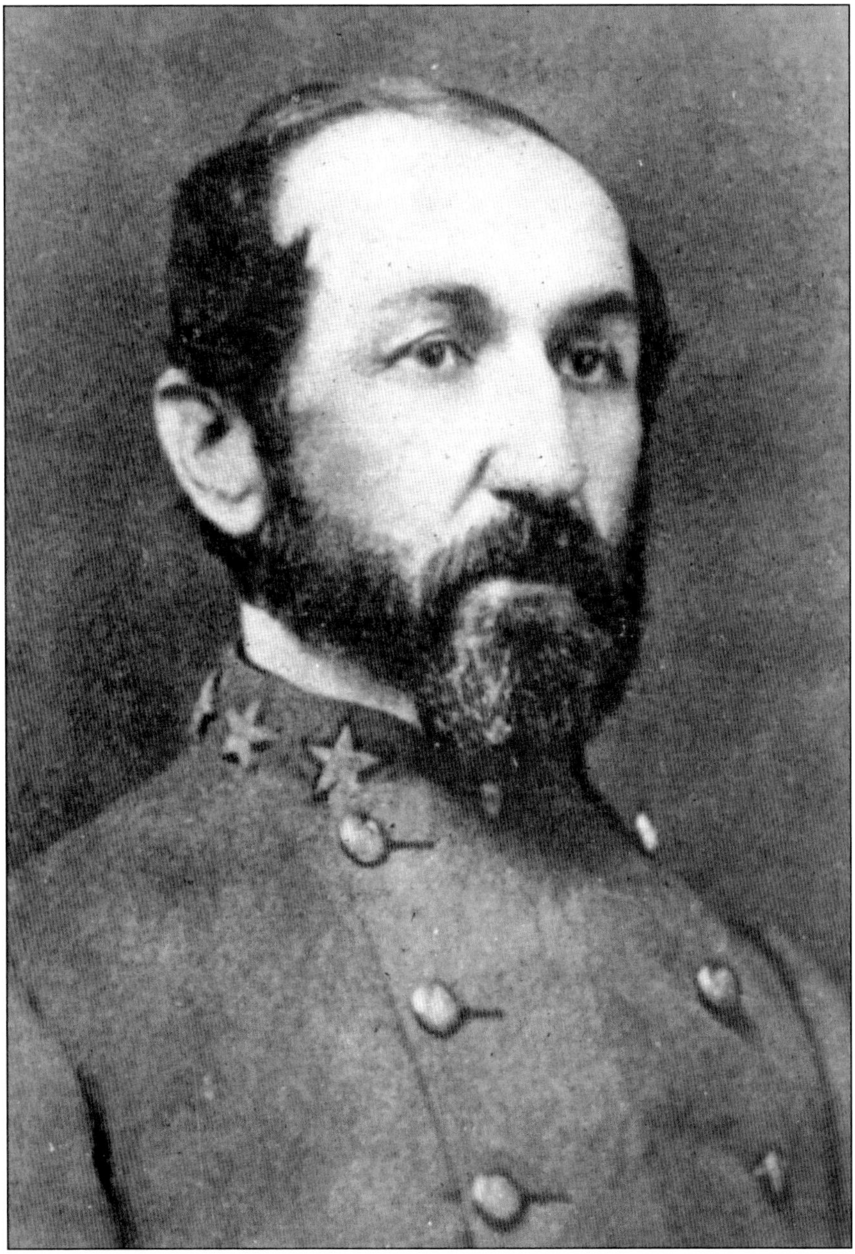

Josiah Gorgas, c. 1861. After his resignation from the US Army, Josiah Gorgas was named chief of the Confederate Ordnance Bureau on April 8, 1861. As part of the Confederate government, Gorgas, along with his family, relocated to the Confederate capital in Richmond, Virginia. When the Civil War began, the Confederacy had little heavy industry to make munitions. To overcome this barrier, Gorgas initiated an innovative multipoint approach. He established shipping lines from Europe, salvaged weapons from battlefields, and developed new production facilities throughout the South. For his ingenuity, Gorgas was awarded the rank of brigadier general on November 10, 1864. In his journal entry dated April 8, 1864, Gorgas recounted, "It is three years ago to-day since I took charge of the Ord. department of the Conf. States at Montgomery—three years of constant work and application. I have succeeded beyond my utmost expectations."

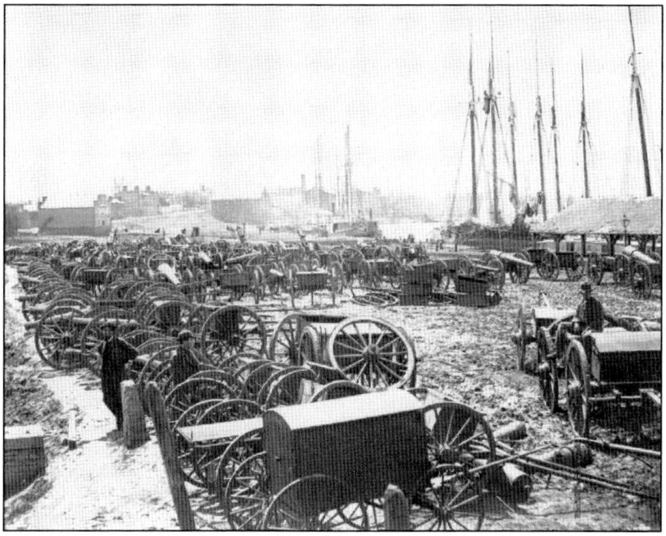

Confederate Artillery, Richmond, Virginia. Although the Confederate soldiers often experienced extended periods of time without adequate food or clothing, they were never without sufficient gunpowder or ammunition. According to Confederate general Braxton Bragg, "[Josiah] Gorgas organized the only successful military bureau during [the Confederate] national existence, and this is the more surprising, as [he] had less foundation to go on than any other." (LOC.)

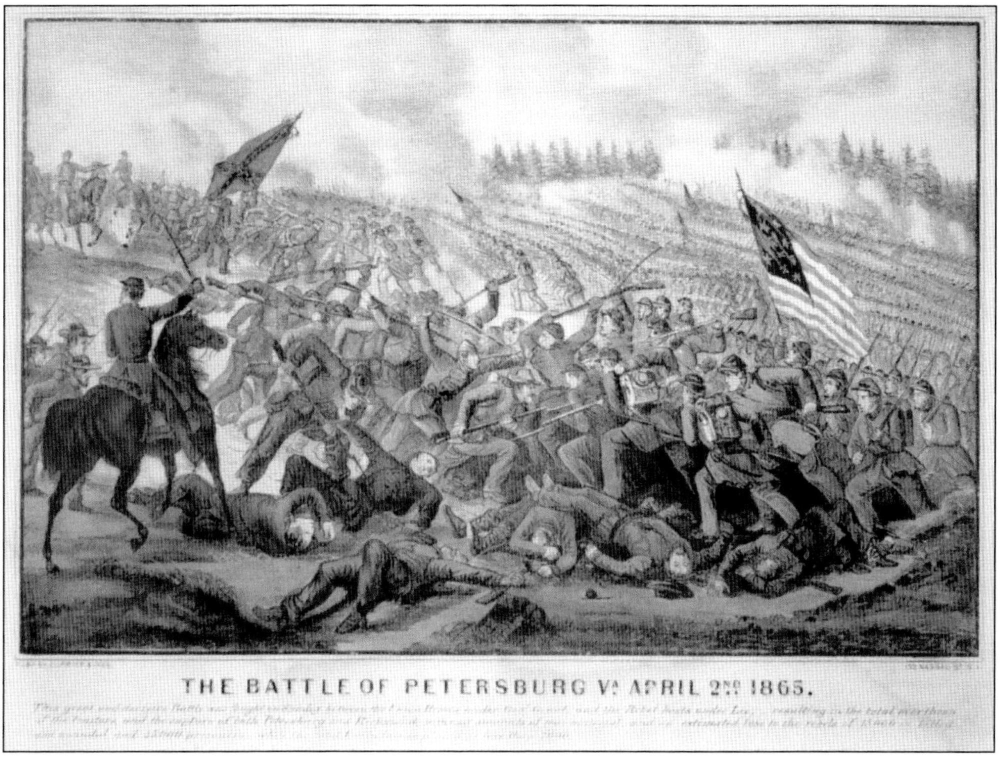

The Fall of Petersburg, Virginia, April 2, 1865. After the fall of Petersburg, Virginia, it was clear that Richmond was next. On April 2, Confederate president Jefferson Davis and his cabinet, which included Josiah Gorgas, left on the last train out of Richmond. Unable to go with them, Amelia Gorgas took their children to stay with her sister Maria Gayle Bayne in Richmond before relocating to Maryland. During the retreat, soldiers set fire to bridges and military targets throughout the city. (LOC.)

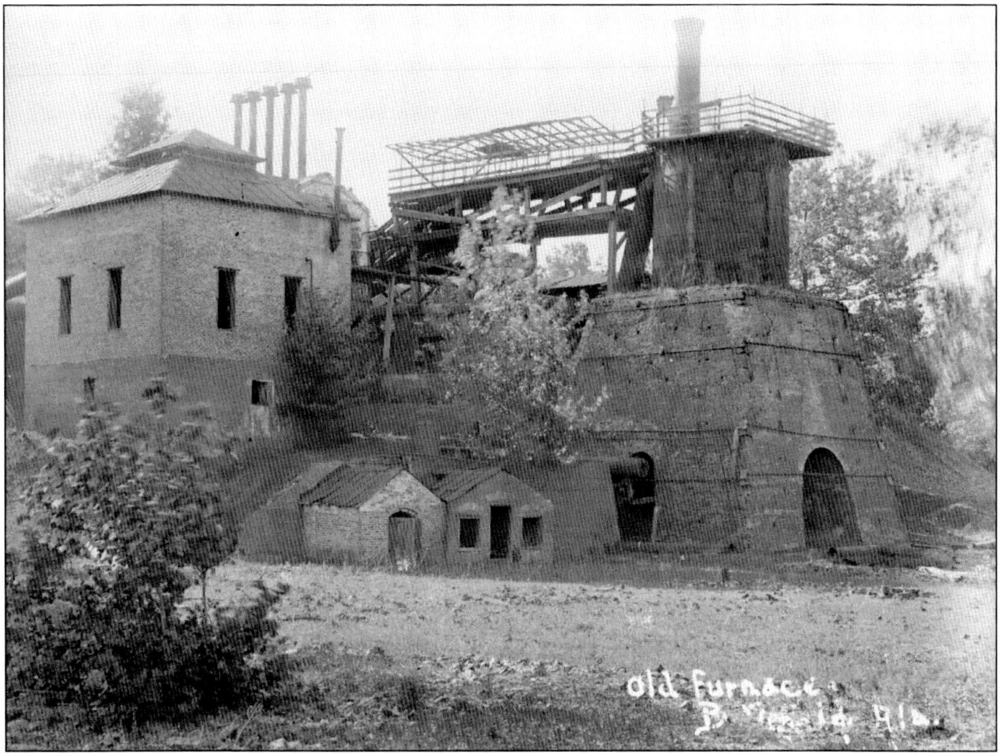

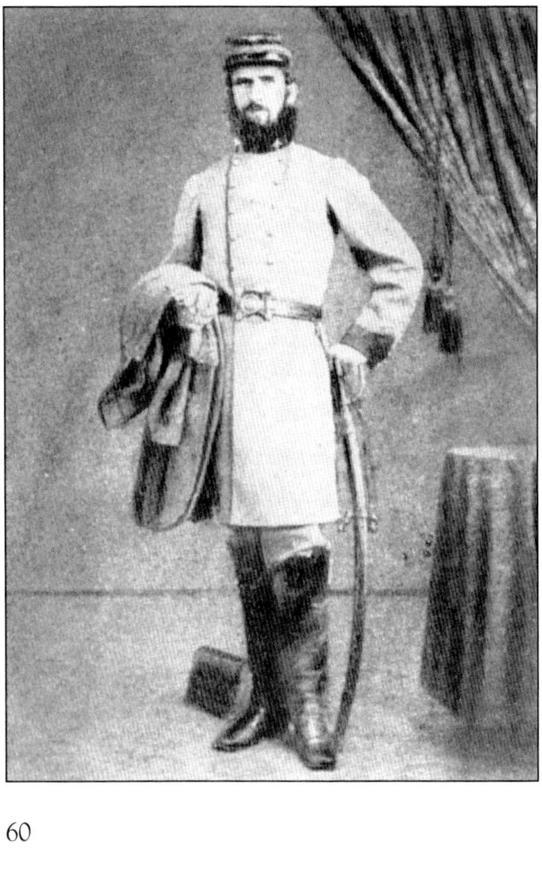

BRIERFIELD FURNACE, BIBB COUNTY, ALABAMA. After the war, Josiah Gorgas and colleagues Francis Strother Lyon, Dr. Bryan Whitfield, John Collins, Dr. James Browder, Frank Griffin, and William Ross founded the Canebrake Company. In 1866, they purchased the Bibb County Iron Company (also called the Brierfield Furnace) for $45,000. Soon thereafter, Gorgas hired John Mallet (left) to help modernize the furnace. Mallet was a nationally renowned scientist, former chemistry professor at the University of Alabama, and former superintendent of the Confederate ordnance in Macon, Georgia. Despite Mallet's assistance, the furnace struggled to earn a profit, and Gorgas suffered financial hardship. (Above, ADAH; left, LOC.)

JOSIAH GORGAS, C. 1872. In 1869, Josiah Gorgas left the ironworks at Brierfield to accept the position of headmaster of the Junior Department at the University of the South in Sewanee, Tennessee. In 1872, Gorgas was promoted to the position of vice-chancellor of the university. (USA.)

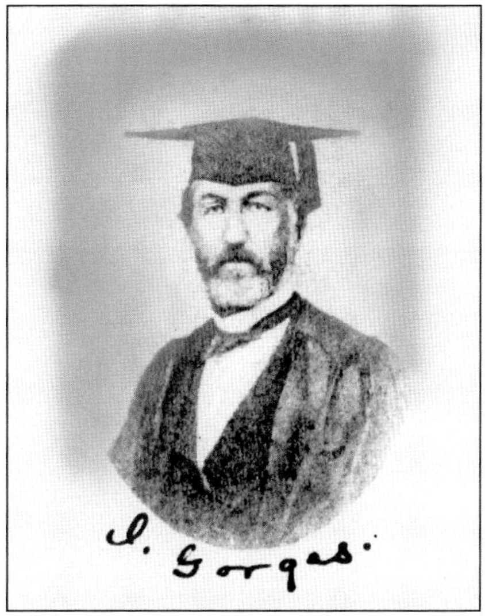

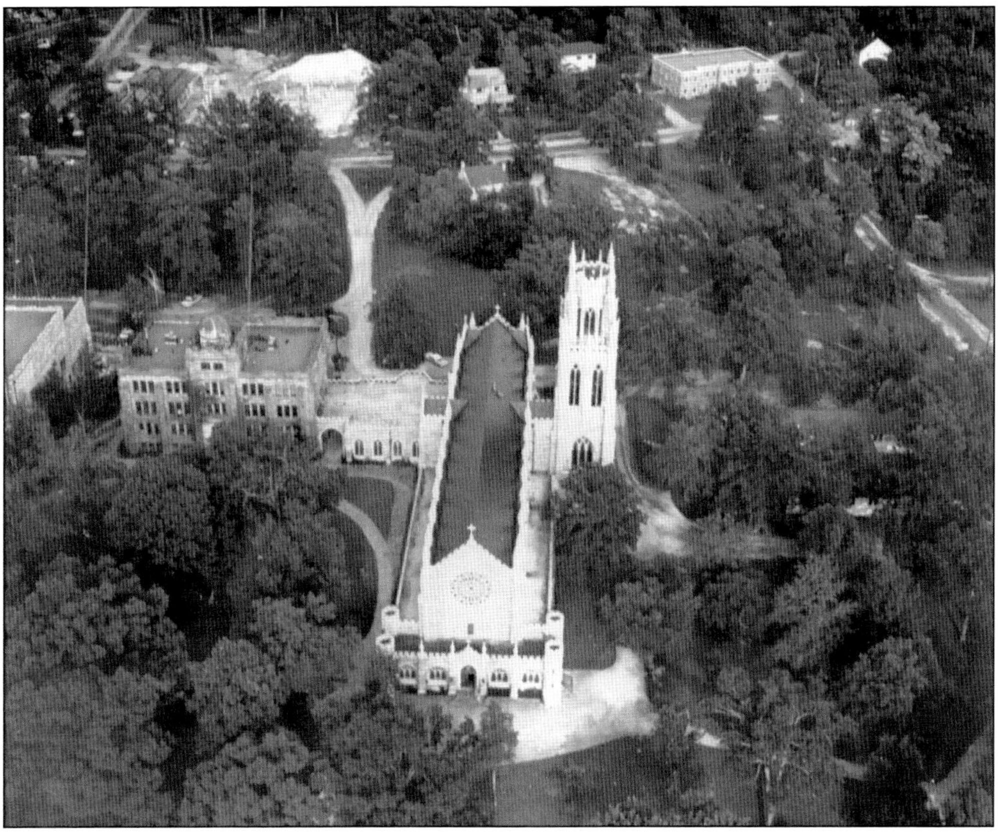

UNIVERSITY OF THE SOUTH, SEWANEE, TENNESSEE. Episcopal delegates from throughout the South founded the University of the South in 1857. The cornerstone was laid in 1860; however, the Civil War delayed the opening until 1868. When Josiah Gorgas was hired in 1869, the trustees hoped his military prestige would benefit the fledgling university. During his tenure, Gorgas's duties included administrative and construction oversights, fundraising, teaching, and the recruitment of students. (TSLA.)

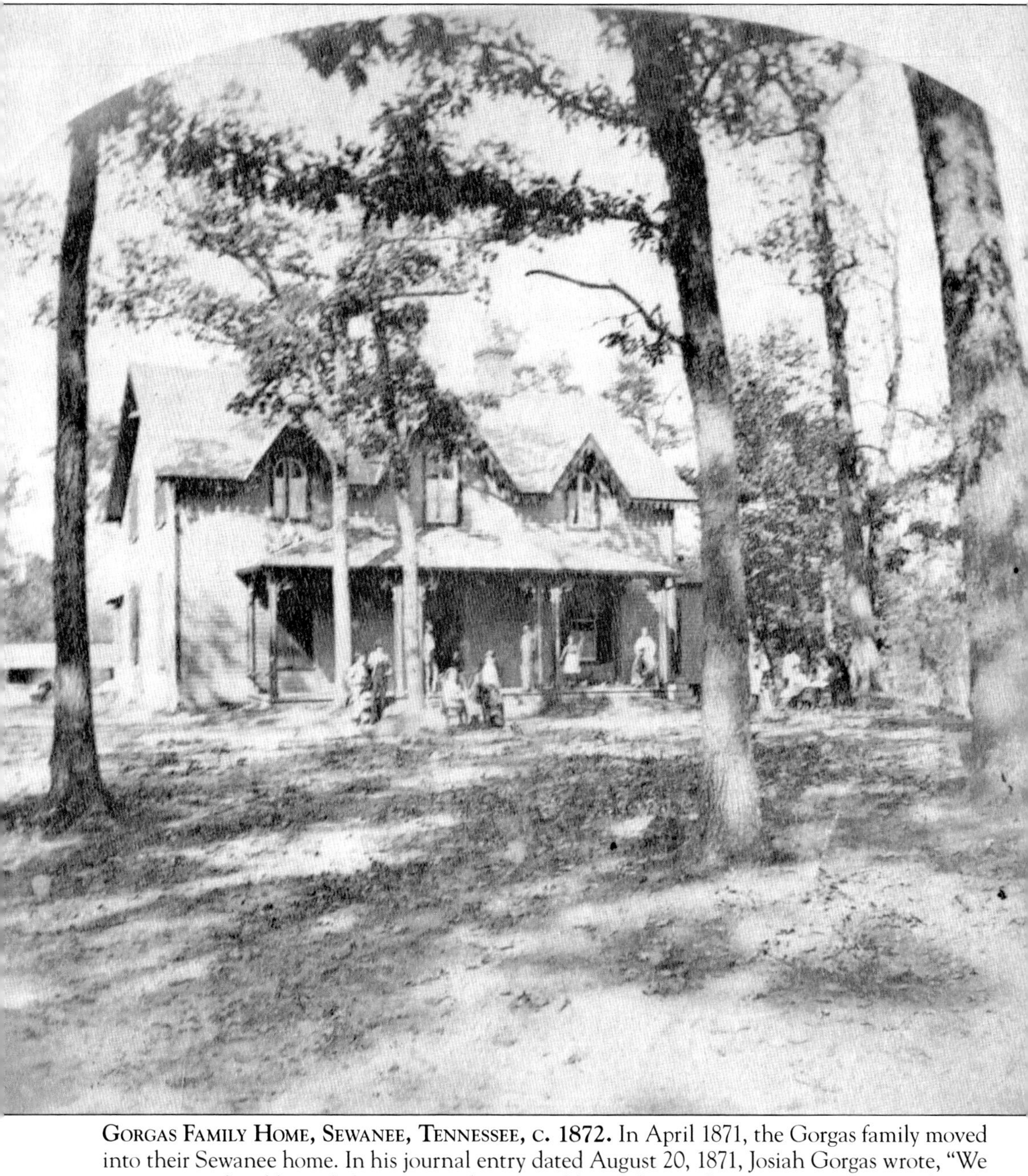

Gorgas Family Home, Sewanee, Tennessee, c. 1872. In April 1871, the Gorgas family moved into their Sewanee home. In his journal entry dated August 20, 1871, Josiah Gorgas wrote, "We are now comfortably settled in our new home, and have plenty of room to entertain our friends during the summer. We have not been without guests since the **1st** of July." Gorgas named the home Brierfield in tribute to the Alabama foundry. (USA.)

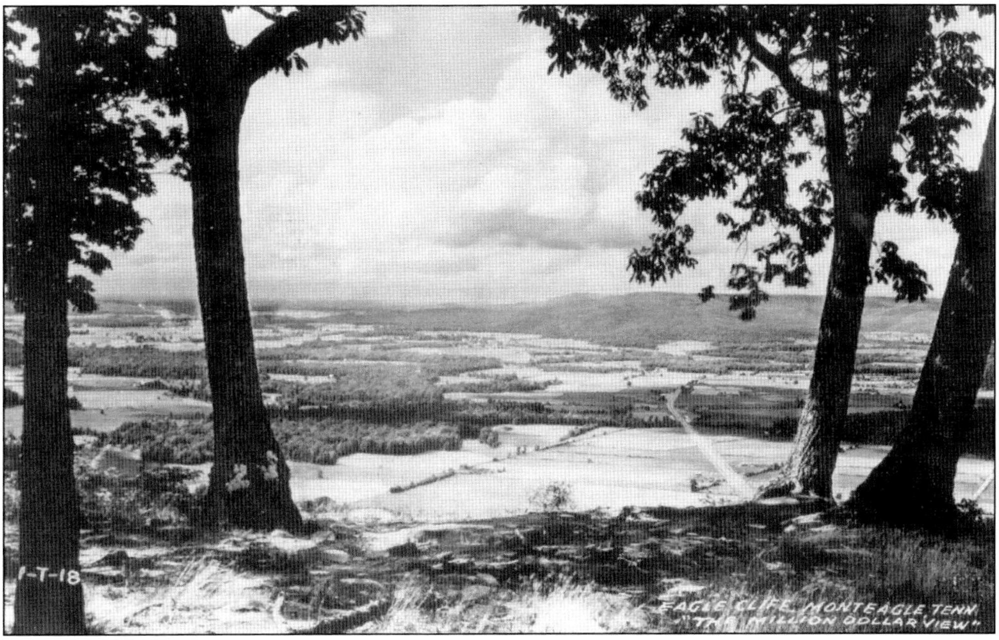

MONTEAGLE, TENNESSEE. In 1873, after attending the Columbia Female Institute, Jessie and Mamie Gorgas, two of Josiah and Amelia's four daughters, enrolled at the newly established Fairmont College in Monteagle, Tennessee. According to Fairmont principal Silas McBee, this female Episcopal college was "for girls what Sewanee [the University of the South] was for young men." From 1886 to 1889, Ria Gorgas, the youngest daughter of Josiah and Amelia Gorgas, taught at Fairmont before attending nursing school in New York. (Authors' collection.)

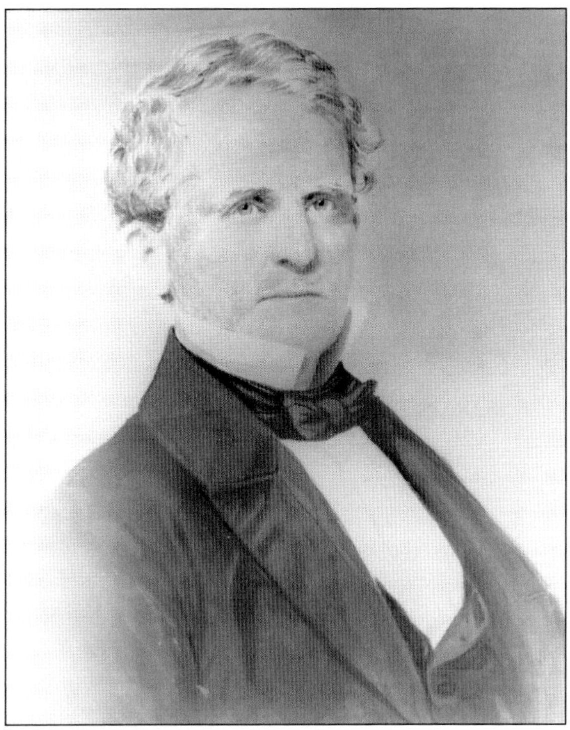

FRANCIS STROTHER LYON. Following graduation, Ria Gorgas remained in New York to care for Amelia Lyon, daughter of Francis Strother Lyon. Francis Lyon was a family friend and former investor in the Brierfield ironworks venture. (ADAH.)

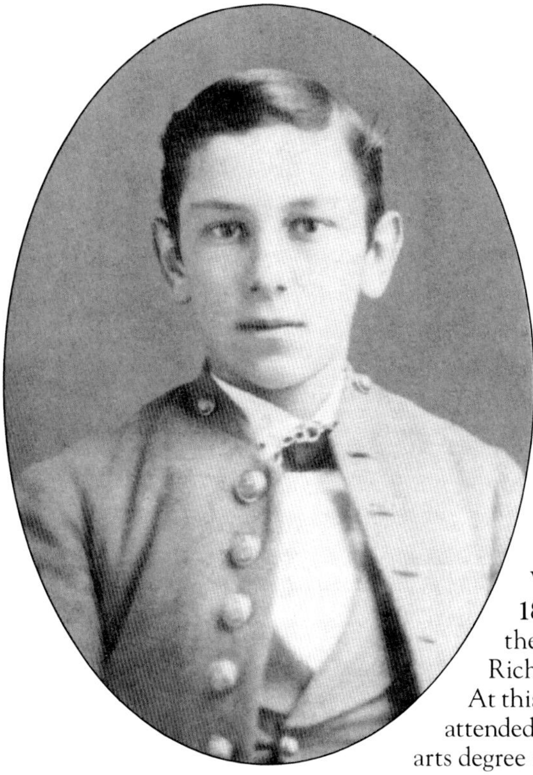

Richard Gorgas (left), c. 1878, and William Crawford Gorgas (below), c. 1875. While Josiah Gorgas was employed at the University of the South, his younger son, Richard, attended grammar school in Sewanee. At this same time, his elder son, William Crawford, attended the university, graduating with a bachelor of arts degree in 1875. (Left, GHM; below, ULDSC.)

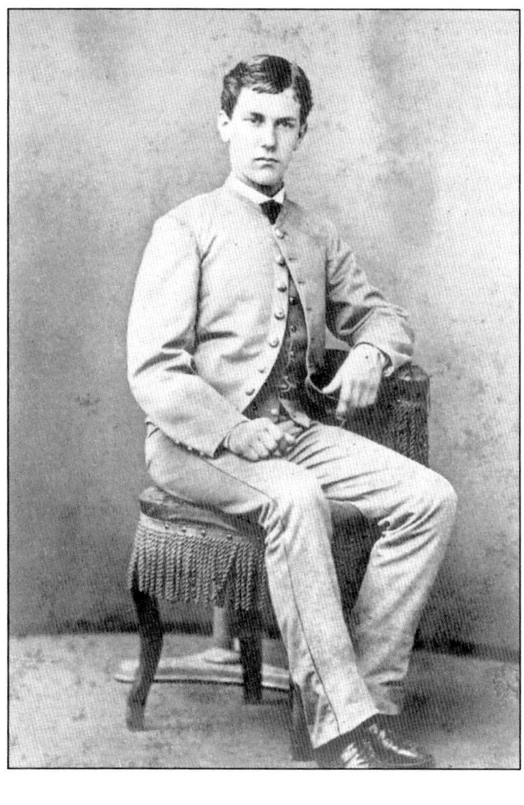

WILLIAM CRAWFORD GORGAS, C. 1876. After graduating from the University of the South, William Crawford Gorgas spent a year working in his uncle's New Orleans law office. Dispassionate about a legal career, he enrolled in the Bellevue Hospital Medical College in New York in 1876.

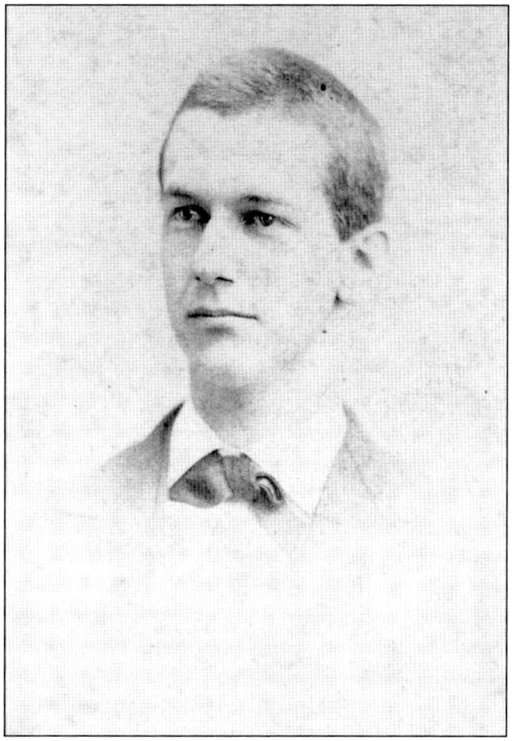

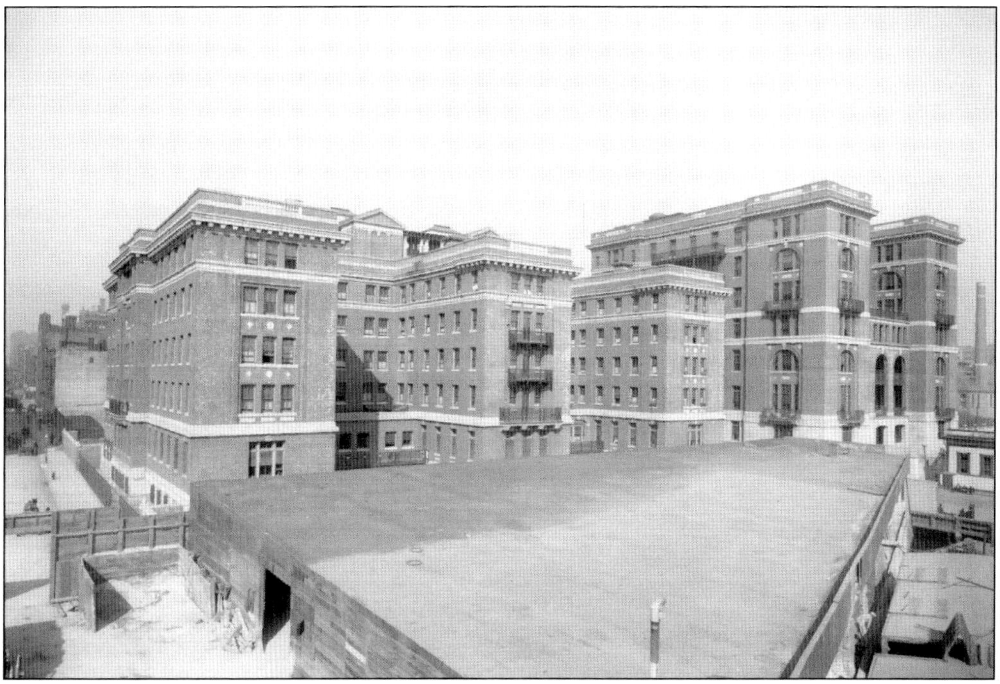

BELLEVUE HOSPITAL MEDICAL COLLEGE. During his senior year at Bellevue Hospital Medical College, William Crawford Gorgas volunteered his services at the New York Insane Asylum on Blackwell's Island (now Roosevelt Island). Gorgas graduated in 1879 and accepted an internship at Bellevue Hospital.

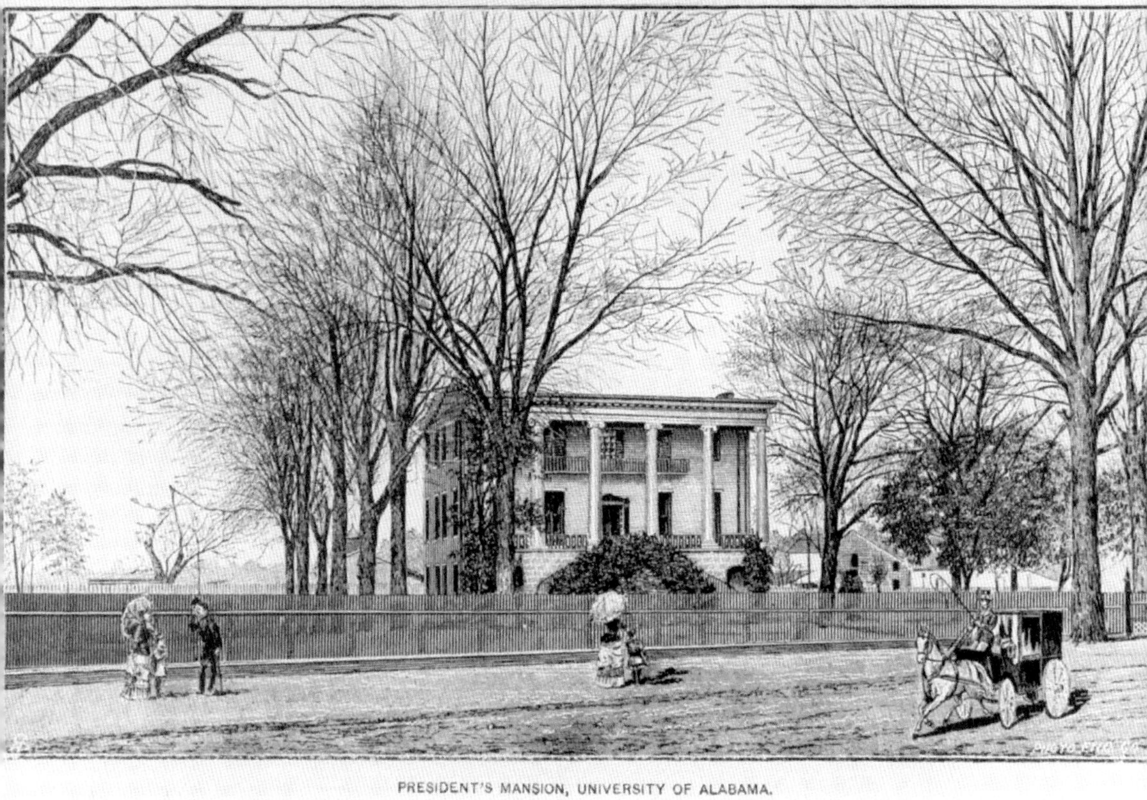

PRESIDENT'S MANSION, UNIVERSITY OF ALABAMA. In July 1878, Josiah Gorgas was selected as the president of the University of Alabama. After the Civil War, the university reopened as a military school and the board of trustees hoped that Gorgas's military experience could restore order to a campus still challenged by disciplinary issues. While serving as president, Gorgas and his family resided in the President's Mansion on the university campus.

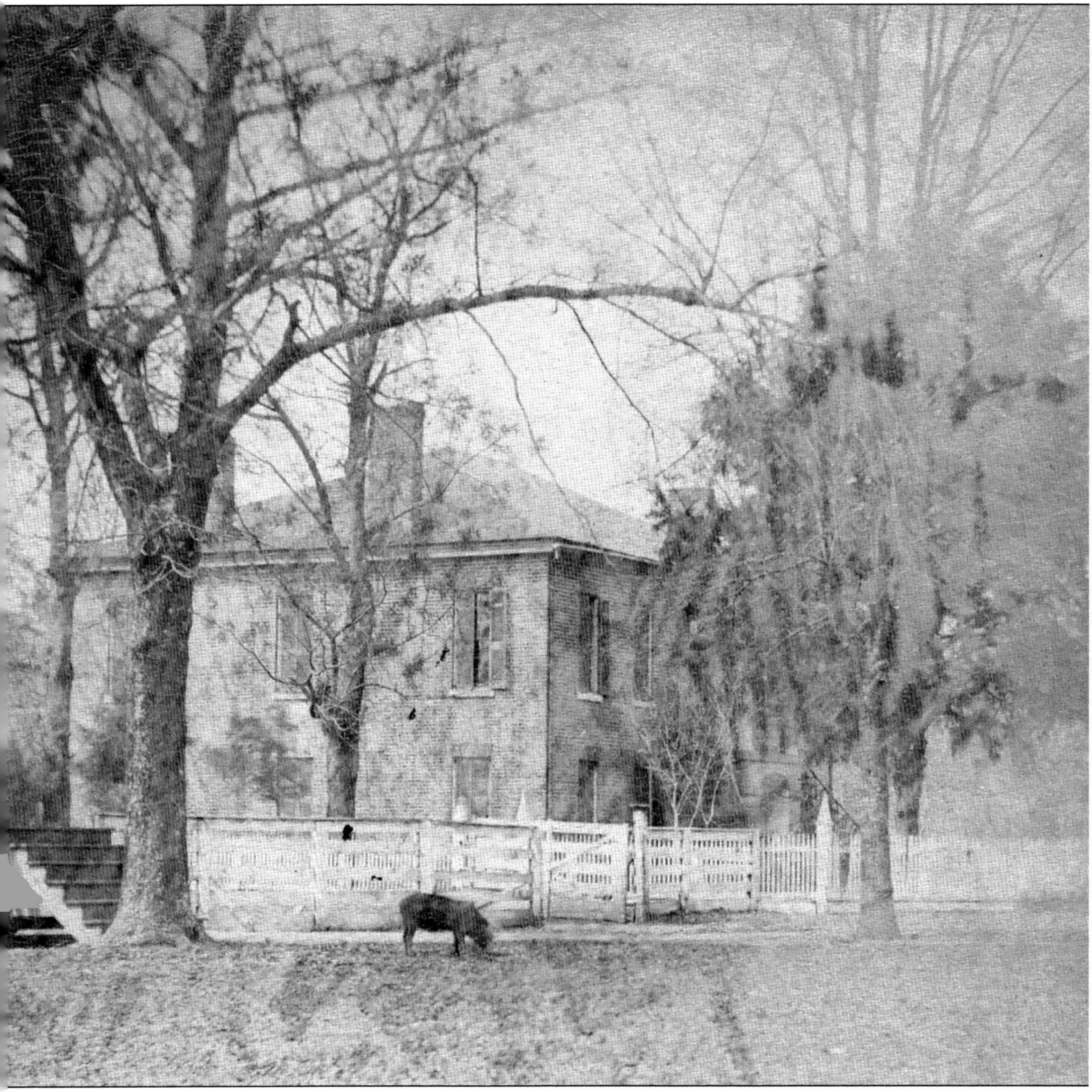

FORMER STEWARD'S HALL, C. 1874. For years, student health had been a recurring problem on the university campus. In the president's report for July 1879, Josiah Gorgas announced, "[An] immediate provision will be made for the care of the sick, by the institution of a permanent hospital department, in charge of a competent matron under the direction of the [university] Surgeon. The upper story of the old Steward's Hall would afford sufficient room, and the services of a lady as matron, could be secured for a salary of $200 per annum, with meals served from the Mess Hall." This is the oldest known photograph of the former Steward's Hall. (ADAH.)

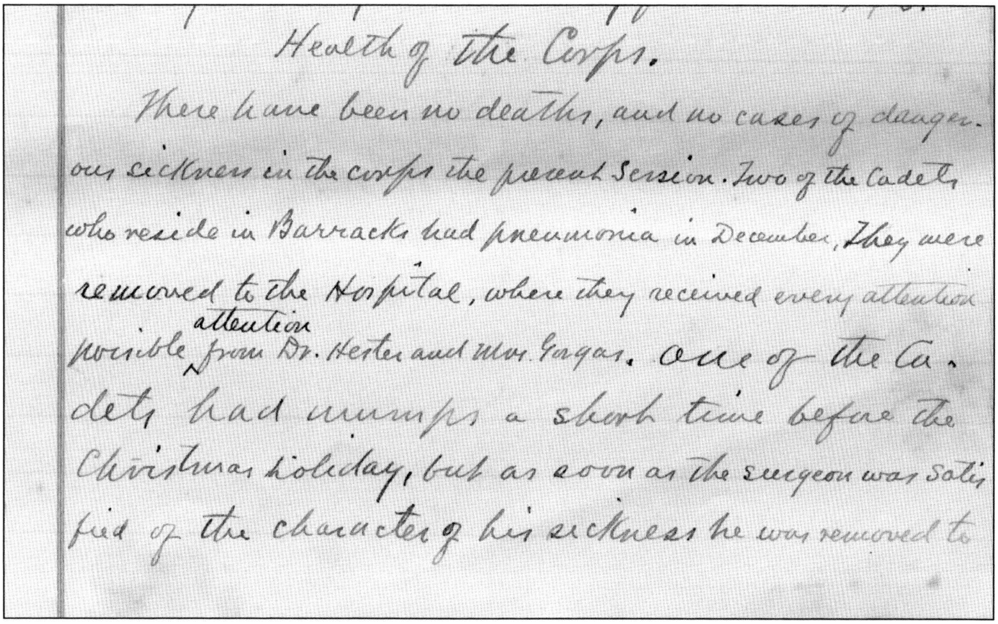

Health of the Corps.

There have been no deaths, and no cases of danger-
ous sickness in the corps the present Session. Two of the Cadets
who reside in Barracks had pneumonia in December, They were
removed to the Hospital, where they received every attention
possible attention from Dr. Hester and Mrs. Gorgas. One of the Ca-
dets had mumps a short time before the
Christmas holiday, but as soon as the surgeon was satis-
fied of the character of his sickness he was removed to

REPORT TO THE BOARD OF TRUSTEES, 1879. The trustees granted Josiah Gorgas's request to have the university infirmary located on the second floor of the former Steward's Hall. In September 1879, his wife, Amelia Gorgas, was selected as the university nurse matron. The ability to segregate sick cadets from their classmates swiftly improved student health.

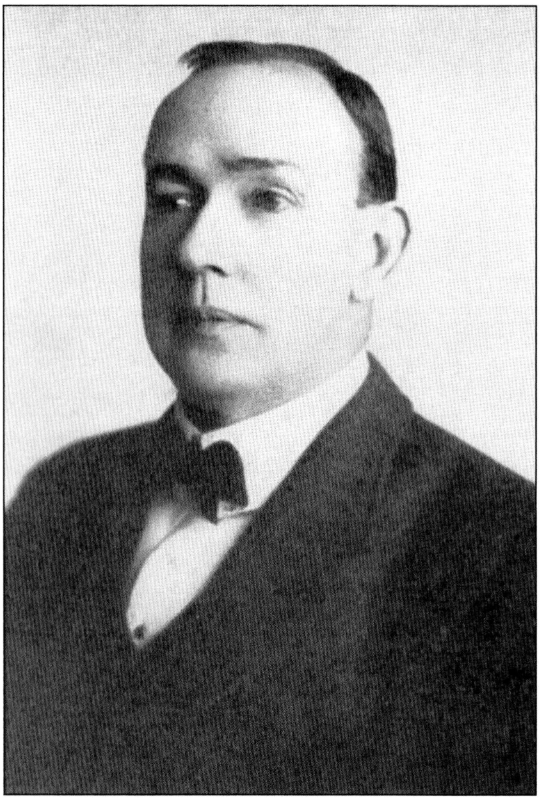

WILLIAM G. SOMERVILLE. Dr. Somerville served as surgeon for the University of Alabama from 1895 to 1896, as well as in 1898 and 1906. Upon Amelia Gorgas's retirement from the university in 1907, she requested that she be relieved of "conducting the college hospital without forfeiting the use of the house in which the hospital was conducted." The university honored her request, and Dr. Somerville cared for the students at his private infirmary.

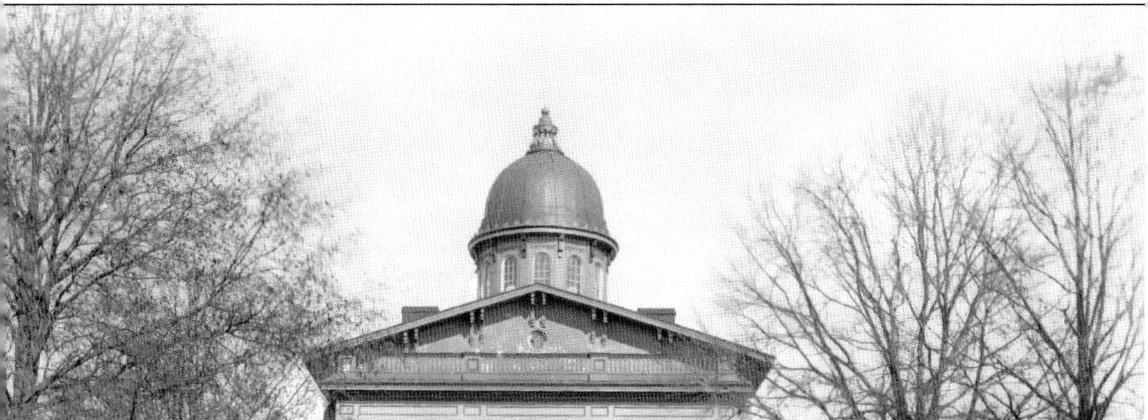

Bryce Hospital. Opened in 1861, the Alabama State Hospital for the Insane in Tuscaloosa is the oldest psychiatric facility in Alabama. Later named for Peter Bryce, a physician and the facility's first administrator, the hospital operated differently from most mental health institutions of the time. Bryce required that all patients be treated with respect and kindness and instituted a work program for patients, which included crafts, farming, and sewing. The Gorgas and Bryce families became close friends during Josiah Gorgas's presidency, when J.T. Searcy, the hospital's second superintendent, served as Josiah's physician.

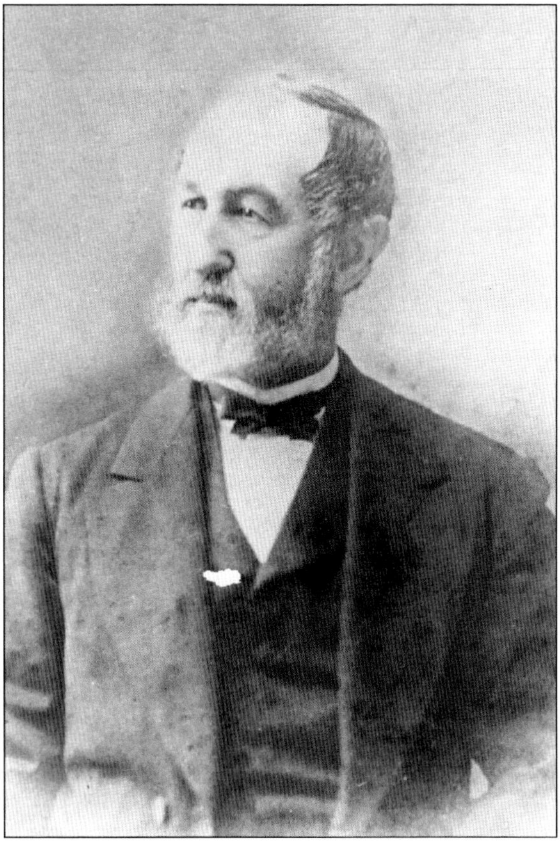

Josiah Gorgas, c. 1878. Due to an extended illness and stroke, Josiah Gorgas resigned as president in 1879. At that time, the board of trustees publicly proclaimed appreciation for "the great improvement he effected in the order and discipline of the Cadets; and particularly, of the admirable system and method which he observed in keeping his books and accounts; and of the clearness and correctness of his business reports to the Trustees." The trustees offered Gorgas a secondary position as the university librarian and a new residence in the former Steward's Hall, where the university hospital was located. The drawing below is from the 1906 edition of university yearbook, the *Corolla*. The President's Mansion and former Steward's Hall both served as campus residences of the Gorgas family.

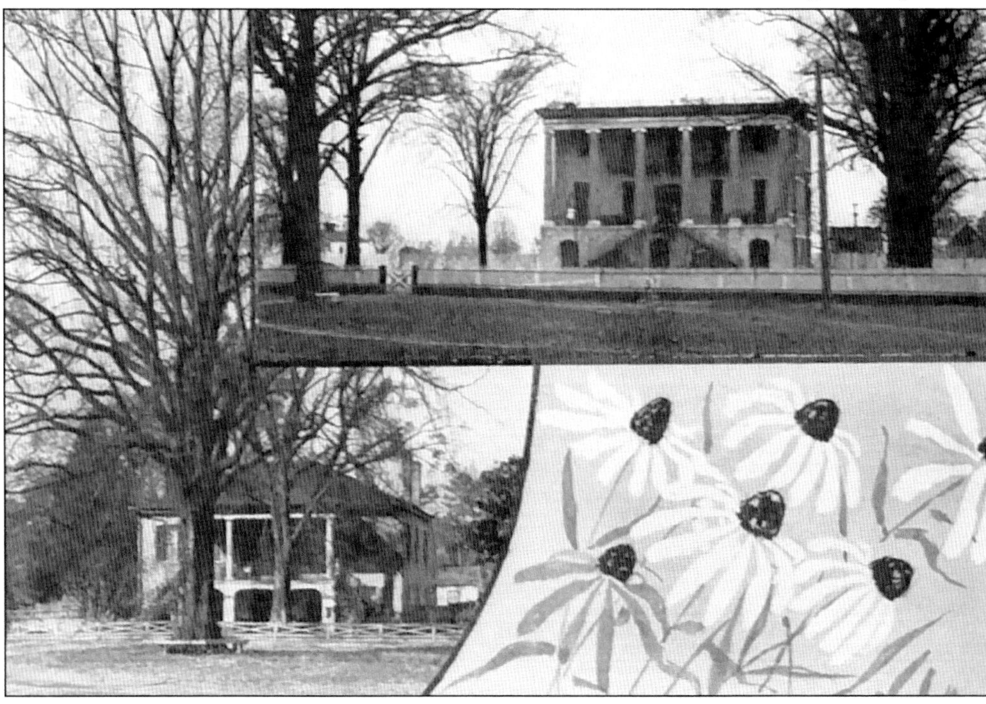

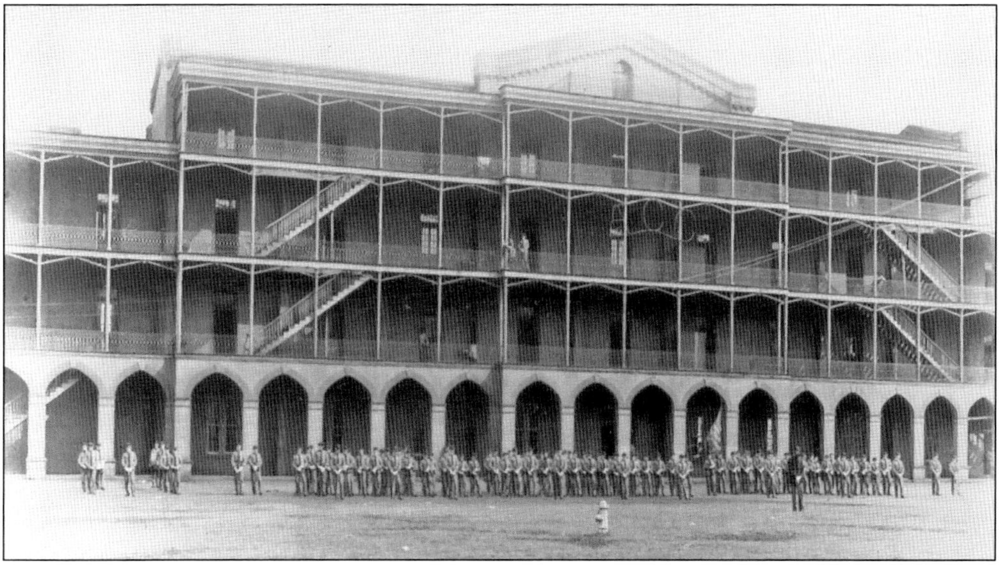

Woods Hall, c. 1890. Josiah Gorgas served as the campus librarian from 1879 until his death in 1883. During this time, the library was housed in Woods Hall, shown here surrounded by university cadets. In 1882, the board of trustees elected Amelia Gorgas to assist as librarian because of her husband's declining health.

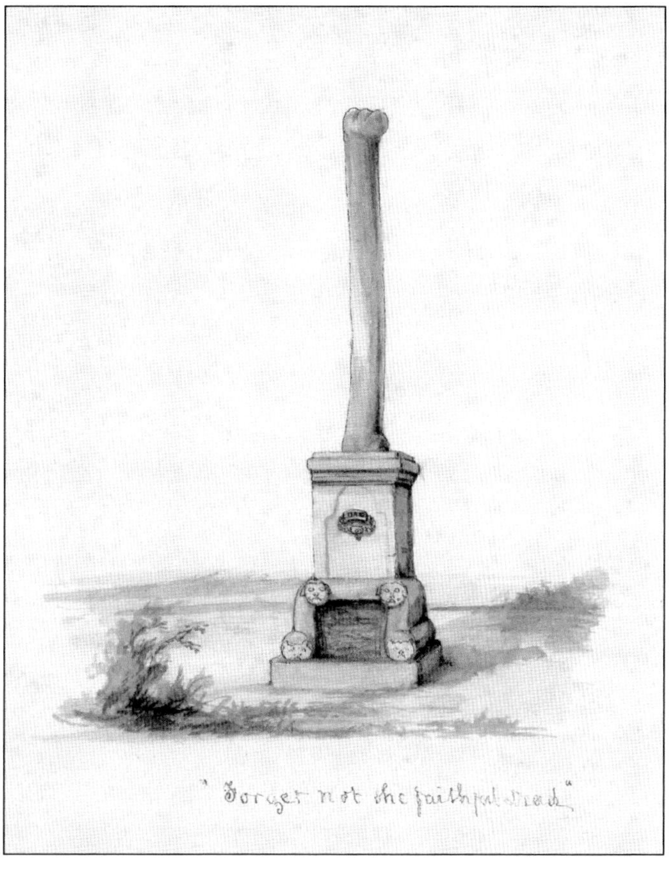

***Forget not the Faithful Dead*, Sketch by Josiah Gorgas.** In 1985, Josiah Gorgas was inducted into the US Army Ordnance Corps Hall of Fame in honor of more than two decades of service, spanning his graduation from West Point in 1841 through the end of the Civil War in 1865. The Hall of Fame was established in 1969 "to recognize and memorialize persons who have made a positive, significant contribution to the U.S. Army Ordnance Corps."

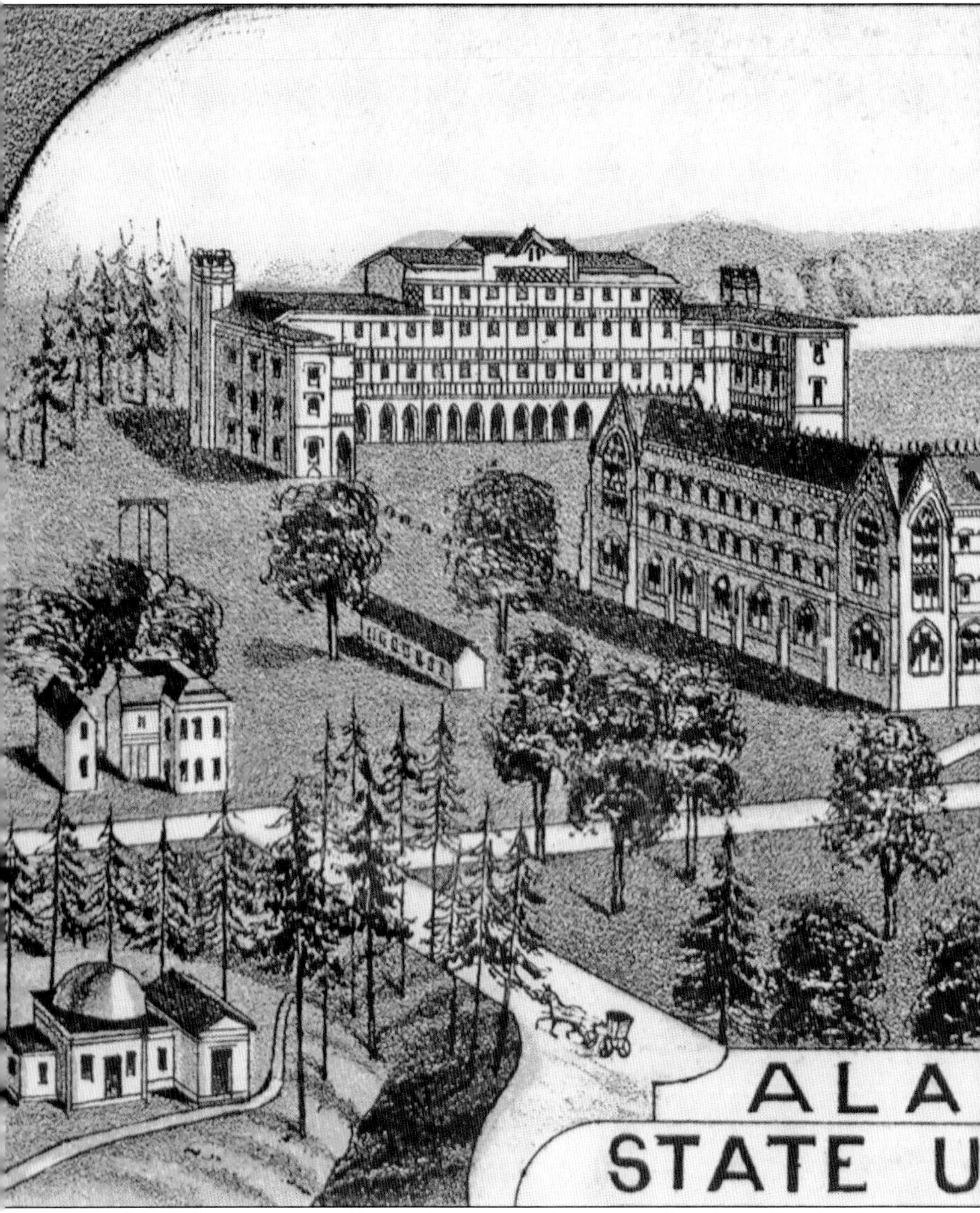

The New Campus, c. 1887. During the tenure of the next president, Burwell Boykin Lewis, the university received a $50,000 grant from the state and 40,000 acres in land grants from the US Congress as part of Civil War reparations secured by Sen. John Tyler Morgan. These resources allowed the university to expand the campus, which included the construction of (from left to

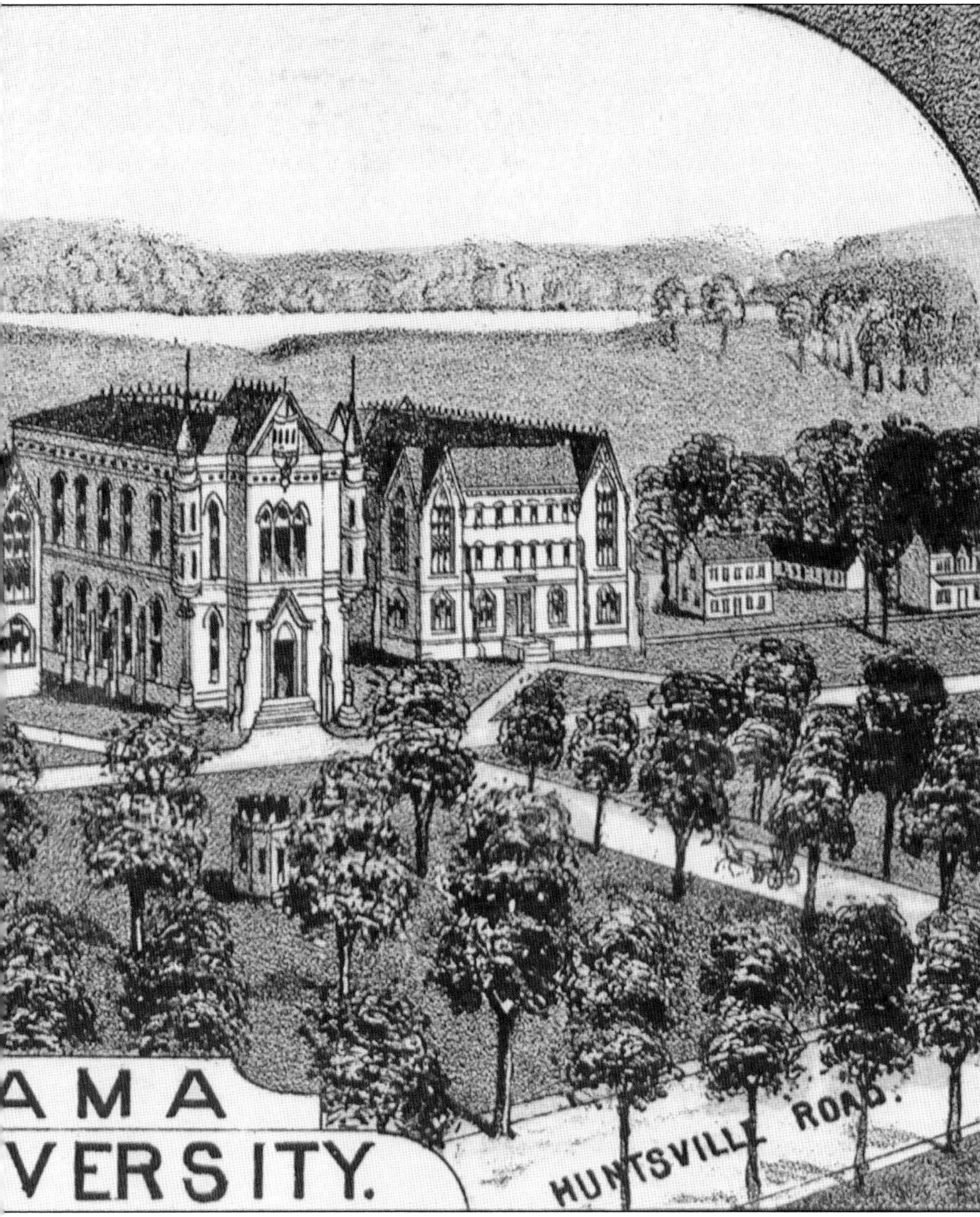

right) Manly, Clark, and Garland Halls, marking the completion of a new Victorian campus. Only one of Nichols's original buildings, the former Steward's Hall or Pratt House (with detached kitchen), survived the campus burning. It is depicted on the left side of the map, above the observatory. (LOC.)

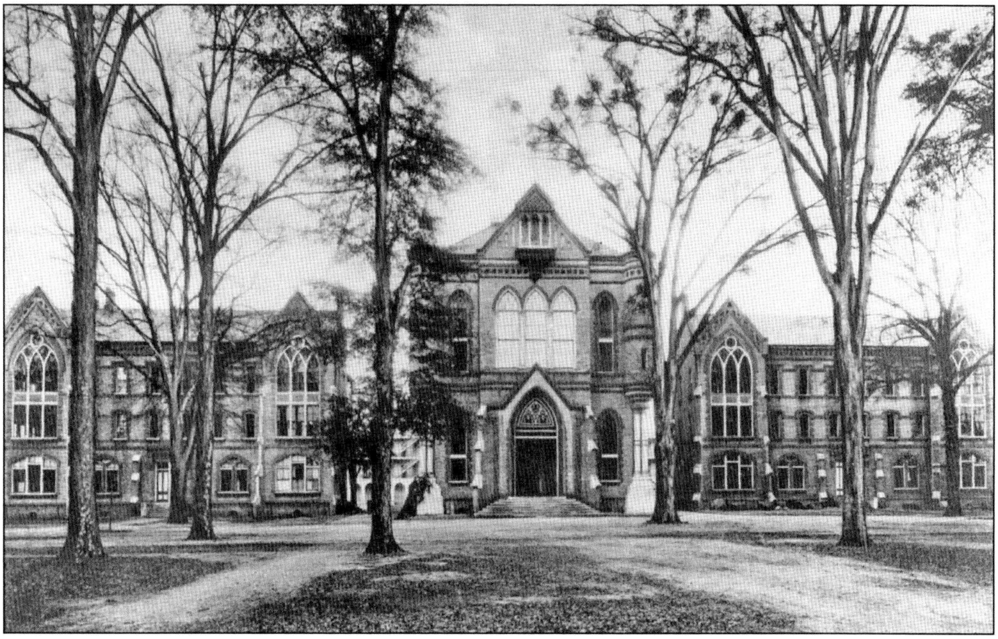

Clark Hall Library. Built between 1884 and 1885, Clark Hall (above) was designed as a multipurpose building that included the main university library (formerly located in Woods Hall). According to a student's description in the 1894 *Corolla*, "The library is open from 11 o'clock until 4 o'clock, during which time you can see a good many boys reading current periodicals with which its tables abound. Those desiring to read books usually draw them and carry them to their rooms, where they can keep them no longer than two weeks." The desks in this photograph (below) were from the Tuscaloosa capitol building and were donated to the university when the state capital was relocated to Montgomery in 1846. One of the desks is on exhibit in the Gorgas House Museum today.

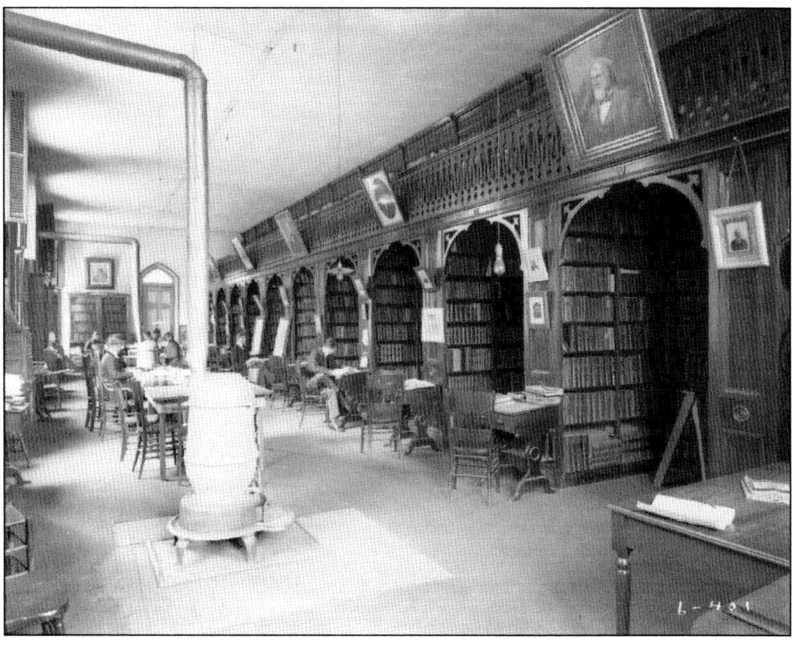

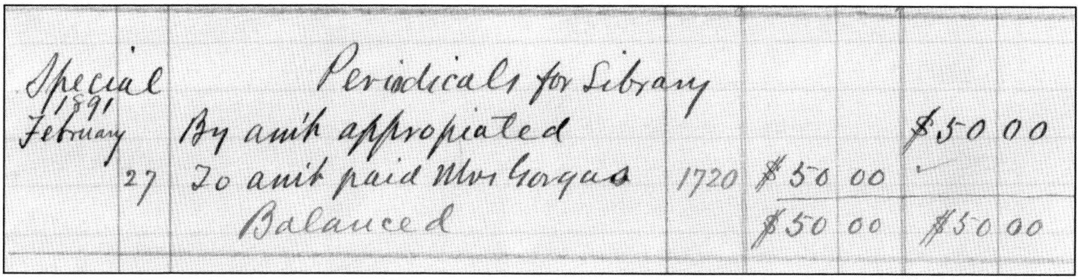

Special 1891		Periodicals for Library					
February		By am't appropriated				$50	00
	27	To am't paid Mrs Gorgas	1720	$50	00		
		Balanced		$50	00	$50	00

UNIVERSITY FUND APPROPRIATIONS, JUNE 1891. During the Civil War, when the rotunda was burned, many of the library's holdings of more than 5,000 volumes were destroyed. Pres. Landon Garland made significant personal efforts to secure book donations to rebuild the library but had little success. During Amelia Gorgas's tenure as librarian, it is estimated that the university library collection grew from 6,000 to 20,000 volumes with the help of funding appropriations. Amelia's business card (below) is preserved in the Gorgas House Museum collection. (Above, ULDSC; below, GHM.)

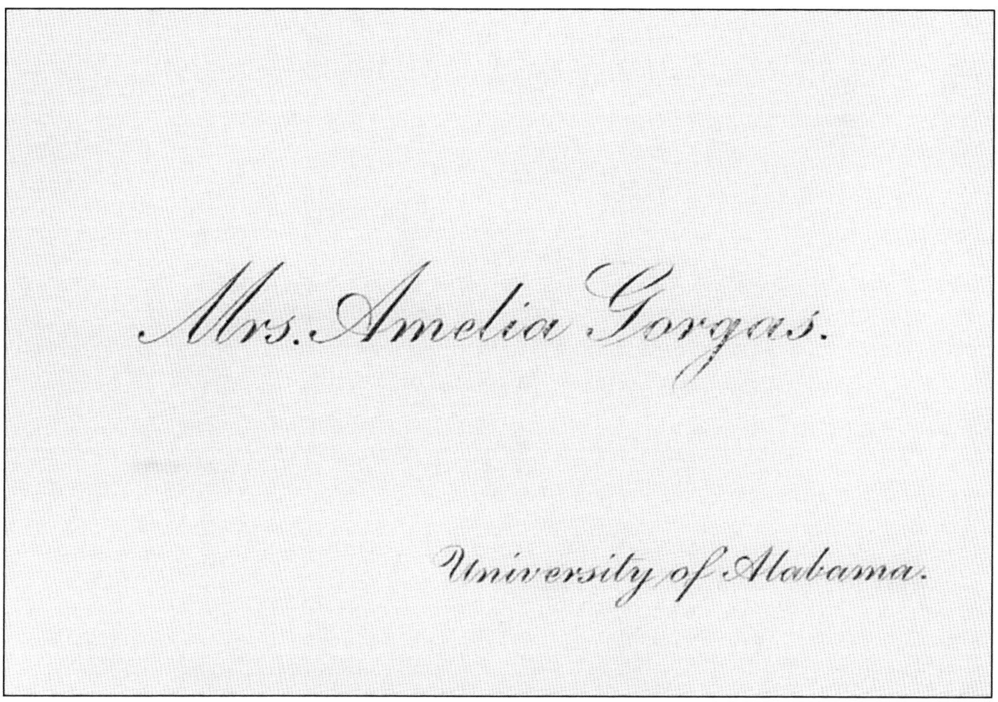

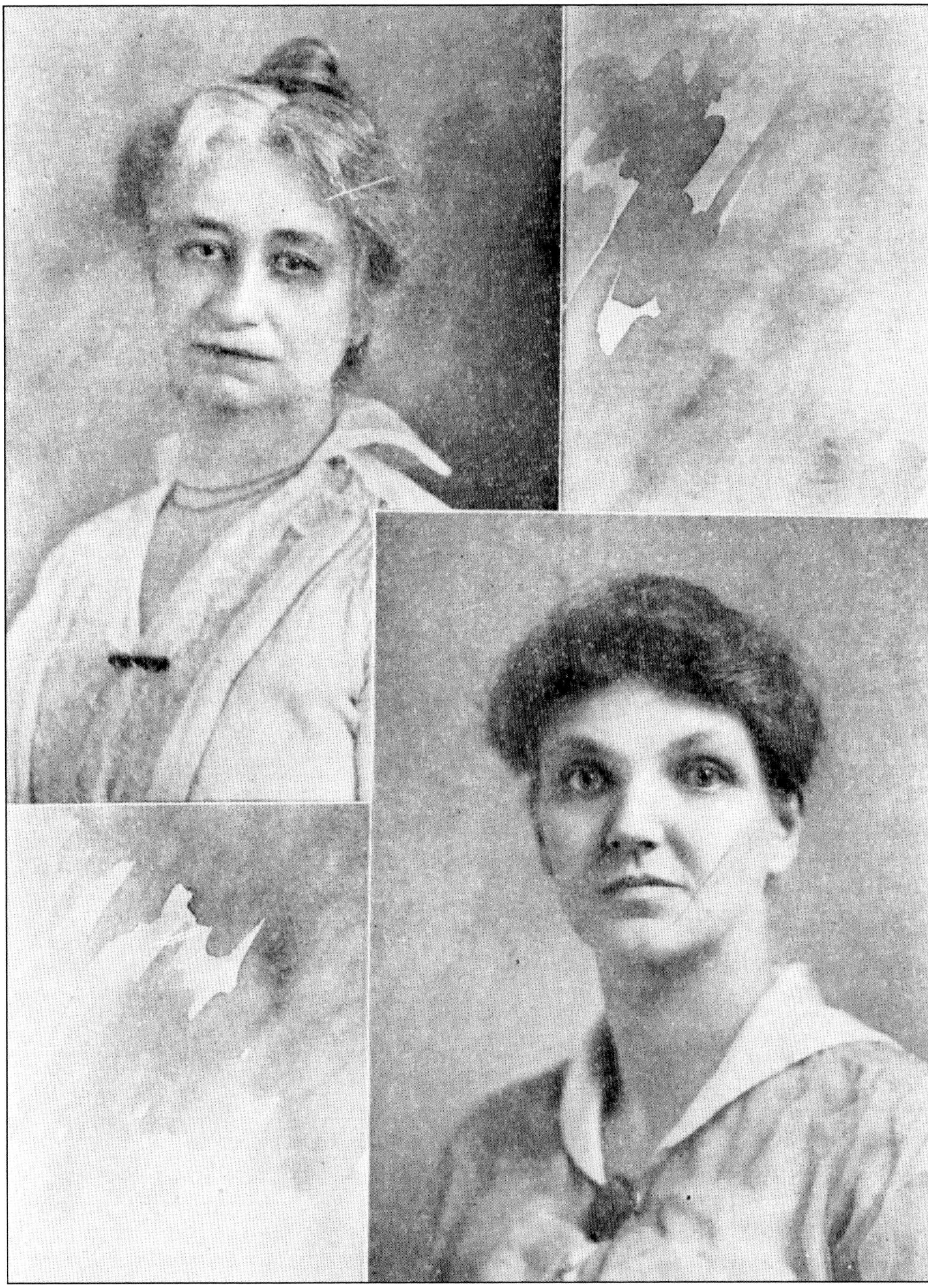

Mary "Mamie" Gorgas, Assistant Librarian. After Josiah Gorgas's stroke in 1879, Mamie Gorgas (left) returned to Tuscaloosa to assist Amelia Gorgas with the household duties. Upon his death, Mamie accepted a teaching position in Talladega, Alabama, but returned to Tuscaloosa in 1886 to assist Amelia with her librarian duties. Following Amelia's retirement, Mamie remained the assistant librarian, working alongside librarian Ora Ioneene Smith (not pictured) and, later, librarian Alice Wyman (right).

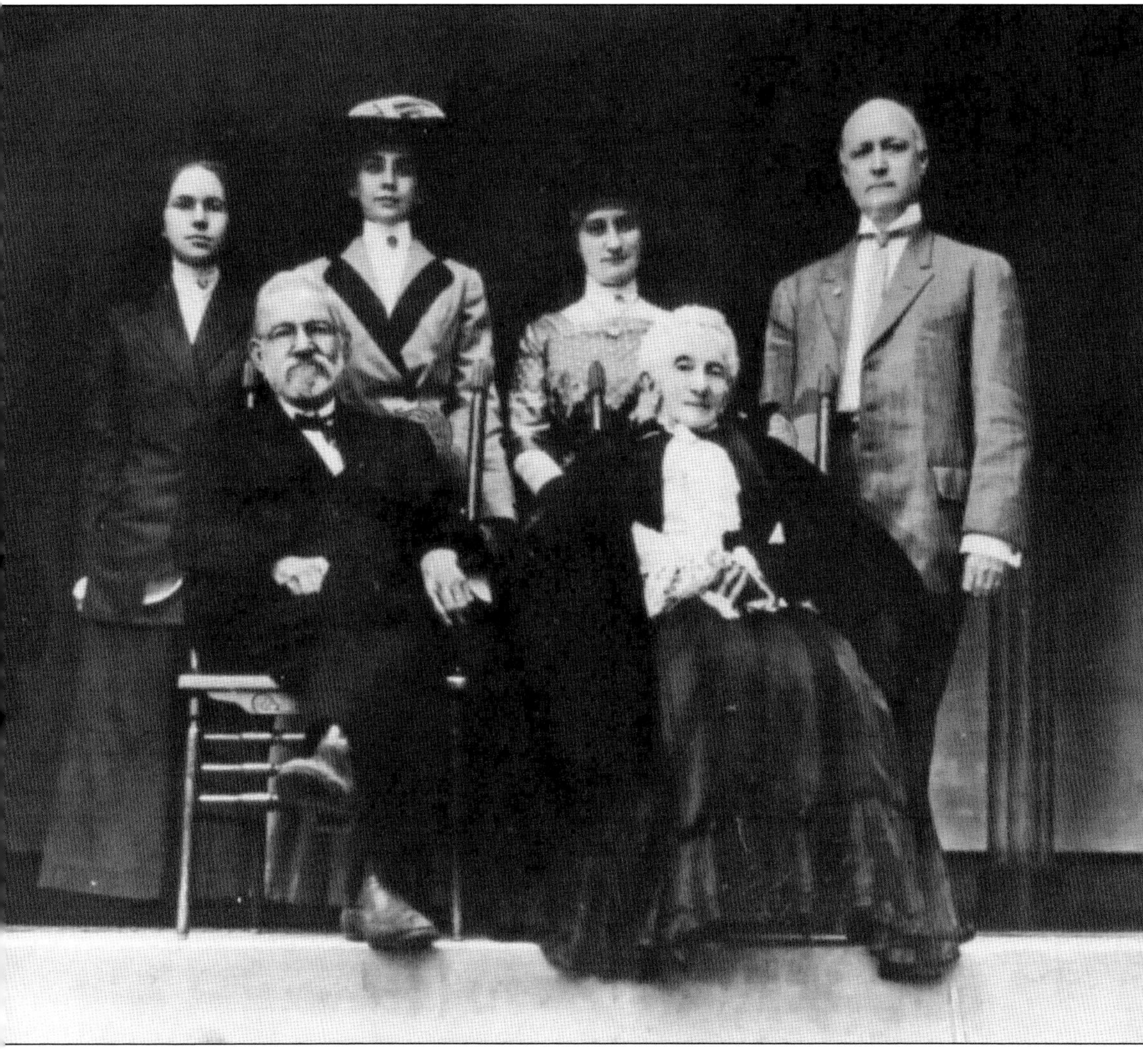

AMELIA AND MARY "MAMIE" GORGAS. In the 1894 *Corolla*, a student wrote the following description of librarian Amelia Gorgas: "As it was only a few minutes until drill when I walked in, I glanced at the latest *North American Review*, also *Puck*, and went over and took my seat by Mrs. Gorgas, for a few moment's chat. In after years, such chats as this will be among my most pleasant college remembrances. In fact I would consider my college course well spent had I gained nothing else outside of my association with her. Should you ever wish to tame the boisterous cadet, to find the *Open Sesame* of his heart, to make him your true friend, simply speak her name." In this photograph taken at the annual meeting of the 1912 Alabama Library Association, Amelia is shown seated, with her daughter Mamie, the assistant university librarian, standing behind her.

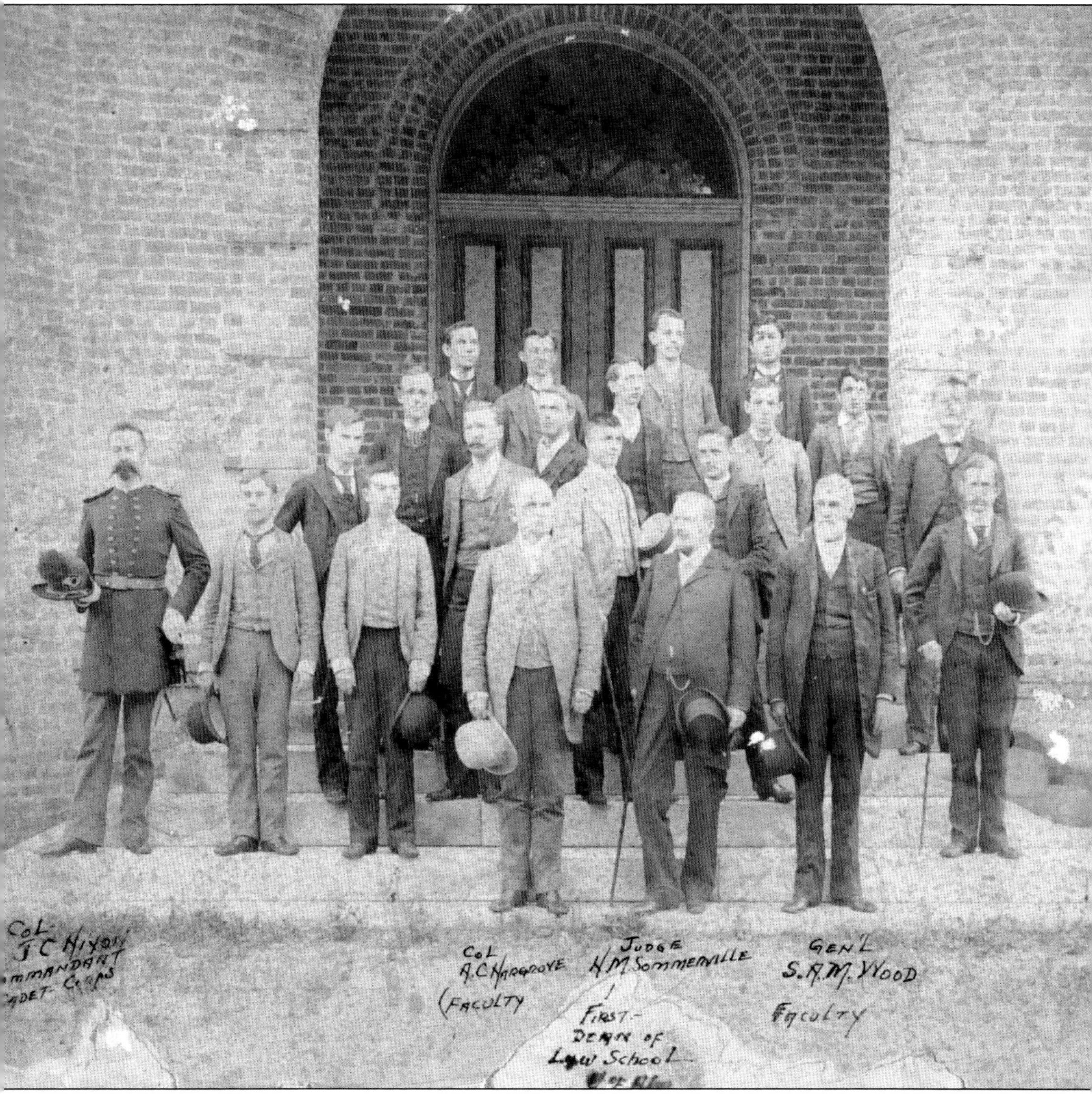

UNIVERSITY OF ALABAMA LAW SCHOOL, 1890. Richard Gorgas, Josiah and Amelia's youngest son, received a bachelor of arts degree from the University of Alabama in 1884 and a law degree in 1890. Richard briefly practiced law in Florence, Alabama, until he began clerking with the City of Montgomery in 1901. This photograph includes the following caption: "Faculty: Col. Andrew C. Hargrove, Prof. Equity Jurisprudence; Judge Henderson M. Somerville, Dean, Prof. Statue & Common Law; General Stering A.M. Wood, Prof. International & Constitutional Law; Graduates Class of 1890: Thomas Garner; Richard Gorgas; Wm. Harris; John Evans; Col. J. Courtney Hixon, Commandant Cadet Corps; Jeter Cullen; Lee Joseph Marx; Martin McAdory; Warren Reese; Herbert Reynolds; Lake Moore; Jeremiah Murphy; Ormand Somerville; Rather Pearsall; Thos. McCorvey Stevens; John Wilkerson; Wiley Tunstall." Gorgas is presumed to be the young man at far left in the back row.

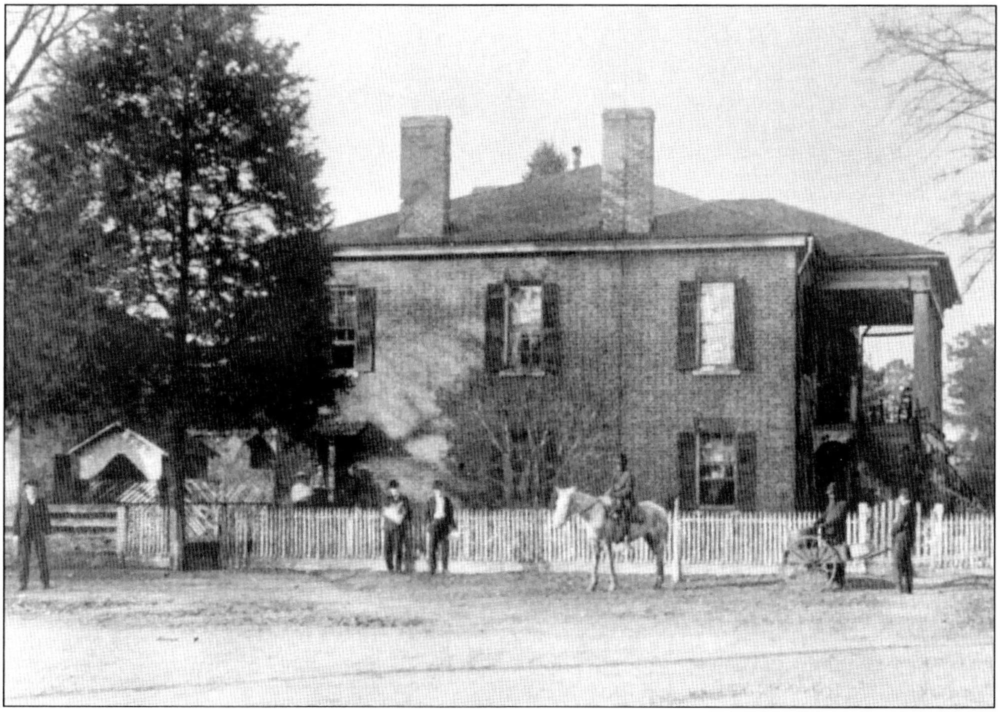

University Post Office. On February 12, 1886, Amelia Gorgas was elected to the federal position of university postmistress, and the post office was operated out of her home. According to Amelia's granddaughter Jessie Palfrey Leake, the post office was first located in "lower front hall, and later in the southwest downstairs room." The image above shows the building in use as a post office. In the image below, the mail slot is still visible in the exterior door of the post office room at the Gorgas House Museum. Upon Amelia's retirement, the university post office was relocated to a room in Woods Hall. (Above, ULDSC; below, authors' collection.)

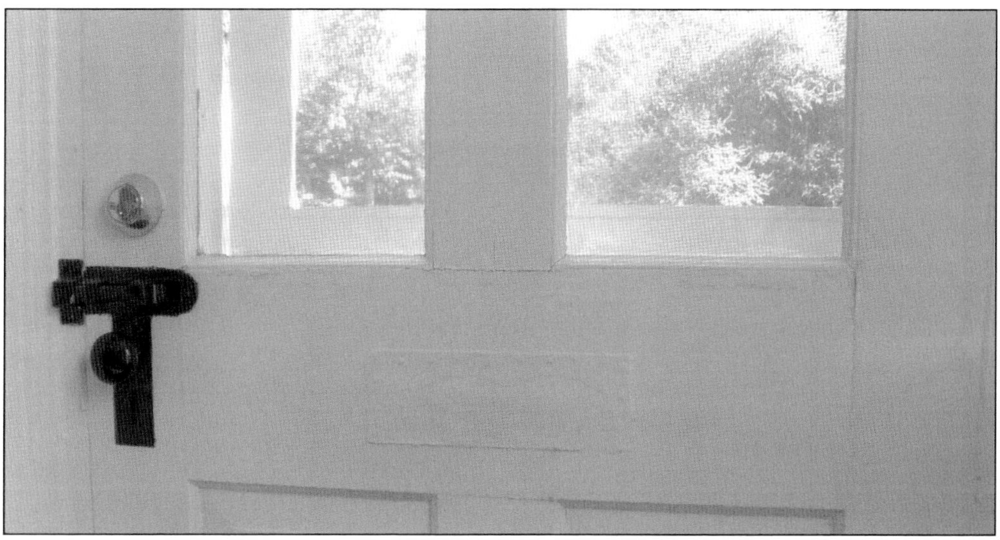

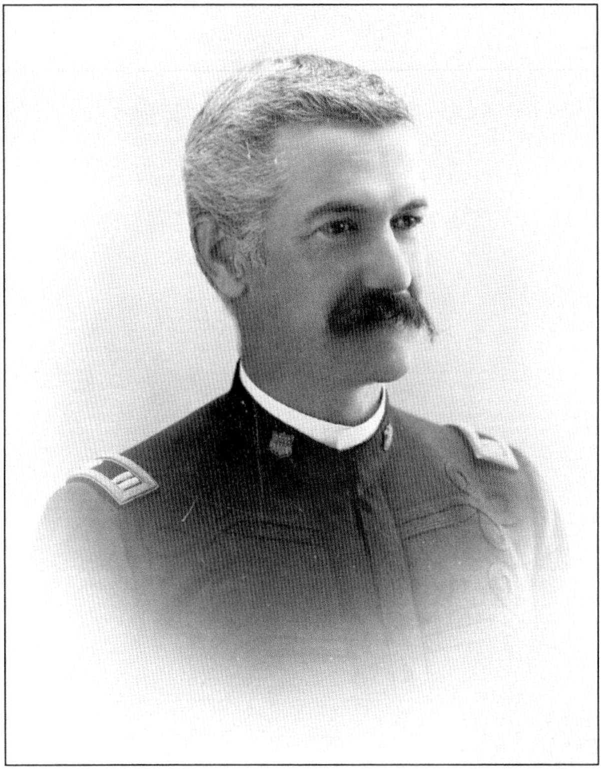

William Crawford Gorgas, US Army Medical Corps. Following his internship at Bellevue Hospital in New York, William Crawford Gorgas entered the US Army Medical Corps in 1880. He served as a physician at military posts in Texas, North Dakota, and Florida. During this time, he began sending money to help support his parents and siblings.

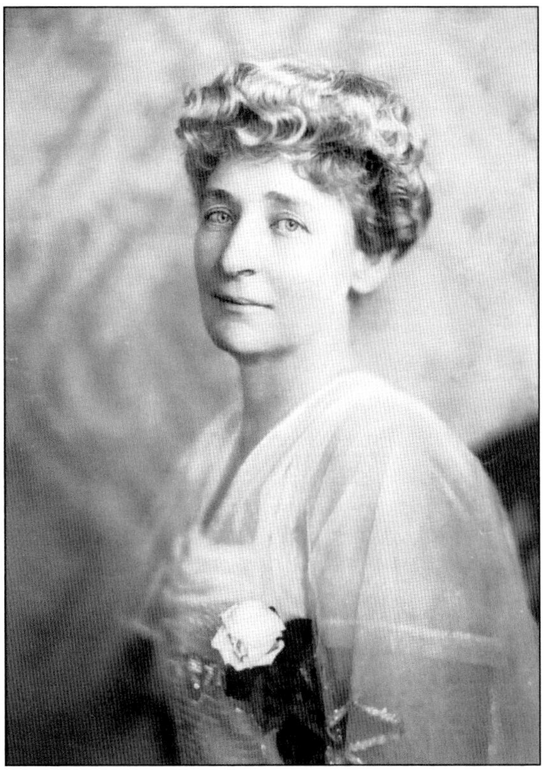

Marie Cook Doughty. In 1882, while stationed at Fort Brown, Texas, William Crawford Gorgas contracted and survived a mild case of yellow fever. During his recovery, he met Marie Doughty, who was also recovering from yellow fever. William and Marie were married on September 15, 1885, and in 1889, they had a daughter, Aileen Lyster Gorgas. Having survived yellow fever, the couple had developed immunity against the virus. As a result, William Crawford was often selected for Army appointments related to the virus.

William Crawford Gorgas. In 1881, Cuban doctor Carlos Finlay developed a hypothesis that mosquitoes could transmit yellow fever. At the time, little was known about the source of yellow fever, and consequently, there were few effective preventative measures. In 1900, the Walter Reed Commission proved Finlay's hypothesis correct. Using this groundbreaking research, William Crawford Gorgas, then the chief sanitary officer of Havana, implemented a sanitation plan that ended a citywide epidemic.

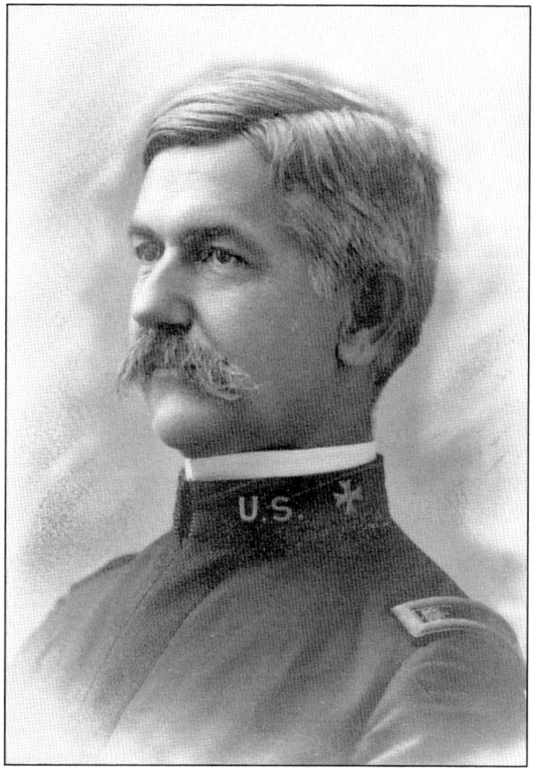

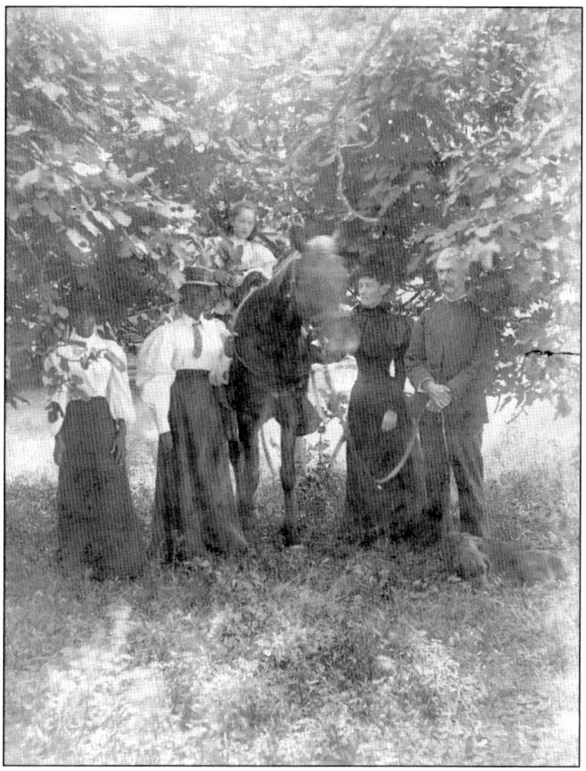

William Crawford, Marie, and Aileen Gorgas in Panama. The success in Havana set William Crawford Gorgas on a path to serve a leading role in public health for the rest of his career. In 1902, during the planning stages of the Panama Canal construction, Crawford was transferred to Washington, DC, to provide his expertise regarding sanitation. Later, in June 1904, he was transferred to Panama to oversee sanitation efforts. In this photograph, Aileen Gorgas is seated on the horse, with her parents, William Crawford and Marie, to her left and two unidentified women to her right.

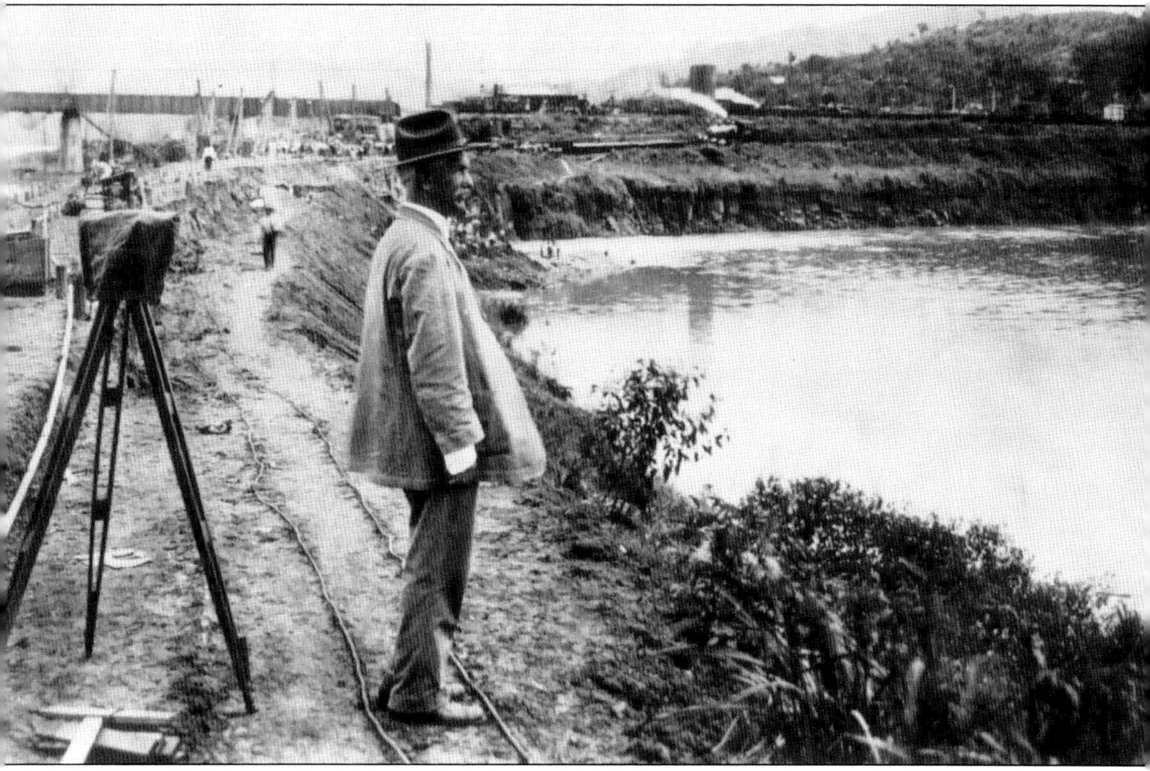

William Crawford Gorgas, Panama. The French, led by engineer Ferdinand de Lesseps, began the early phases of the construction of a canal through Panama in 1879. Throughout the next two decades, it is estimated that over 20,000 people died, with the majority of deaths from disease. In 1904, the United States purchased the French assets and took control of the Panama Canal Zone. Within a year, William Crawford Gorgas presented Pres. Theodore Roosevelt with a mosquito abatement plan at a cost of $1 million. Gorgas believed the plan would free Panama from mosquito-borne diseases, including yellow fever, and allow the canal to be built. At the urging of his personal physician, President Roosevelt granted the funding. Gorgas's plan was a success. The final death from yellow fever in the Panama Canal Zone occurred in 1906. (NLM.)

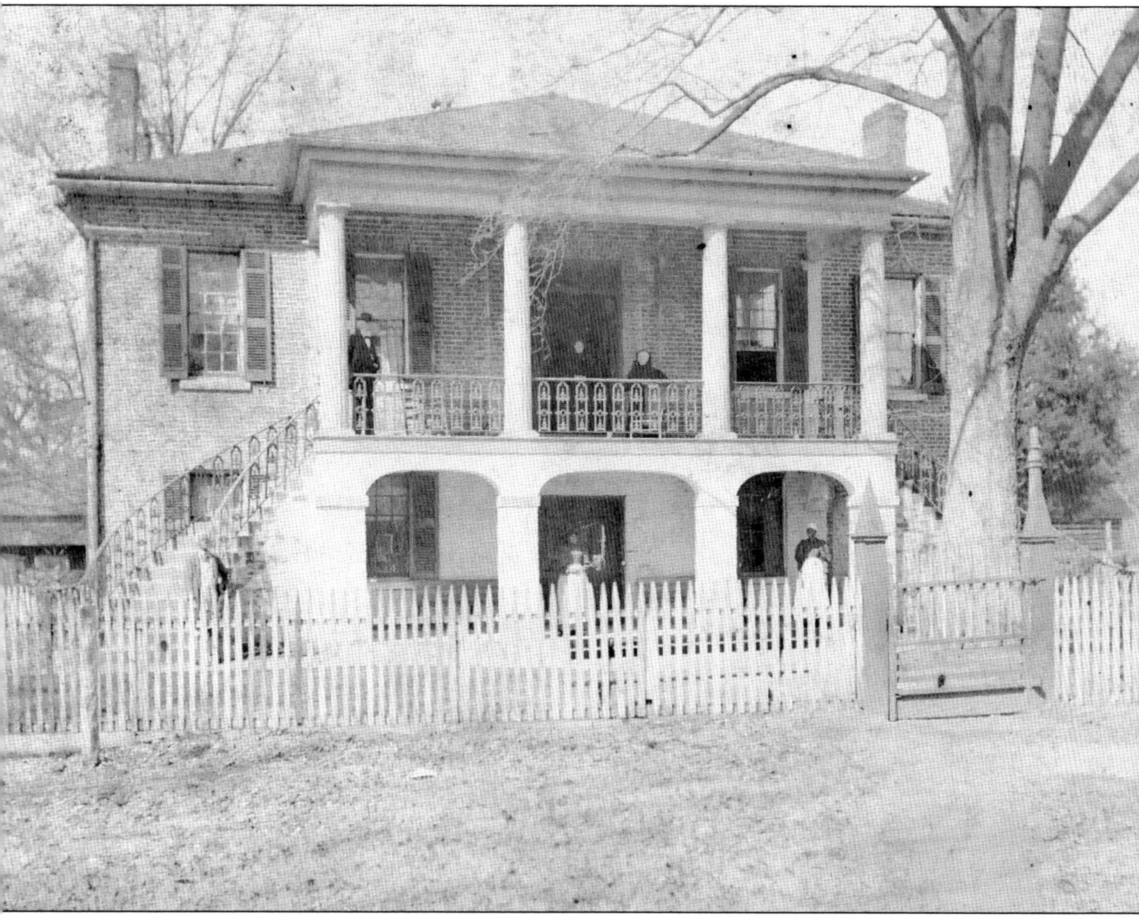

GORGAS HOUSE, C. 1895 TO EARLY 1900s. In 1895, the front of Amelia Gorgas's home was renovated to provide her with a second-story porch that extended the full width of the home. Robert Hardaway, a university professor of engineering, provided oversight for the renovation. The individuals in the photograph are unidentified but may include Amelia on the upper porch and university employees on the lower level.

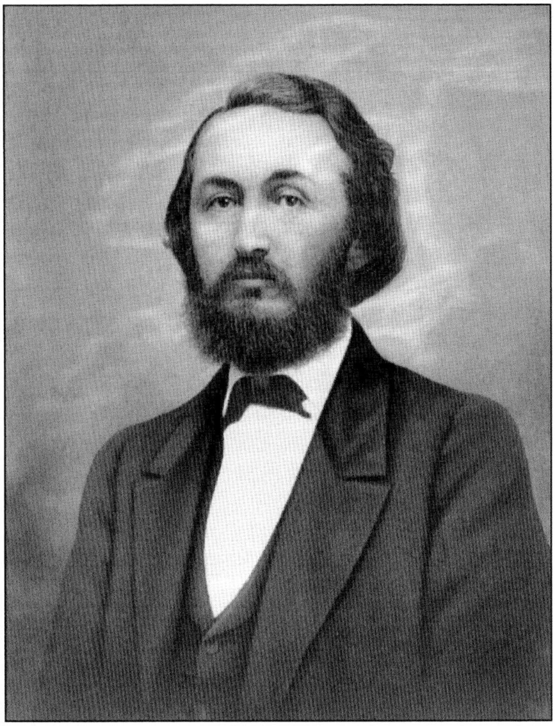

Robert Archelaus Hardaway. Born in Georgia in 1829, Robert Hardaway served in the US Army during the Mexican War. He joined the Confederacy during the Civil War, achieving the rank of lieutenant colonel in 1864. After the war, Hardaway taught engineering at Auburn University and later accepted a position at the University of Alabama, where he served as a professor from 1882 to 1897 and helped to establish the Department of Engineering. The University of Alabama museum collection records indicate that Professor Hardaway lent furniture to the Gorgas family prior to his death. The photograph below shows what is now known as the Hardaway Room at the Gorgas House Museum, which contains some of Hardaway's furniture that was donated by his son Benjamin Hardaway.

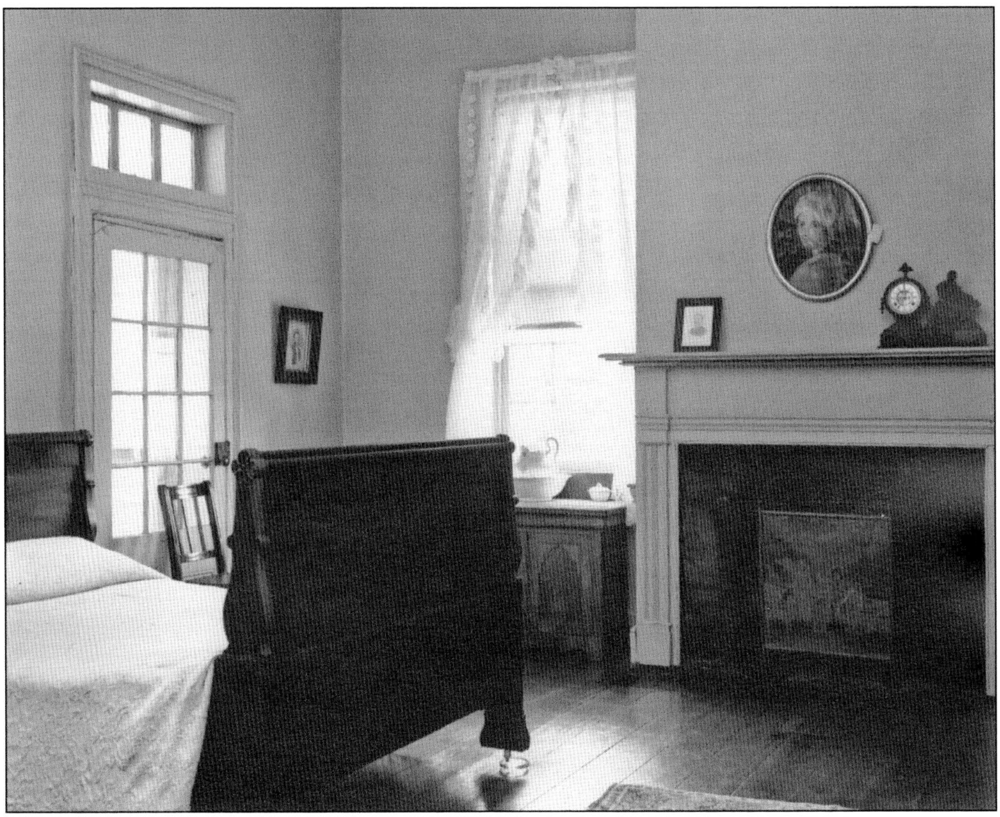

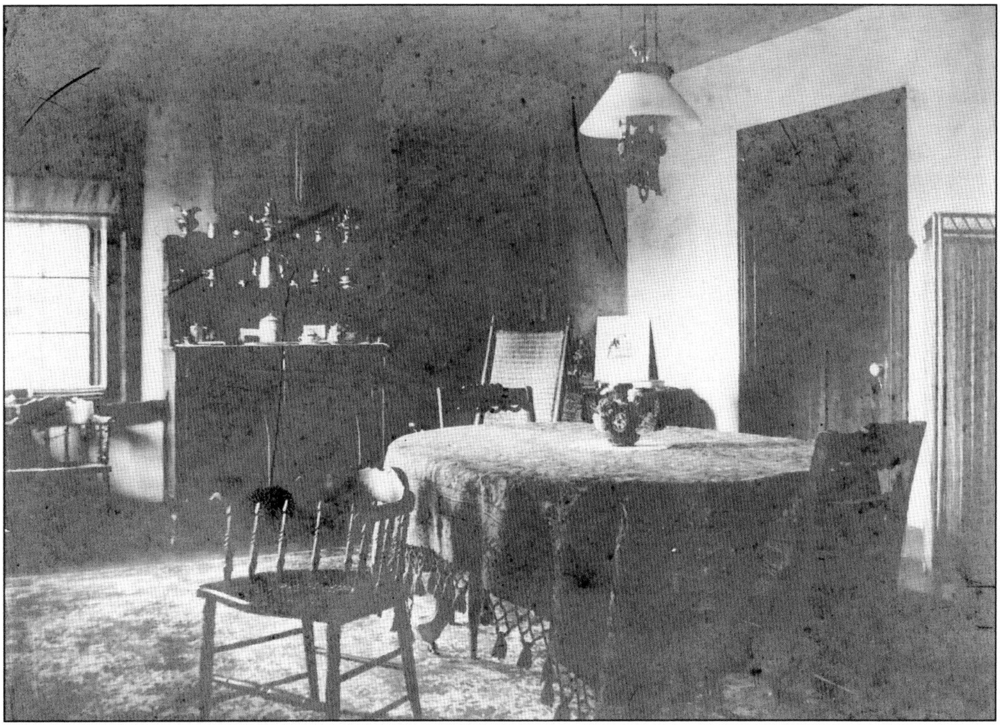

GORGAS HOUSE, EARLY 20TH CENTURY. These are the two oldest known photographs of the interior of the Gorgas House. Many of the furnishings owned and used by the Gorgases, including the chairs and ceiling lamp in the dining room (above) and the étagère, table, and chairs in the parlor (below), are still on display at the Gorgas House Museum.

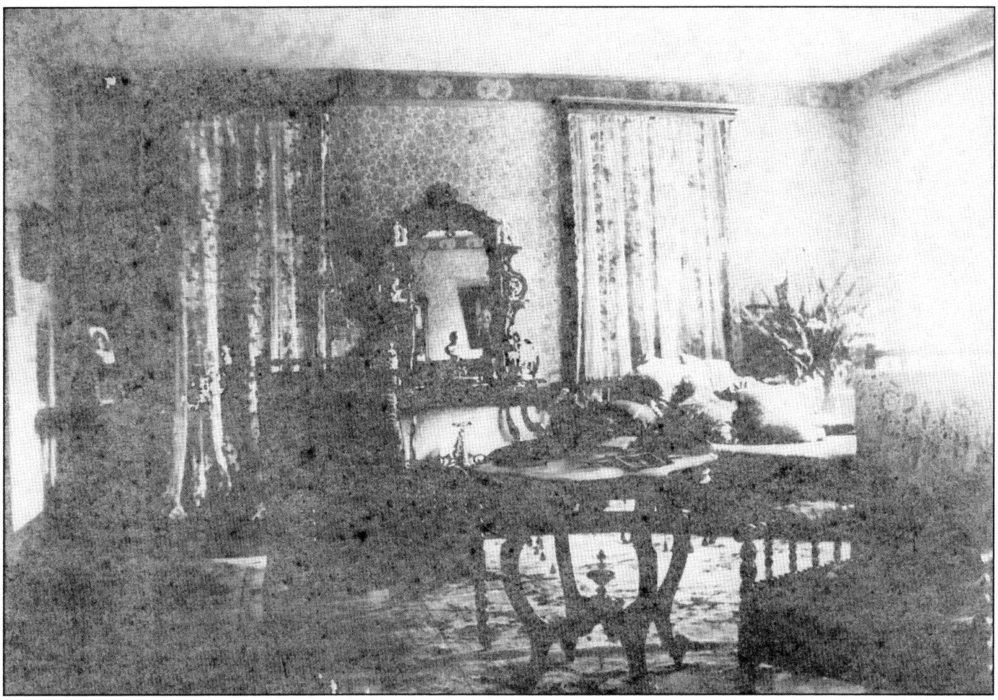

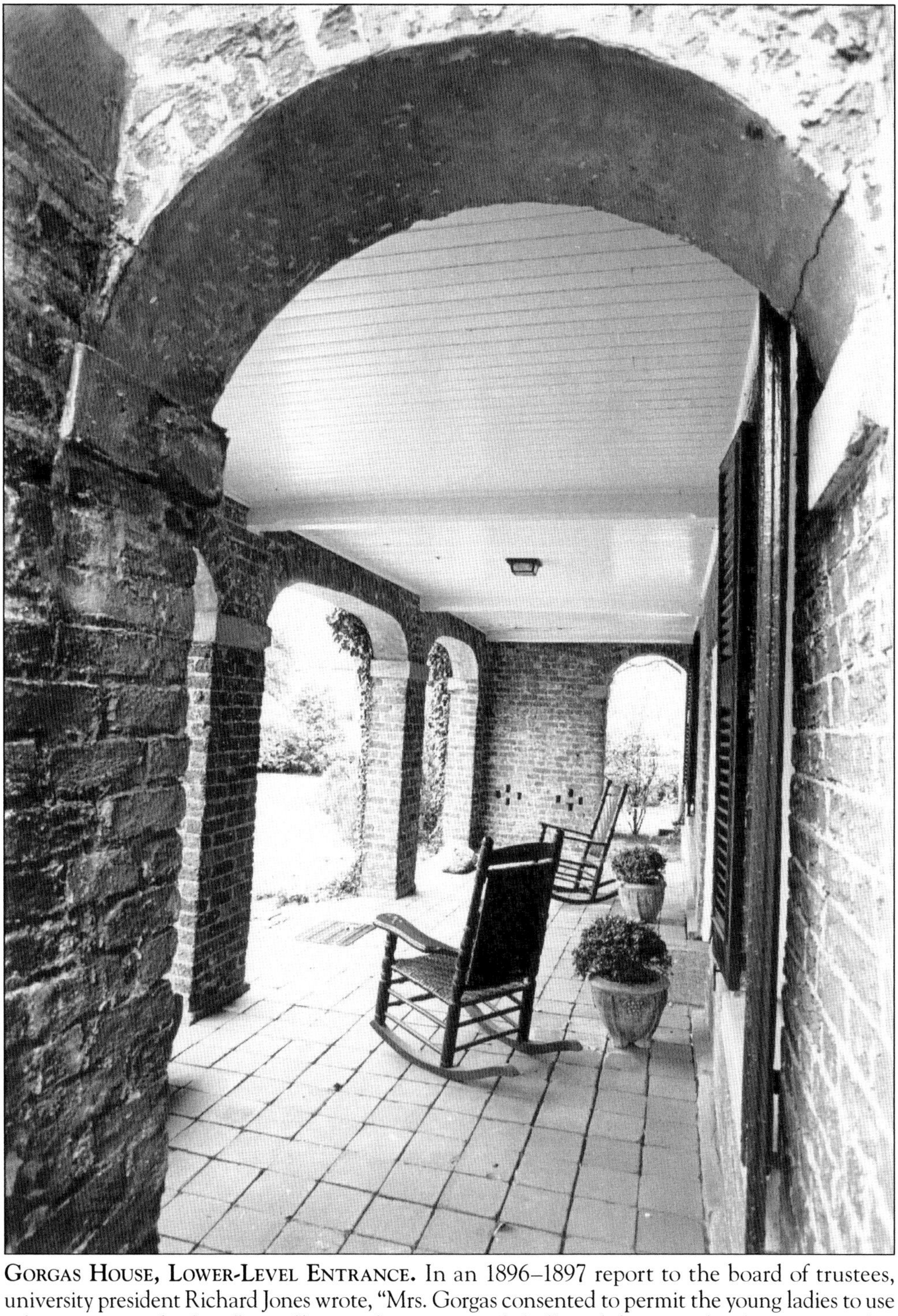

Gorgas House, Lower-Level Entrance. In an 1896–1897 report to the board of trustees, university president Richard Jones wrote, "Mrs. Gorgas consented to permit the young ladies to use a front room on the first floor of her residence as a study hall, and this room has been assigned to them for that purpose. The young ladies were directed by me, under no circumstances to entertain visitors in their study room, or under the porch of Mrs. Gorgas's residence."

COROLLA DEDICATION, 1906. In 1896 and 1906, the *Corolla* yearbooks were dedicated to Amelia Gorgas. The second dedication was in recognition of her years of service to the university. The university alumni also awarded Amelia with the university's first-ever loving cup, as seen in the photograph at the bottom of this page.

To Mrs. Gorgas

Many men of many minds,
All our hearts are one,
They are fixed upon the right,
They can vary none.
Fixed on virtue, fixed on truth,
Fixed on purity,
Fixed on excellence and worth,
Fondly fixed on thee.

You for years, day in, day out,
'Midst our smiles and tears,
You have stood our constant friend,
Through the changing years;
You, in sickness, you in health,
You, a mother stood,
Stood in place of her we left,
Of our bone and blood.

In this little book of ours,
Love in every line,
In its spotless heart of hearts,
We thy name enshrine;
Steadfast guide and monitor,
Each succeeding morn,
There is ne'er a nobler name
Can its page adorn.

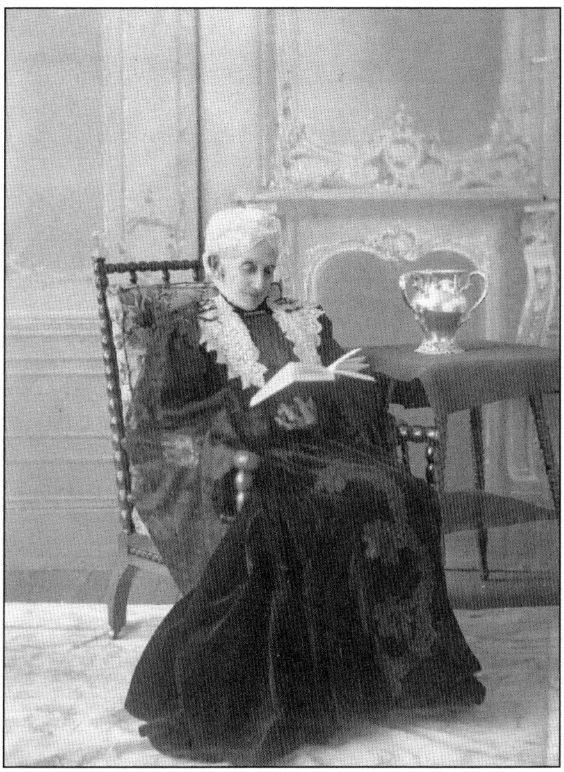

AMELIA RETIRES FROM THE UNIVERSITY. On December 10, 1906, Amelia Gorgas was awarded a retirement allowance by the Carnegie Foundation for her long service to education in Alabama. Amelia officially retired from the university at the age of 80 in January 1907.

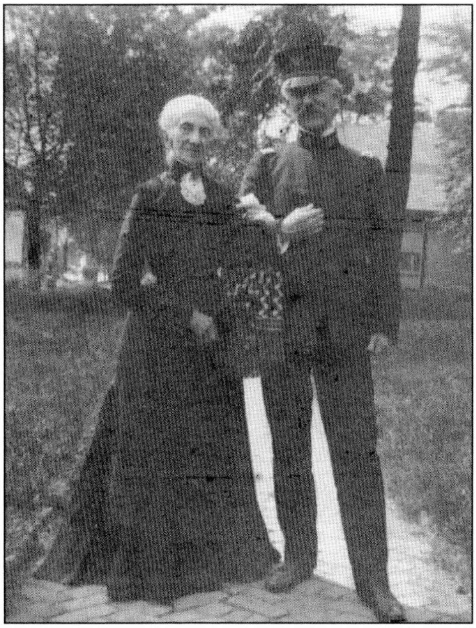

Amelia and William Crawford Gorgas. Amelia Gorgas continued to live in her campus residence until her death at the age of 86 on January 3, 1913. Her funeral was held in the Morgan Hall auditorium, and she was buried in the Gorgas family plot in Tuscaloosa's Evergreen Cemetery, seen below. At right, Amelia is pictured with her eldest son, William Crawford Gorgas. William Crawford never lived in the Tuscaloosa residence but often visited his family. In 1977, Amelia was inducted into the Alabama Women's Hall of Fame in recognition of her 25 years of service and influence at the University of Alabama. Established at Judson College in 1970, the Hall of Fame provides a "permanent place of honor for Alabama's most outstanding women and a place for people to visit and learn about the significant contributions that these women have made to our state and nation." (Left, ULDSC; below, authors' collection.)

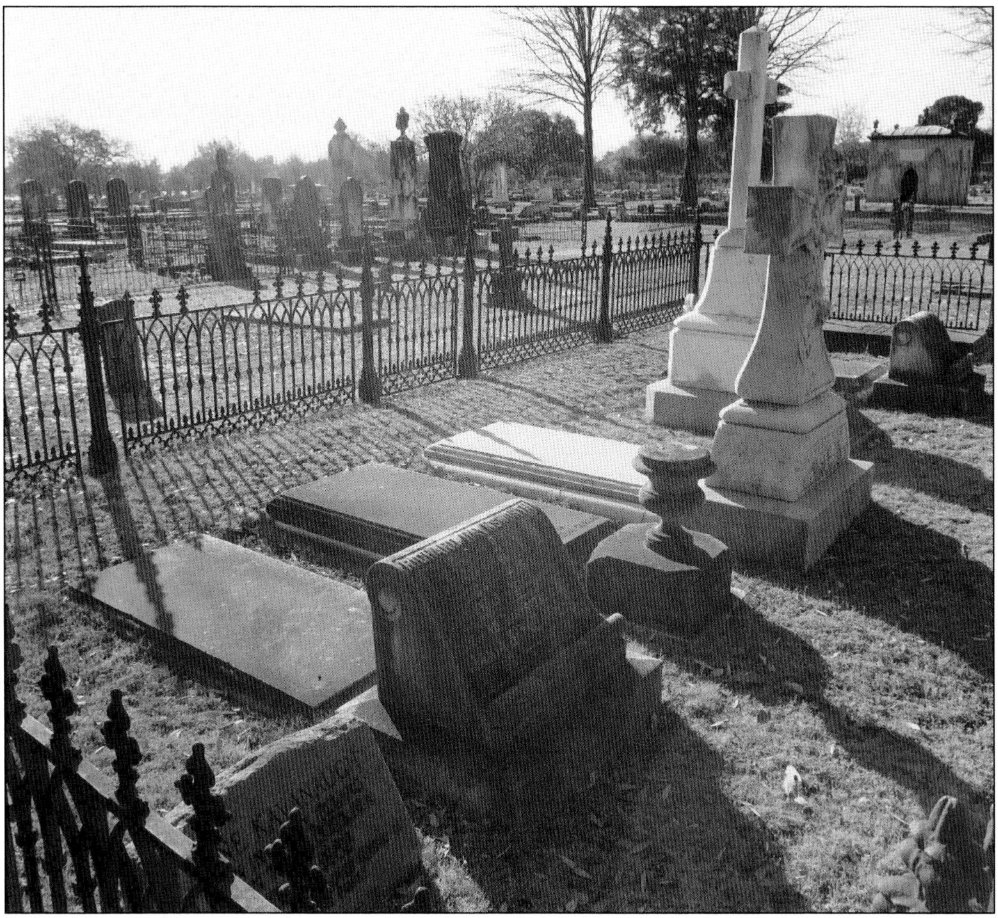

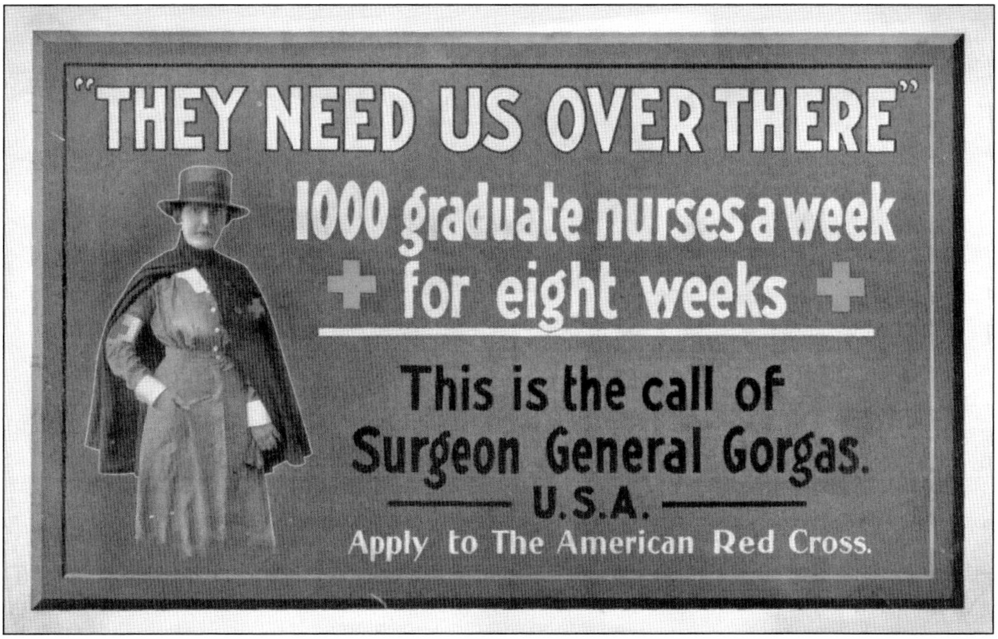

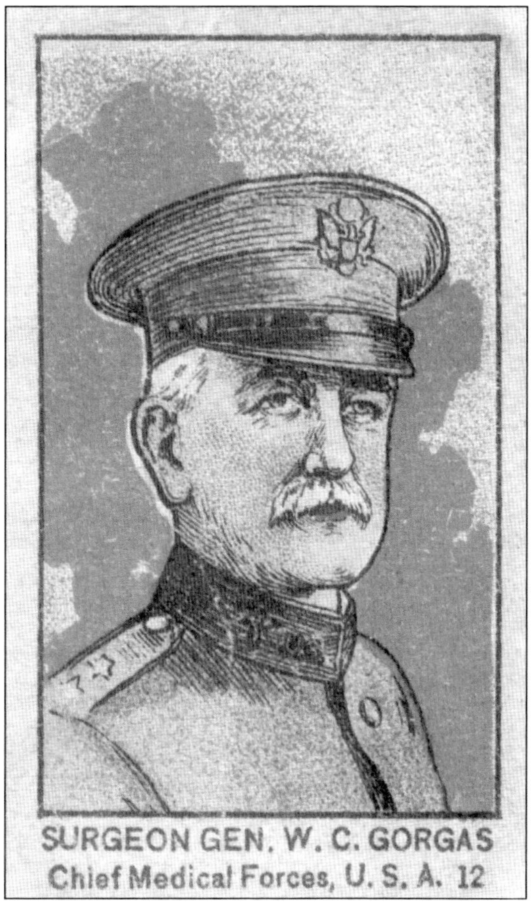

William Crawford Gorgas, US Army Surgeon General. Following his work in Panama, William Crawford Gorgas accepted consulting projects involving sanitation and health in Africa and Central and South America. In January 1914, he was appointed as US Army surgeon general, and in March 1915, he was promoted to major general. (Above, LOC; right, GHM.)

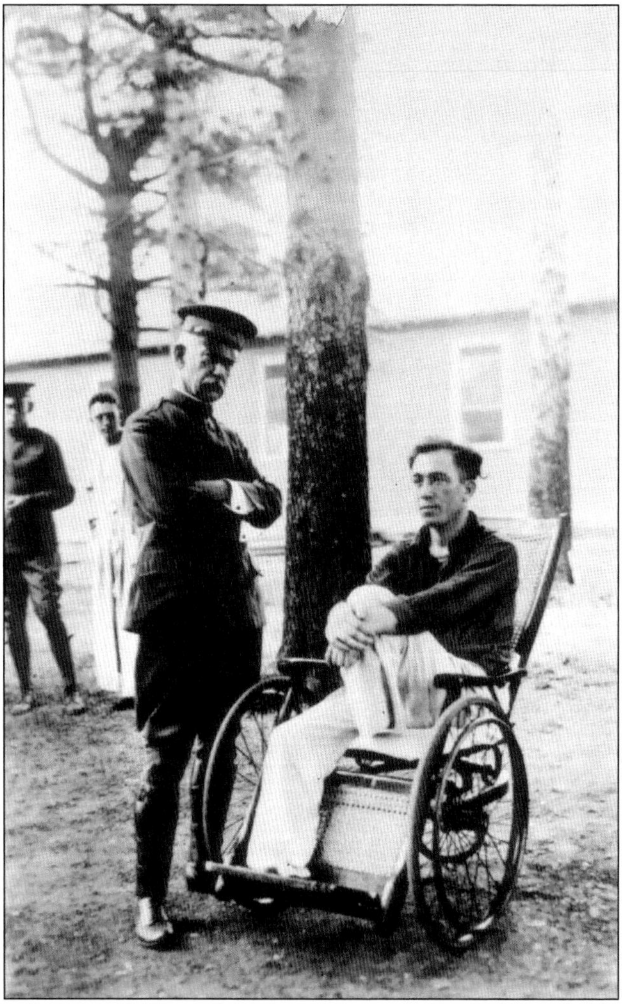

Dr. William Gorgas, Walter Reed Hospital. On April 6, 1917, days after the United States had entered World War I, William Crawford Gorgas was called upon to lead the US Army Medical Corps. Following his inspection of Army camps and battlefield trenches, he fought for changes, including the reduction of overcrowded camps and increased numbers of medical officers. These changes led to improved health and survival rates for soldiers injured in combat. (LOC.)

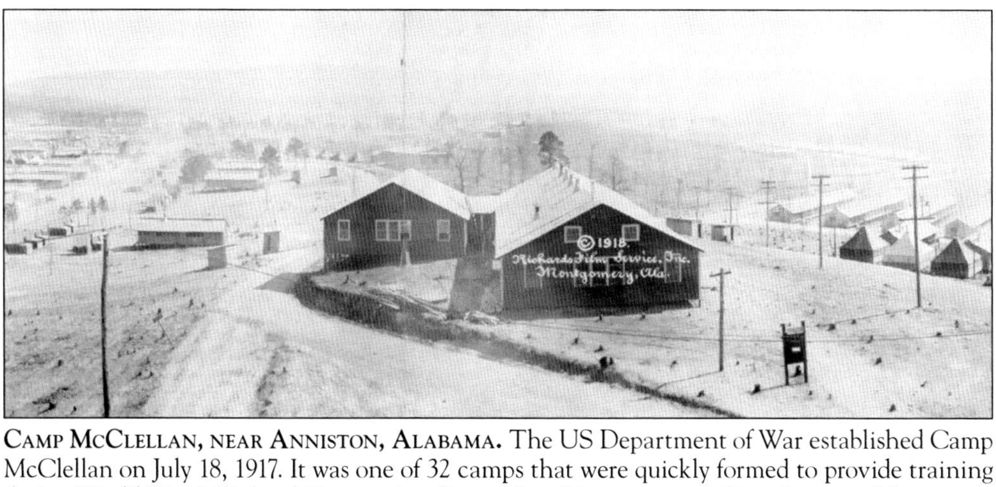

Camp McClellan, near Anniston, Alabama. The US Department of War established Camp McClellan on July 18, 1917. It was one of 32 camps that were quickly formed to provide training during World War I. Richard Gorgas, Amelia and Josiah's youngest child, volunteered for service and was stationed at Camp McClellan with the Sanitary Corps. (LOC.)

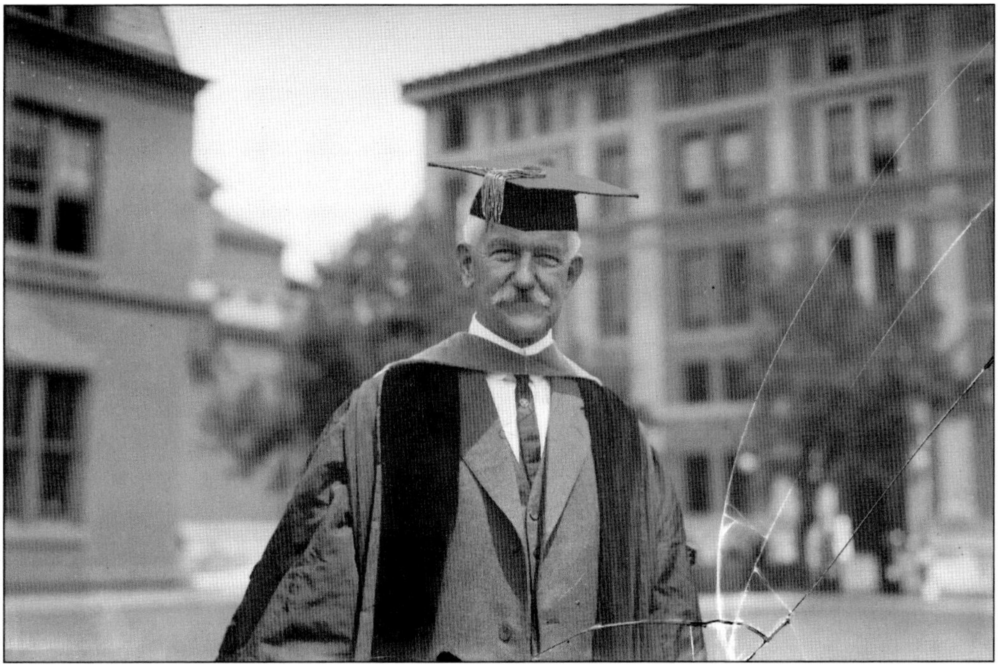

WILLIAM CRAWFORD GORGAS, COLUMBIA UNIVERSITY, JUNE 4, 1913. William Crawford Gorgas's dedication to the medical profession and public service was evident in his many appointments, promotions, and honors, including president of the American Medical Association from 1910 to 1911, receipt of the French Legion of Honor in 1919, and honorary degrees from University of the South, Harvard, Brown, University of Pennsylvania, Johns Hopkins, Oxford, and Columbia. (LOC.)

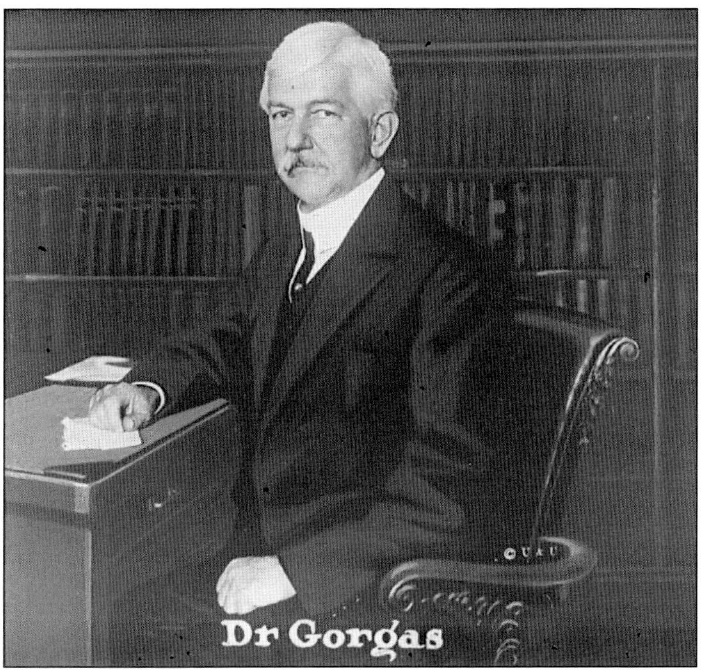

DR. WILLIAM CRAWFORD GORGAS. Due to age limitations, 64-year-old William Crawford Gorgas was forced to retire from the military on October 3, 1918. Gorgas returned to work in the public health sector with the International Health Board of the Rockefeller Foundation. In 1920, he was asked to investigate a yellow fever outbreak in Africa. Prior to his trip, he attended the International Hygiene Conference in Brussels, and upon his return to London, he suffered a stroke. (GHM.)

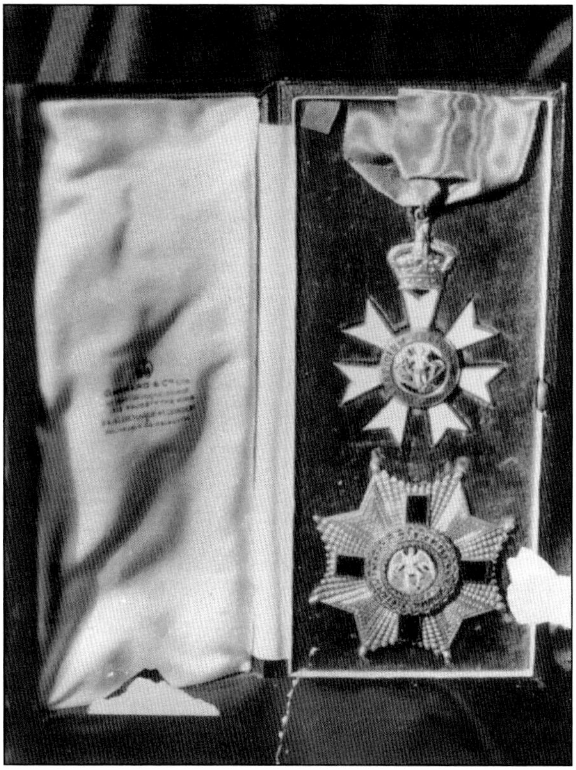

Medals of Knighthood. Following his stroke, William Crawford Gorgas was hospitalized in London. There, he was visited by King George V and knighted to the Order of St. Michael and St. George for his lifetime of public service. Gorgas died on July 3, 1920, and at the request of King George V, he received a state funeral at St. Paul's Cathedral in London. In addition, a service was held at the Church of the Epiphany in Washington, DC, before Gorgas was buried in Arlington National Cemetery. (NLM.)

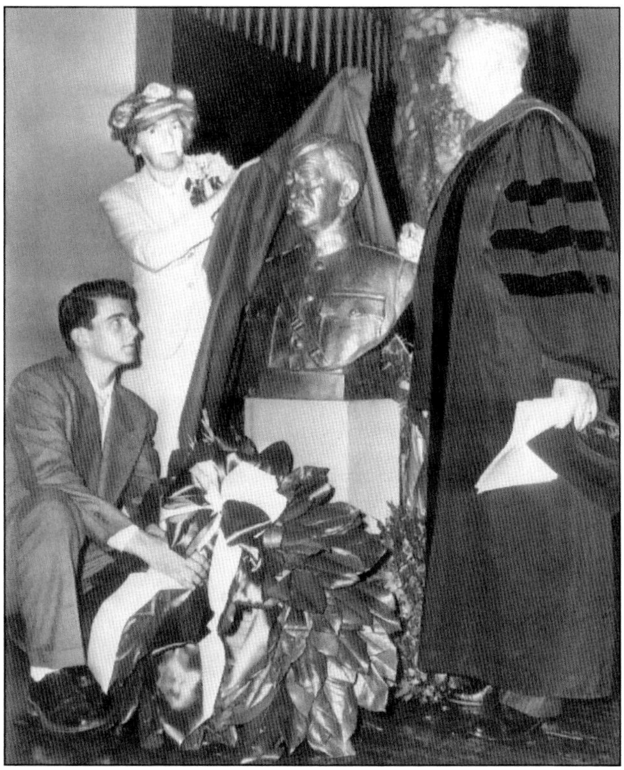

Bust of William Crawford Gorgas. On May 24, 1951, a bust of William Crawford Gorgas, modeled by Bryant Baker, was unveiled by his daughter Aileen Gorgas Wrightson and great-grandson Roger Gabriel Jr. at the New York University Hall of Fame for Great Americans. Established in 1900, the Hall of Fame selects inductees who "by wealth of thought, or else by mighty deed, [have] served mankind in noble character. In worldwide good they live forever more." (GHM.)

Three

The Legacy of the Gorgas House 1934–Present

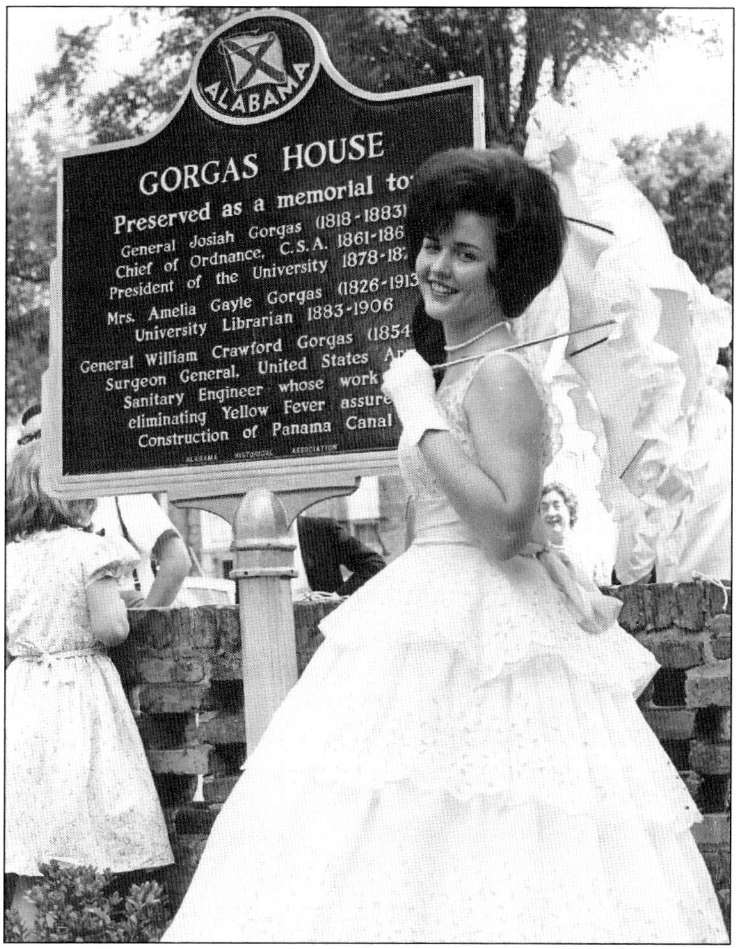

Gorgas House as a Museum. The Gorgas family lived in their campus residence until 1953. The following year, the university dedicated the building as a museum in honor of the family. Today, under the auspices of the University of Alabama Museums, the Gorgas House Museum preserves and shares the Gorgas family and historic campus legacies that are integral to the history of the state. (GHM.)

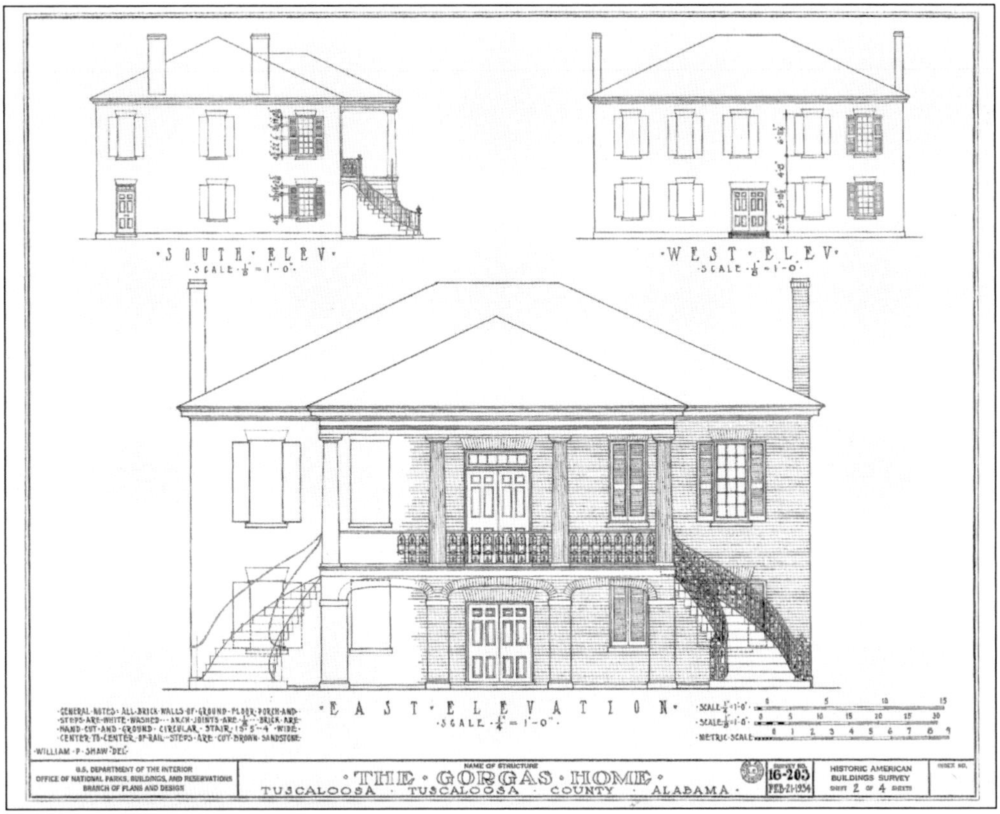

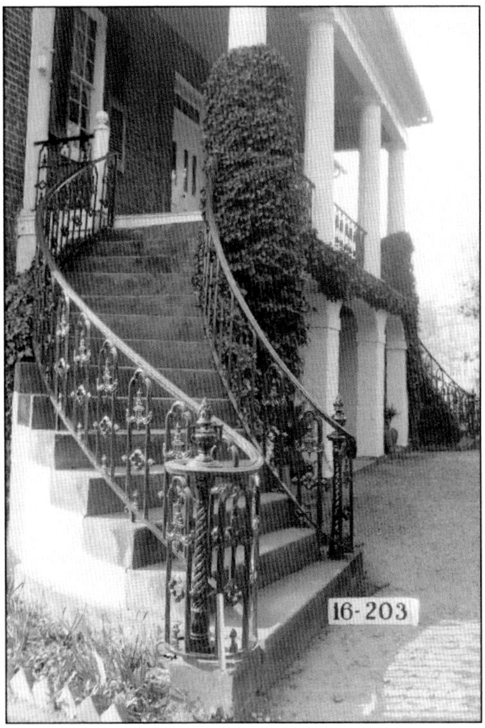

ARCHITECTURAL SURVEY. In 1934, the Gorgas House was among the first buildings selected for inclusion in the Historic American Buildings Survey (HABS), a national program created during the Great Depression to provide work for jobless architects and photographers. According to HABS founder Charles E. Peterson, "If the great number of our antique buildings must disappear through economic causes, they should not pass into unrecorded oblivion." While many buildings were selected for their architectural uniqueness, Peterson recognized there were a "great number of plain structures which by fate of accident are identified with historic events" that also deserved recognition. The drawing (above) and photograph (left) document the exterior porch renovations from 1895. (Both, LOC.)

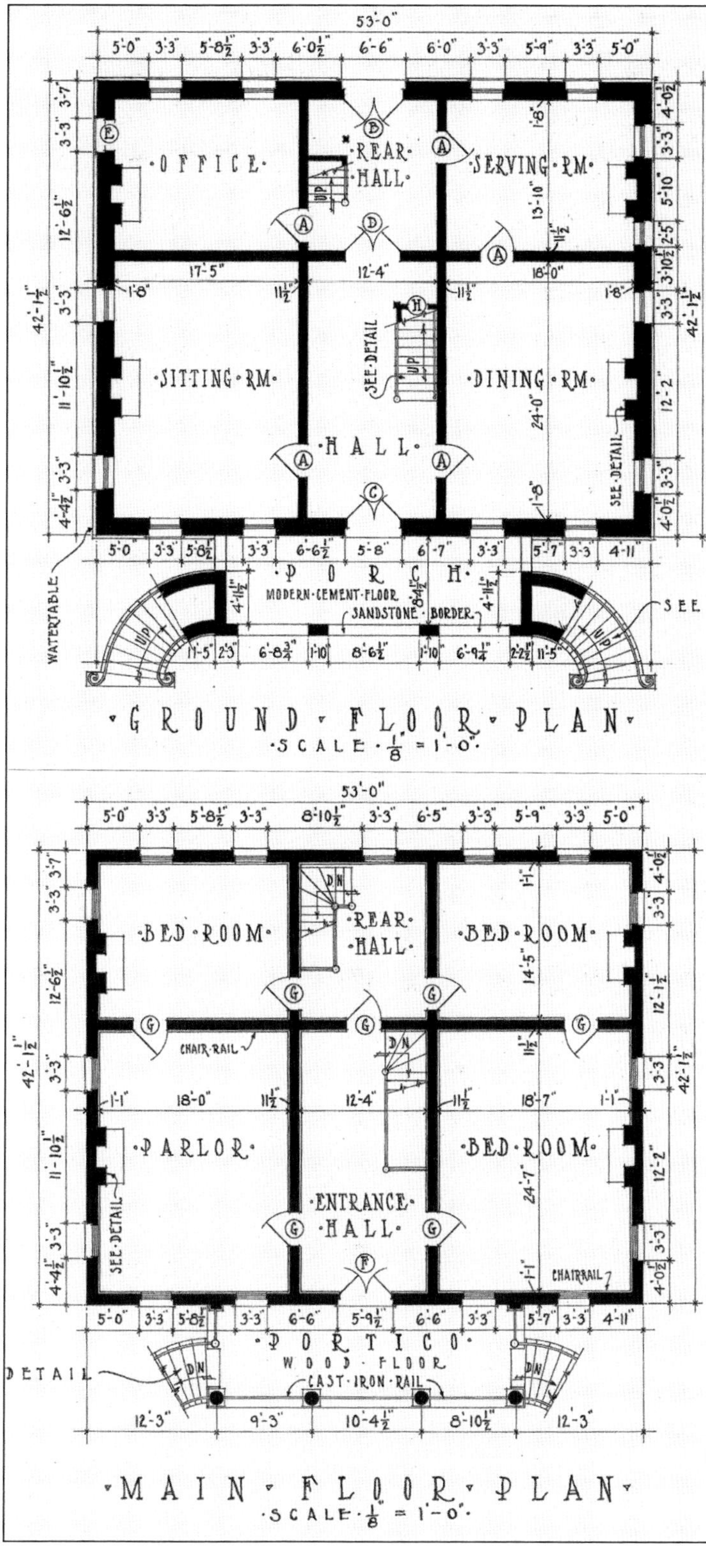

Gorgas House, Floor Plans. HABS delineator William P. Shaw drew this floor plan on February 21, 1934. It illustrates the layout of both the upper and lower levels during the time that Mamie, Ria, and Minnie, the three surviving Gorgas daughters, were still living in the home. HABS district administrator E. Walter Burkhardt stated, "This home, apart from its historic interest, is of special interest on account of the double exterior iron stairs, giving the whole building a very unusual and graceful appearance. The proportions of the two-story portico treatment are very good, and very consistent with the mass of the building as a whole. This type of raised building represents a strong Mississippi Valley influence." (LOC.)

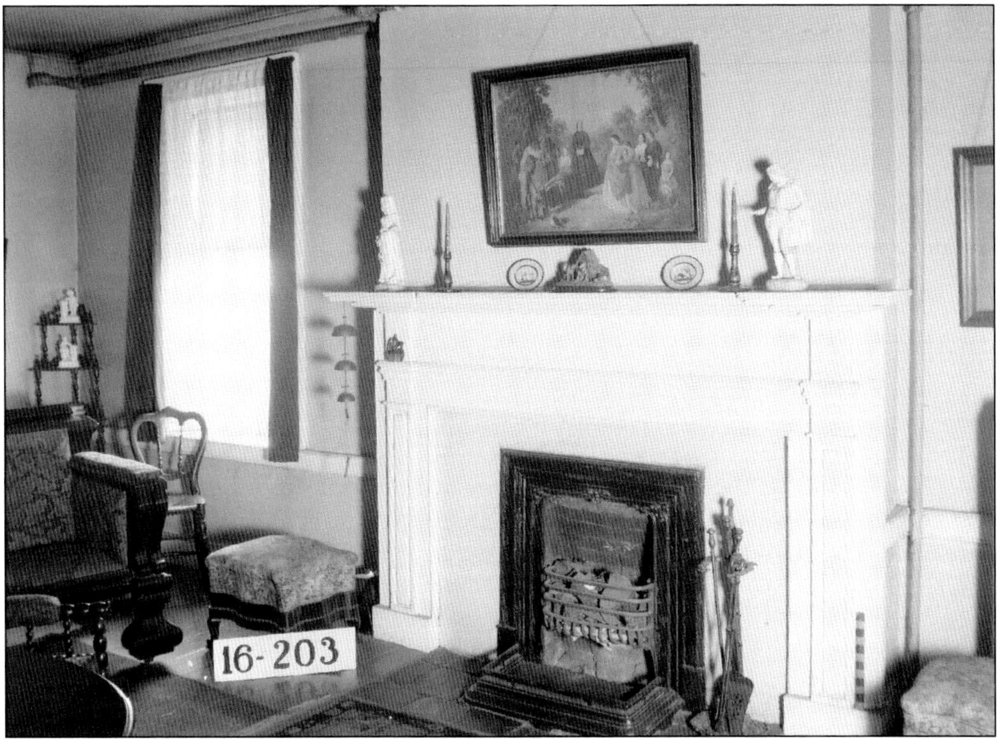

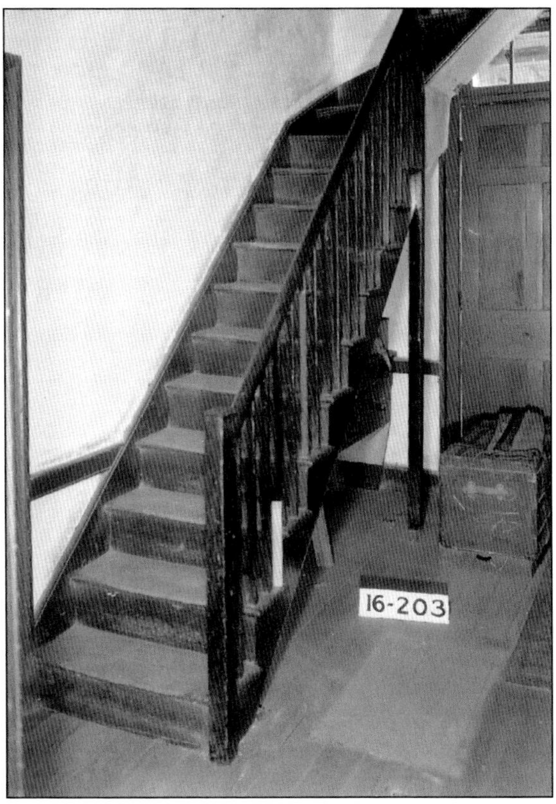

HABS Photographs, 1934. Taken by HABS photographer Alex Bush, these photographs document one of the building's sitting areas (above) and the original staircase (left), which were located at the rear of the house. According to Jessie Palfrey Leake, the granddaughter of Josiah and Amelia Gorgas, "One charm of the Gorgas house has been its simplicity. The plain painted walls—there was no [wall] paper until after 1900—the few pieces of furniture, the feeling of space and tranquility—these were its charms. No wealthy people ever lived there, so it stayed simple." (Both, LOC.)

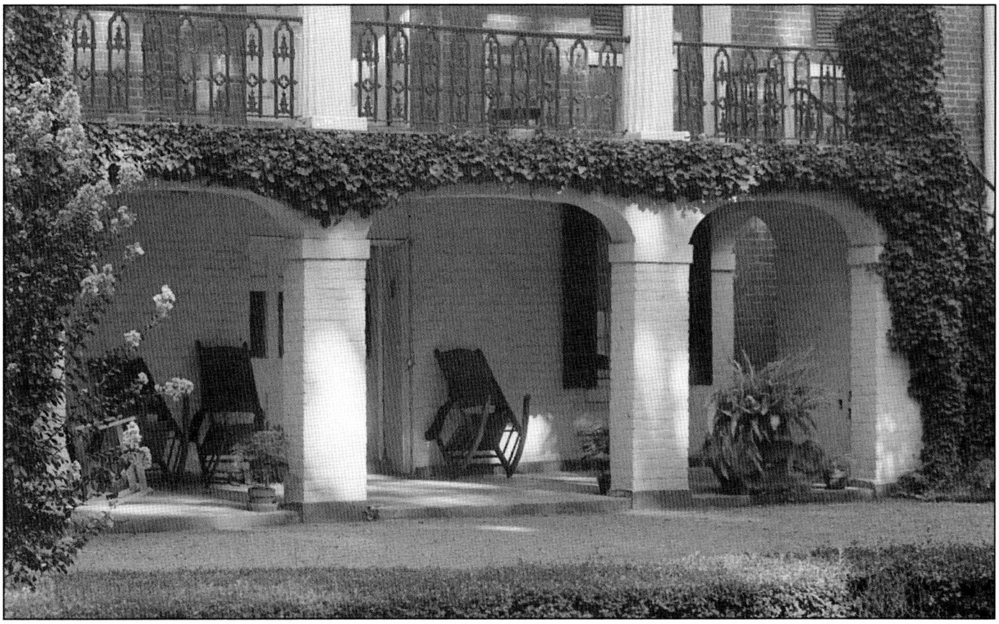

Gorgas House, 1934. In this photograph of the lower-level porch (above), also taken by Alex Bush, a ruin from William Nichols's rotunda is on display beneath the fern. The rotunda had 24 paired Ionic columns around its exterior. Carved from locally quarried sandstone, the capital fragment (below) is currently on display at the W.S. Hoole Special Collections Library. (Above, LOC; below, ULDSC.)

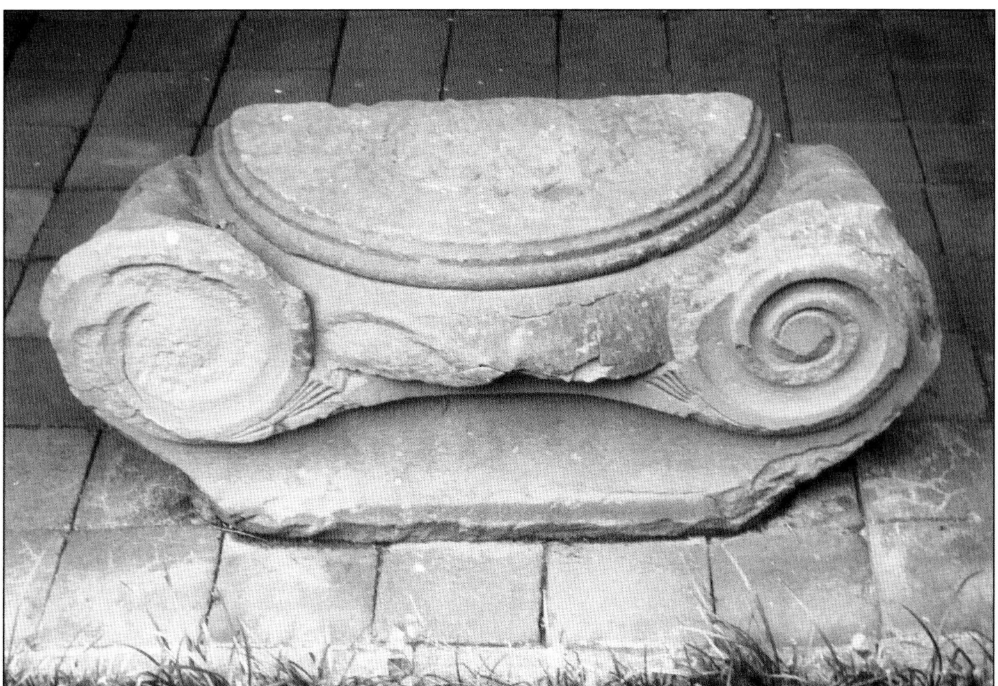

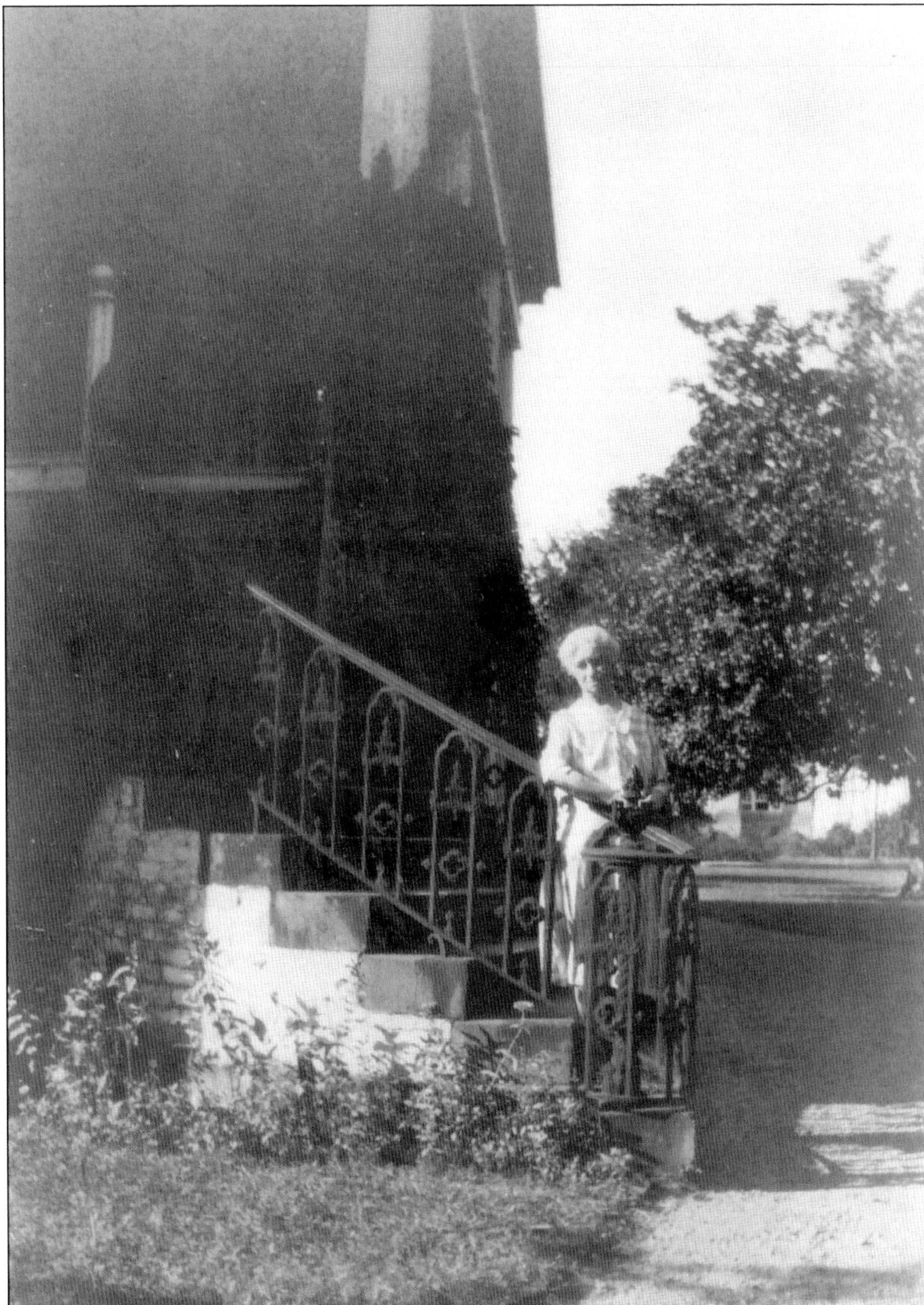

Gorgas House, c. 1931. This image is likely one of the Gorgas daughters—Mamie, Ria, or Minnie—who was living in the home at the time this photograph was taken. The daughters are known to have welcomed visitors to the lower level of their home to share the legacy of the house and family. (GHM.)

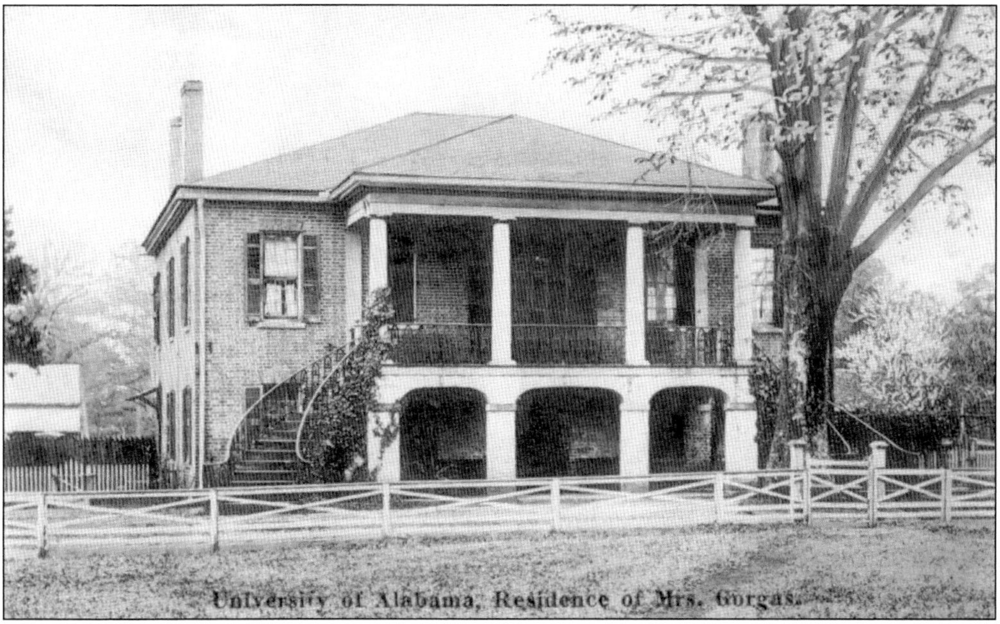

GORGAS HOUSE POSTCARDS. In 1944, the Alabama Legislature dedicated the Gorgas family house as a state shrine to Josiah, Amelia, and William Crawford Gorgas. Used as a post office, study room, and infirmary, the Gorgas's home was integral in the lives of countless university students for more than 25 years. Beginning in the early 1900s, souvenir postcards were printed depicting the Gorgas House, first as Mrs. Gorgas's residence (above) and later as a state shrine and museum (below). In 1943, the Gorgas Memorial Board was formed to oversee the care and preservation of the home. Over time, the board also developed marketing materials and museum displays. The Gorgas House became a favorite site for visitors to learn about the history of the University of Alabama campus and the Gorgas family. (Above, GHM; below, authors' collection.)

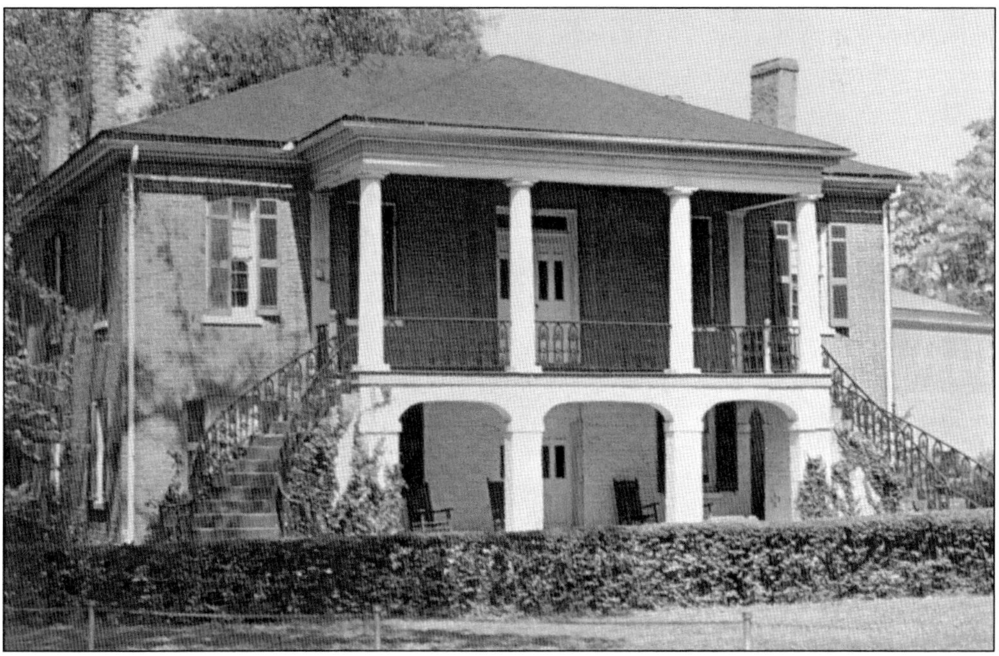

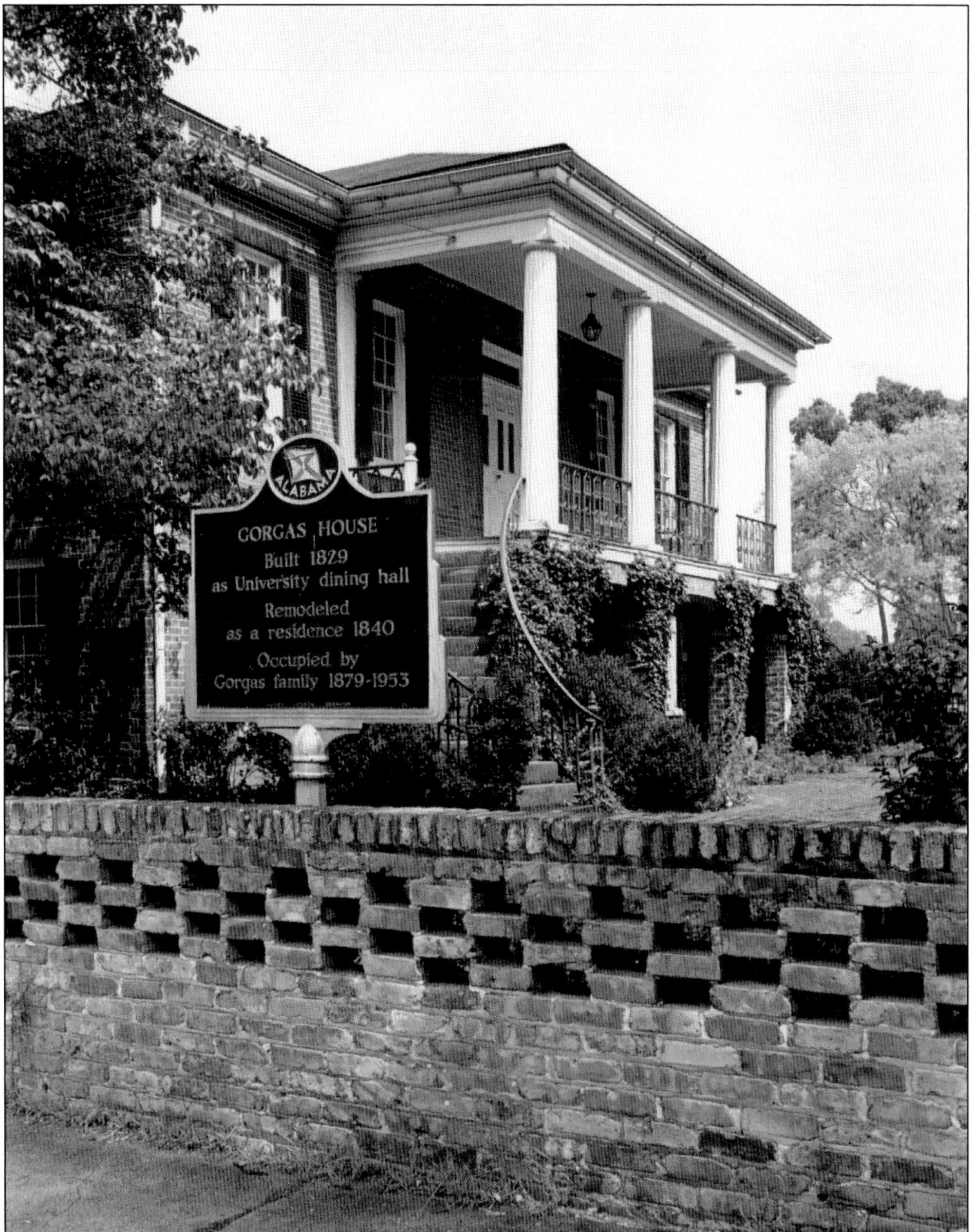

ALABAMA HISTORICAL ASSOCIATION MARKER. On May 29, 1966, the Alabama Historical Association recognized the significance of the Gorgas House with the dedication of the marker pictured here. The marker reads, "Gorgas House. Built 1829 as University dining hall. Remodeled as a residence 1840. Occupied by Gorgas family 1879–1953. Preserved as a memorial to: General Josiah Gorgas (1818–1883), Chief of Ordnance, C. S. A. 1861–1865, President of the University 1878–1879; Mrs. Amelia Gayle Gorgas (1826–1913), University Librarian 1883–1906; General William Crawford Gorgas (1854–1920), Surgeon General, United States Army, Sanitary engineer whose work in eliminating Yellow Fever assured Construction of Panama Canal."

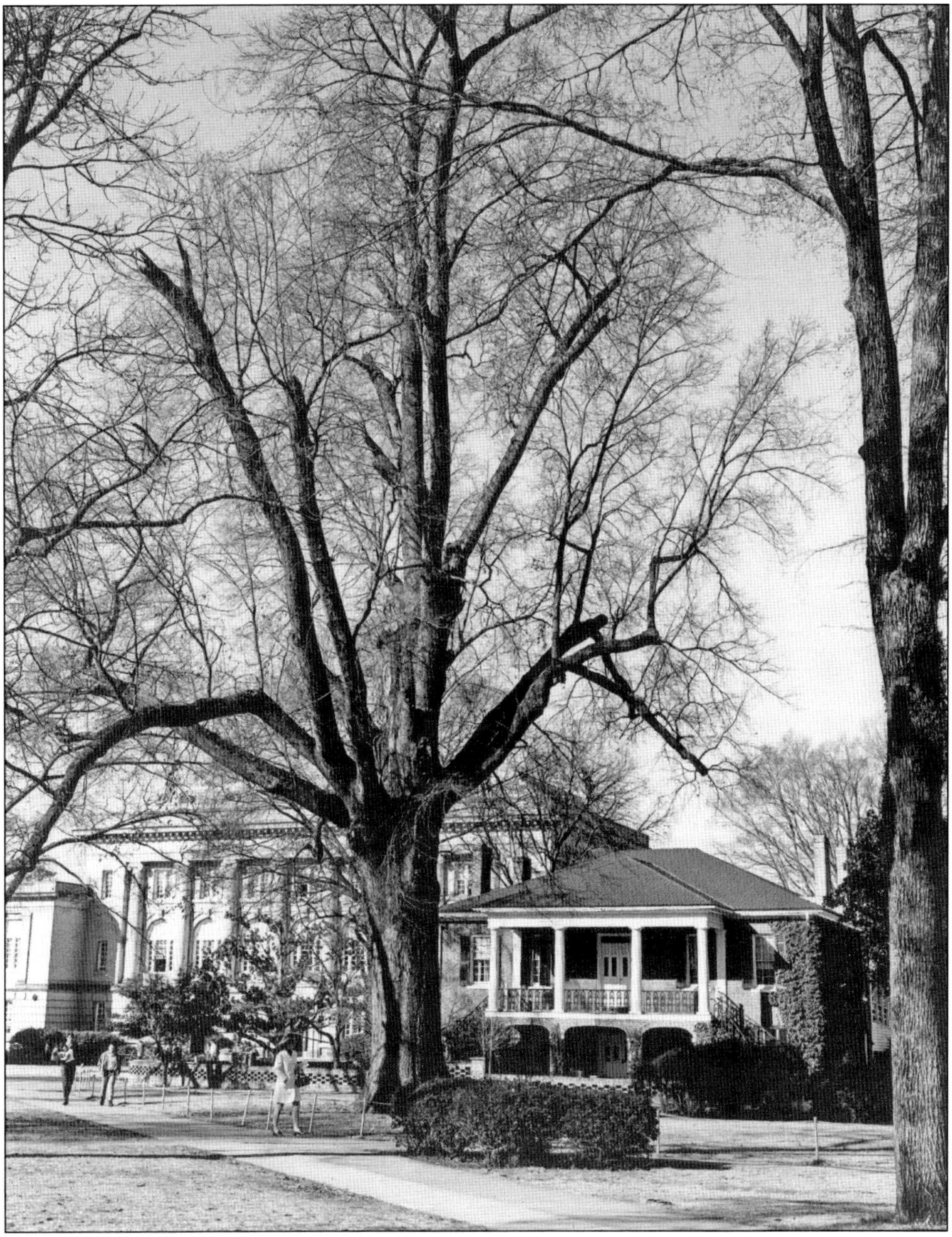

GORGAS OAK, UNIVERSITY OF ALABAMA. In 1978, the American Foresters Association placed the Gorgas Oak (*Quereus phellos*) on a list of famous trees. Honored for its size and historical significance, the tree was presumed to be at least as old as the university. Unfortunately, lightning struck the tree in 1981, requiring its removal. A seedling from the tree was replanted near the original location, where it is marked with a plaque noting its significance.

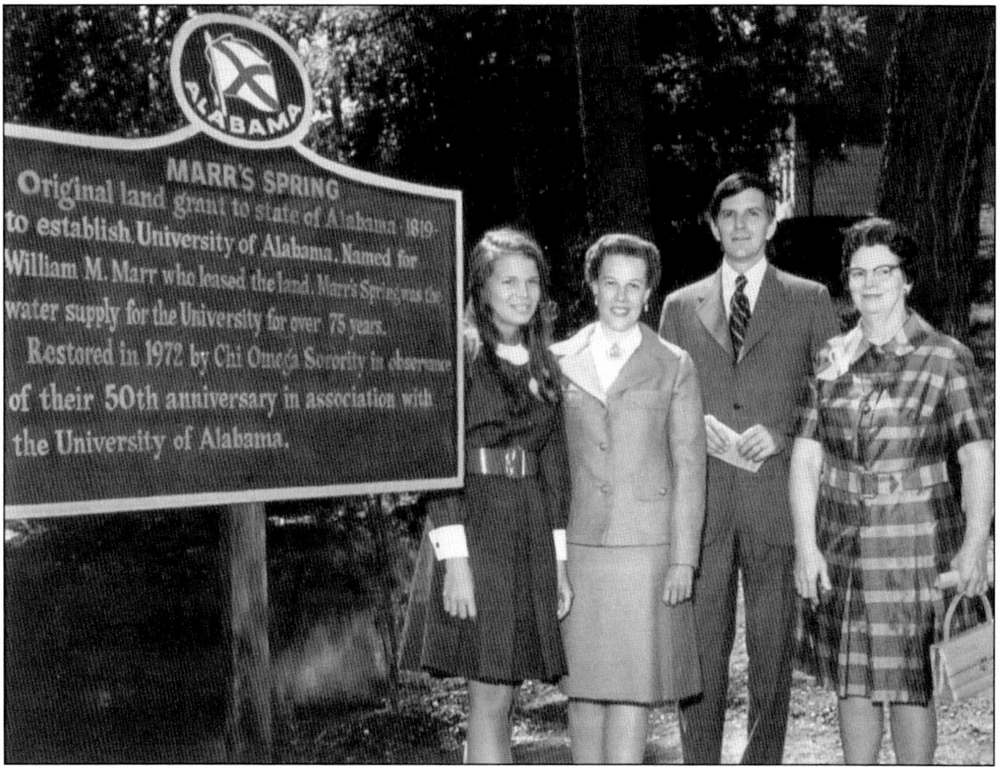

MARR'S SPRING CISTERNS. Marr's Spring served as the primary water supply for the campus for more than 100 years. Eventually, the needs of the university increased, and the spring no longer fully sustained the campus. In 1972, the Chi Omega sorority worked collaboratively with the university to recognize the historical significance of the spring. A historical marker was erected on the site, as seen above with university president F. David Matthews. In 2011, the university's facilities and grounds department revived the spring by restoring the lower portions of the cisterns, seen below, to create a new green space. The bricks for the cisterns were reclaimed from the 1950s-era Gorgas House fence. (Above, ULDSC; below, authors' collection.)

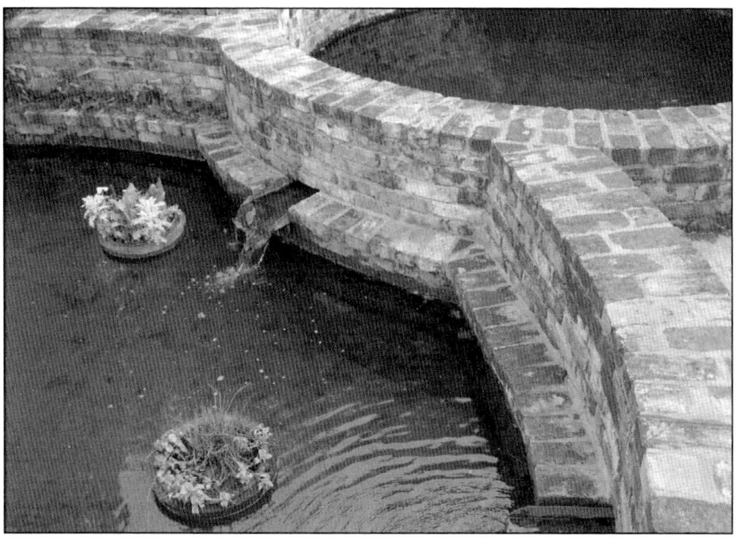

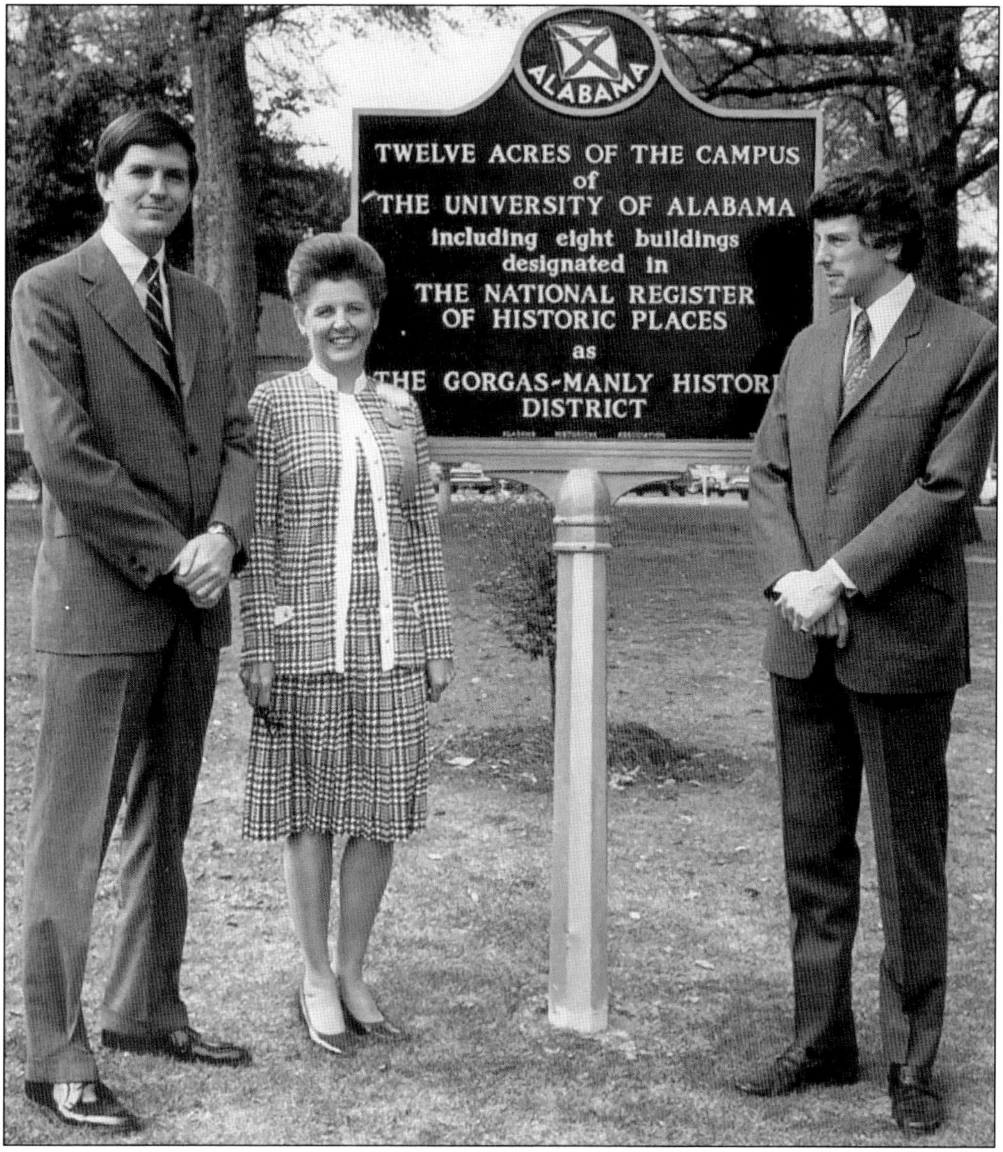

GORGAS-MANLY DISTRICT. On July 14, 1971, the Gorgas House was added to the National Register of Historic Places as part of the 12-acre Gorgas-Manly Historic District on the University of Alabama campus. Also included in the district are the Little Round House (guardhouse) and Woods, Clark, Manly, Garland, Tuomey, and Barnard Halls. The eight buildings included in the district represent the core of the early university campus. University of Alabama president F. David Matthews (1969–1980) is shown here at the far left in the photograph.

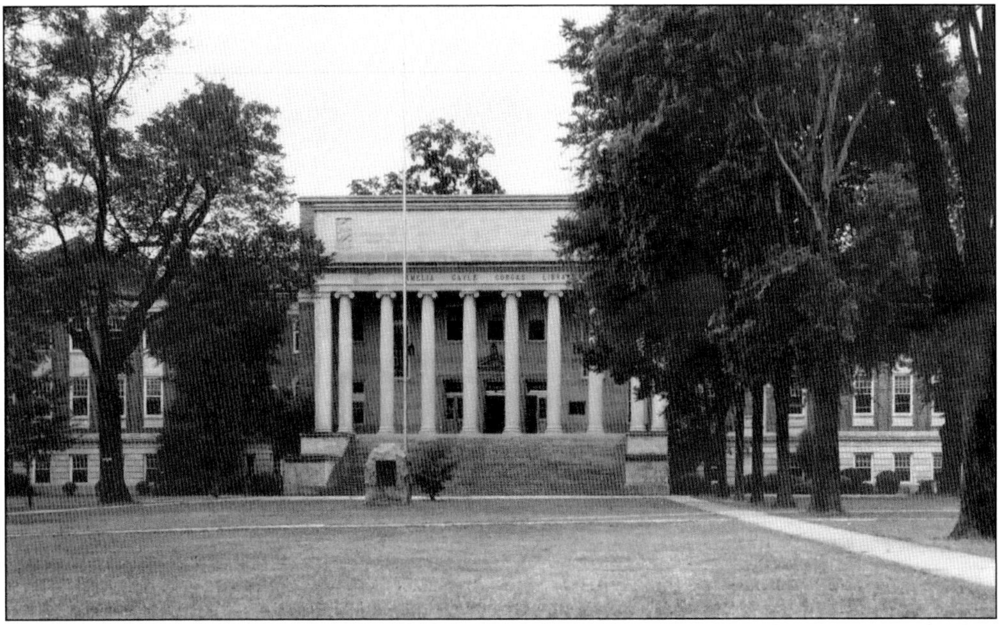

AMELIA GAYLE GORGAS LIBRARY AND ROTUNDA EXCAVATION. Amelia Gayle Gorgas was the first female campus librarian and the first woman to have an academic building named in her honor at the University of Alabama. Built in 1925, the initial Amelia Gayle Gorgas Library was located on the second floor of what is now Carmichael Hall. This small library was only temporary while funds were raised for a permanent building to house the main university library. At the time of its completion in 1939, the official Amelia Gayle Gorgas Library (above) was the largest library in the state. The front staircase of the library opens onto the foundation of the original rotunda (below), where the first university library was located.

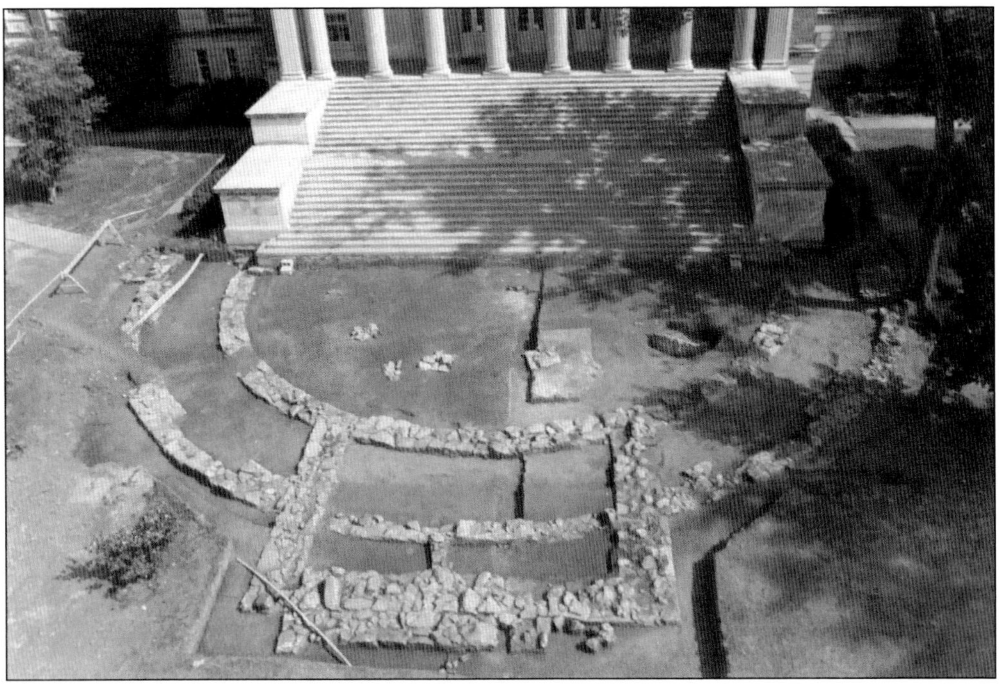

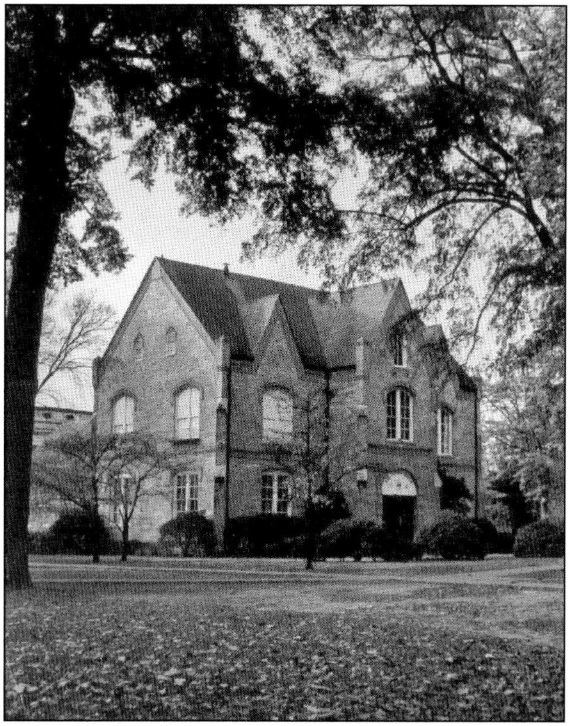

Barnard Hall, c. 1945, and Tuomey Hall, c. 1970. Several buildings at the university have been named for faculty members associated with the Gorgas House. Barnard Hall (right) was named for Frederick A.P. Barnard, who lived in the house from 1844 to 1847. Tuomey Hall (below) was named for Michael Tuomey, who lived in the house beginning in 1847. Both Barnard and Tuomey Halls were designed by Montgomery architect W.A. Crossland in the late 1880s. Another campus building, Hardaway Hall (not pictured), was named for Robert Hardaway, who was the first full-time professor of civil engineering and served as the university's acting architect, during which time he supervised the renovation of the Gorgas House porch in 1895.

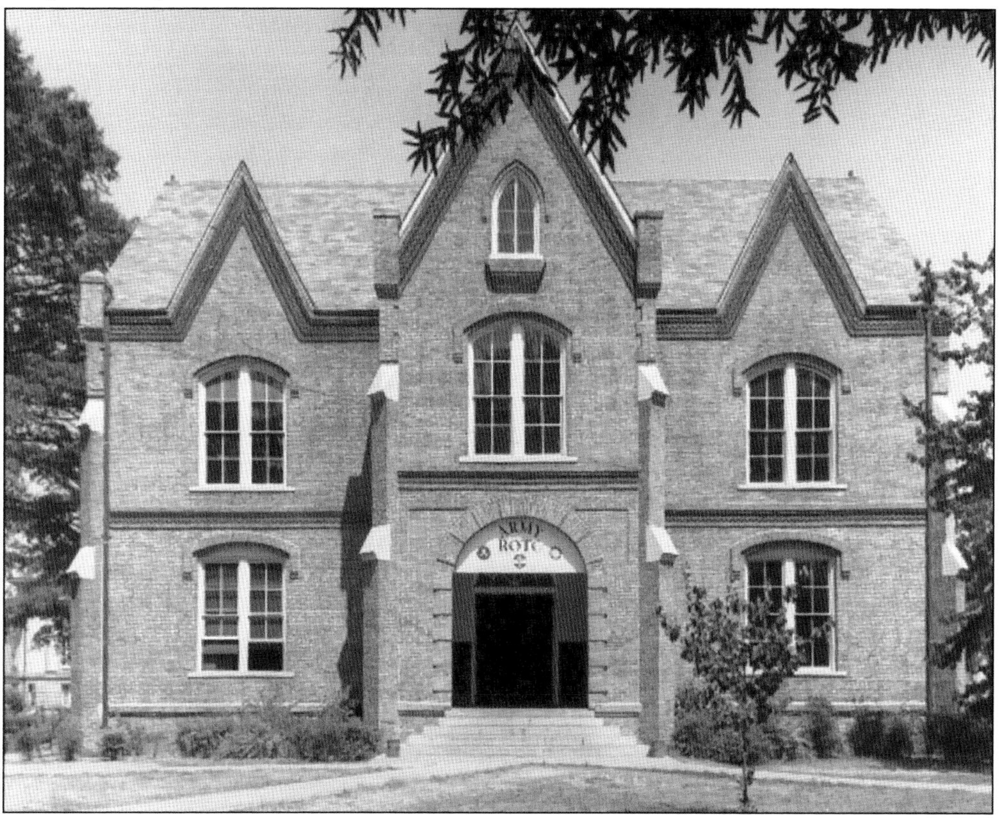

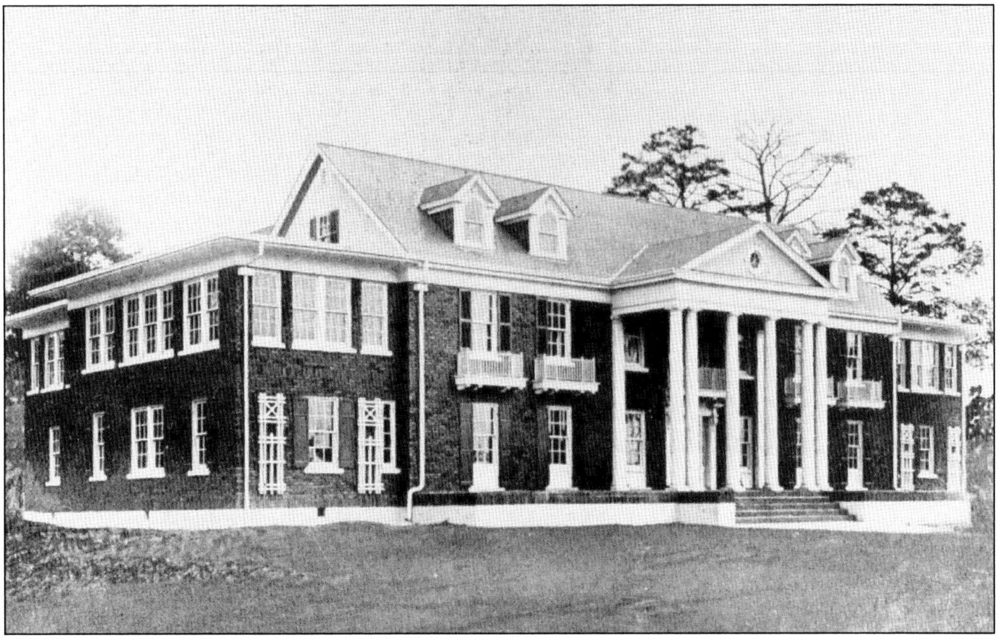

Gorgas Hall, University of Alabama. Named for Josiah Gorgas, Gorgas Hall at the University of Alabama was erected as a men's dormitory in 1921. In the 1960s, the building was converted for use by the university's police department. The Delta Kappa Epsilon fraternity house replaced the building in 2005.

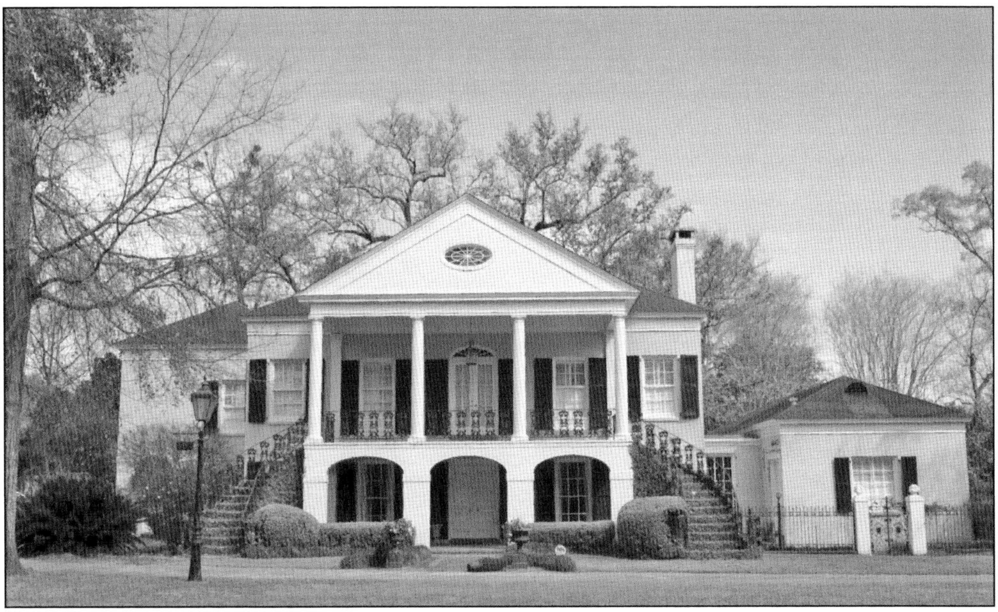

Private Residence, Mobile, Alabama. The architecture of the Gorgas House has been an inspiration for other university buildings, as well as private homes and businesses in Tuscaloosa and more distant communities throughout the state and the country. One example is the private home in Mobile shown here. In 1956, this home won an award from the Historic Mobile Preservation Society for the congruence of the architectural design with historical Southern style. (Authors' collection.)

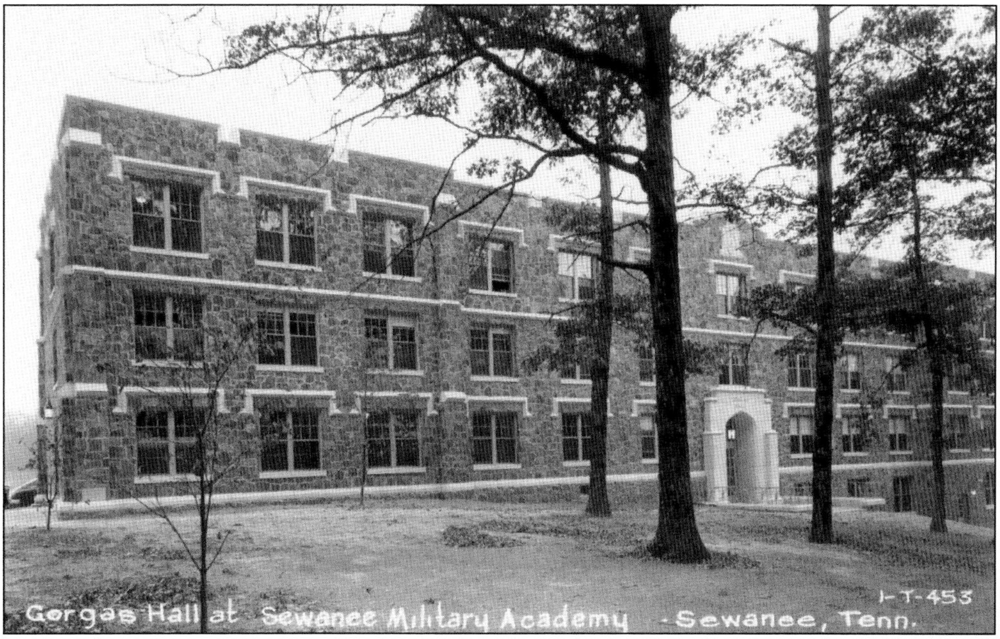

Gorgas Hall, University of the South. Gorgas Hall at the University of the South in Sewanee, Tennessee, was built in 1952 to serve as a student residence hall. Its name honored Josiah Gorgas, the university's second vice chancellor, and his son William Crawford Gorgas, one of the most renowned alumni of the university. (USA.)

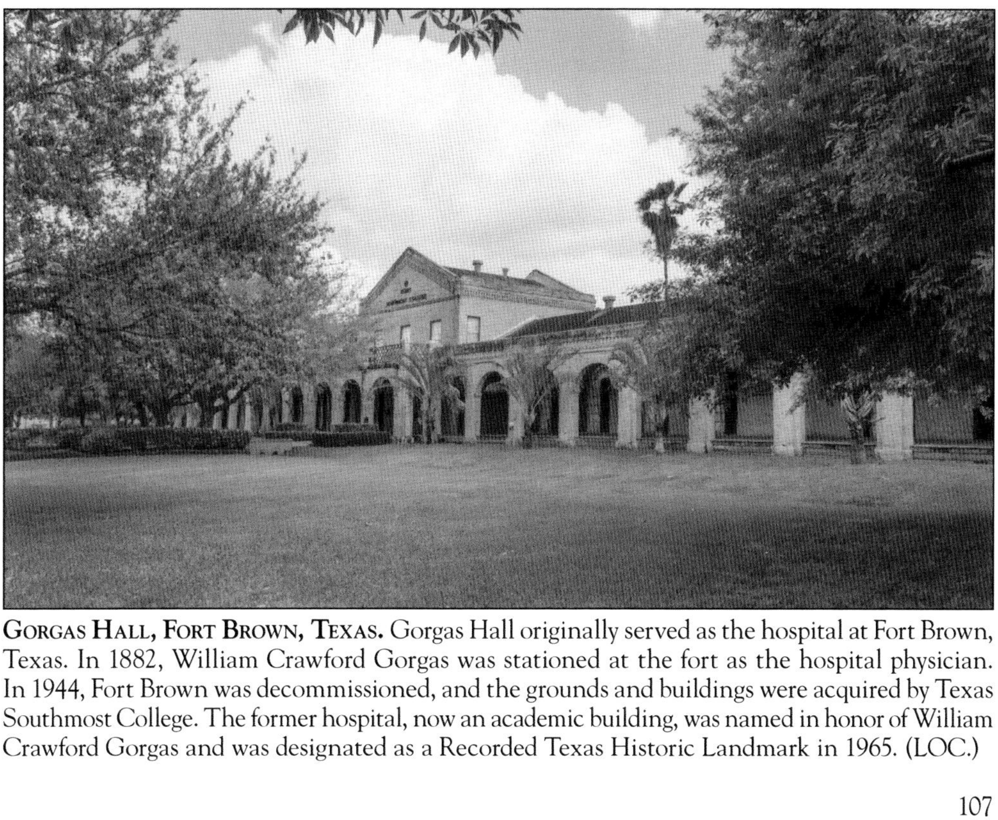

Gorgas Hall, Fort Brown, Texas. Gorgas Hall originally served as the hospital at Fort Brown, Texas. In 1882, William Crawford Gorgas was stationed at the fort as the hospital physician. In 1944, Fort Brown was decommissioned, and the grounds and buildings were acquired by Texas Southmost College. The former hospital, now an academic building, was named in honor of William Crawford Gorgas and was designated as a Recorded Texas Historic Landmark in 1965. (LOC.)

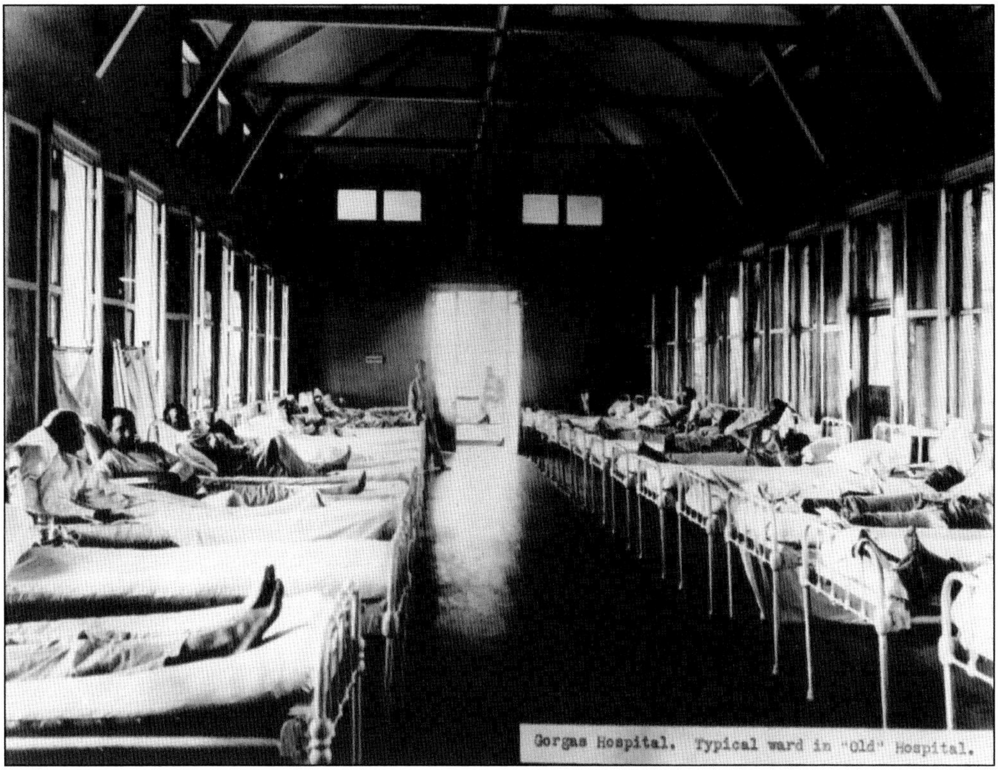

GORGAS HOSPITAL, PANAMA. During his years in Panama in the early 1900s, William Crawford Gorgas recommended improvements to Ancon Hospital, including screened doors and windows, as part of his overall sanitation plan for the Panama Canal Zone. In 1928, the hospital was renamed in his honor. In 1977, the Gorgas Hospital was transferred from US Army to Panamanian control via the Torrijos-Carter Treaties. In 1999, the building became home to the Instituto Oncologico Nacional, a hospital specializing in the treatment of cancer. (NLM.)

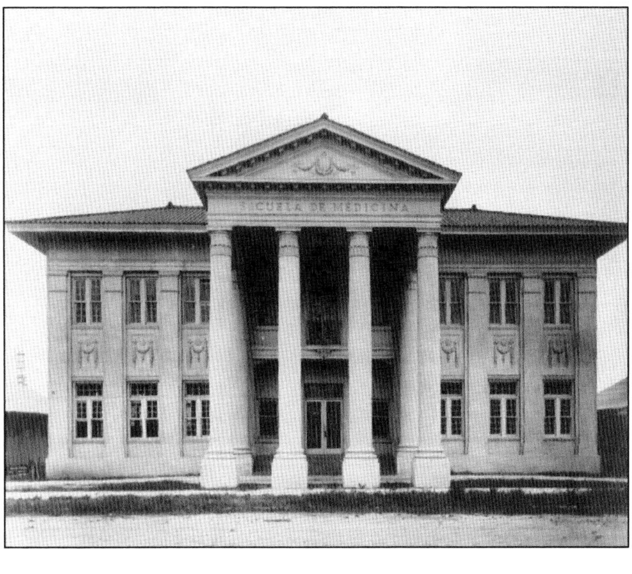

GORGAS MEMORIAL INSTITUTE. In 1921, Panamanian president Belisario Porras Barahona proposed the creation of an Institute of Tropical and Preventative Medicine. Dedicated to William Crawford Gorgas, the laboratory and institute focused on the treatment of parasitic diseases and viruses common to tropical environments. The institute lost congressional funding in 1990 and was relocated to the University of Alabama at Birmingham in 1992. (NLM.)

THE GORGAS COURSE IN CLINICAL TROPICAL MEDICINE, LIMA, PERU. In 1995, the University of Alabama at Birmingham School of Medicine, in conjunction with the Universidad Peruana Cayetano Heredia, reintroduced the Gorgas Course in Clinical Tropical Medicine. The nine-week diploma course, taught in Peru, includes lectures, case studies, bedside rounds, and diagnostic laboratory experience with guest faculty from the United States, Canada, and Africa. The Gorgas Course is recognized as one of the world's premier training programs in tropical medicine. (NLM.)

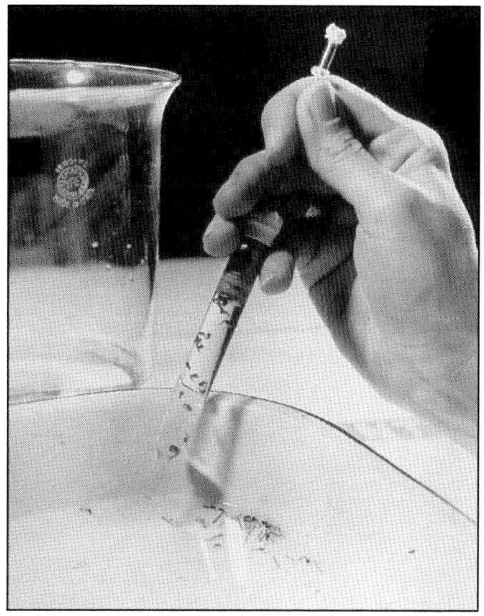

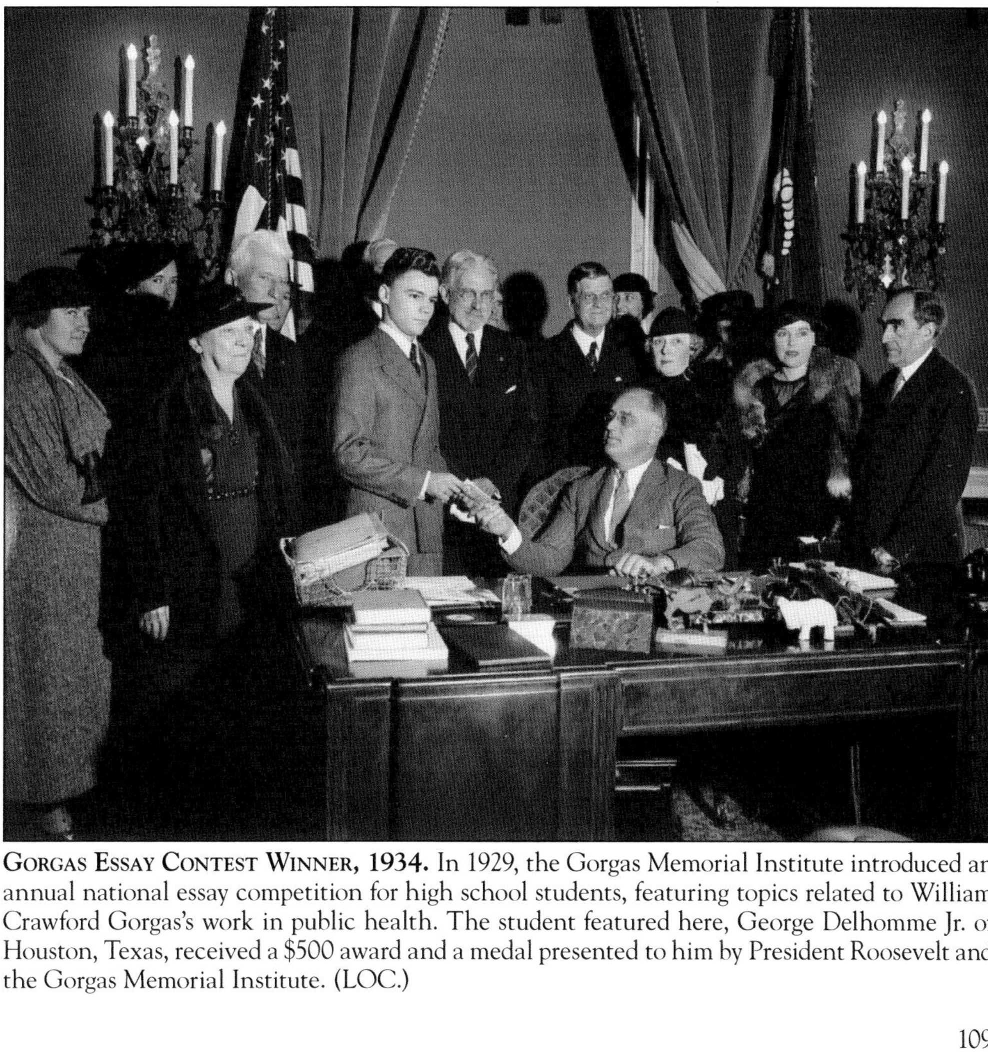

GORGAS ESSAY CONTEST WINNER, 1934. In 1929, the Gorgas Memorial Institute introduced an annual national essay competition for high school students, featuring topics related to William Crawford Gorgas's work in public health. The student featured here, George Delhomme Jr. of Houston, Texas, received a $500 award and a medal presented to him by President Roosevelt and the Gorgas Memorial Institute. (LOC.)

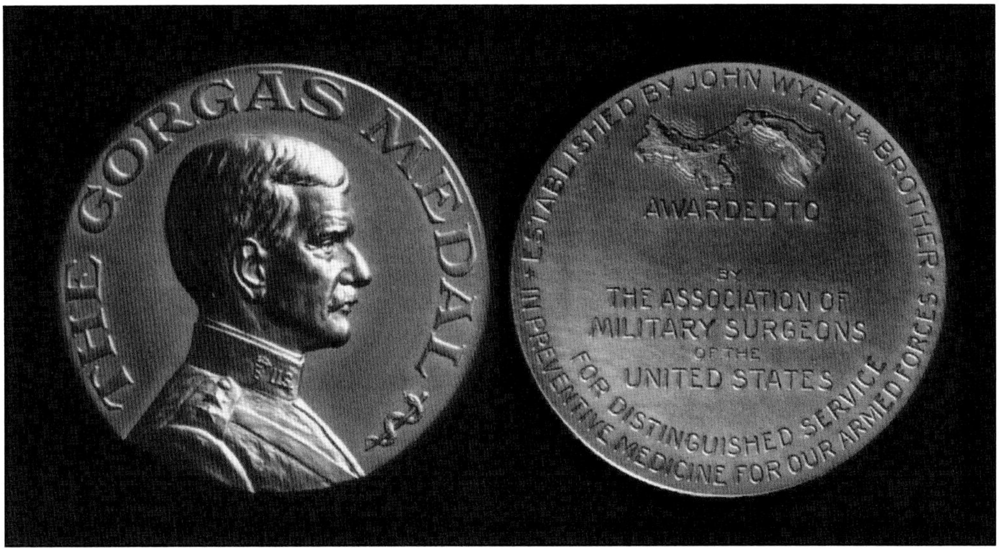

GORGAS MEDAL. Established in 1915, the Gorgas Medal was awarded to winners of a writing competition hosted by the Medical Research Corps Association. Wyeth Laboratories assumed management of the award in 1942, granting it to individuals who performed distinguished work in preventative medicine. Honorees included Frederick Russell, for the development of a typhoid vaccine, and Charles Shepard, one of the discoverers of the bacteria that cause Legionnaires' disease. In 2010, the award was restructured and renamed the William Gorgas Preventive Medicine Award. (NLM.)

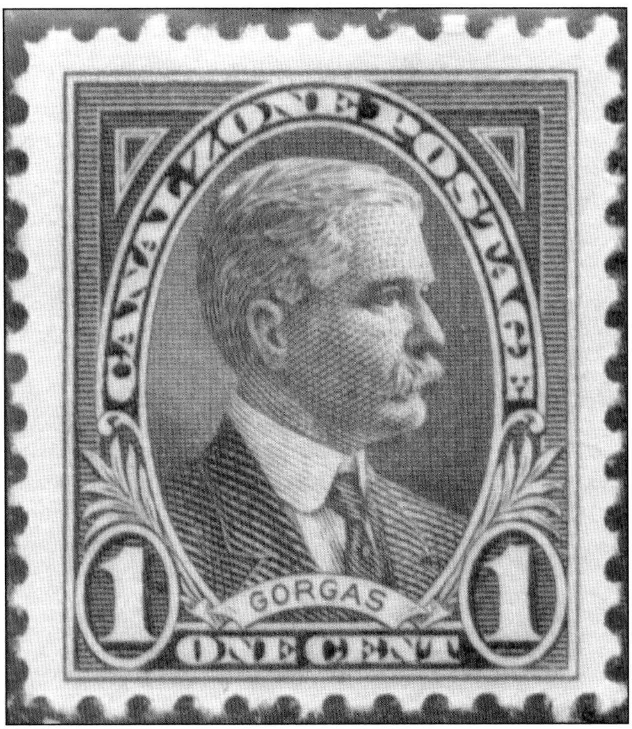

WILLIAM C. GORGAS STAMP. The one-cent Gorgas stamp was first issued on October 3, 1928. It was the second stamp issued by the Panama Canal Zone post office under a policy of issuing stamps directly related to the men, activities, or history of the Panama Canal Zone construction. At one time, the one-cent Gorgas stamp was believed to be the "oldest stamp in the world in terms of continuous use." Following the Torrijos-Carter Treaties, the final Panama Canal Zone stamp was issued on October 25, 1978. (Courtesy of Dennis Pappas Sr.)

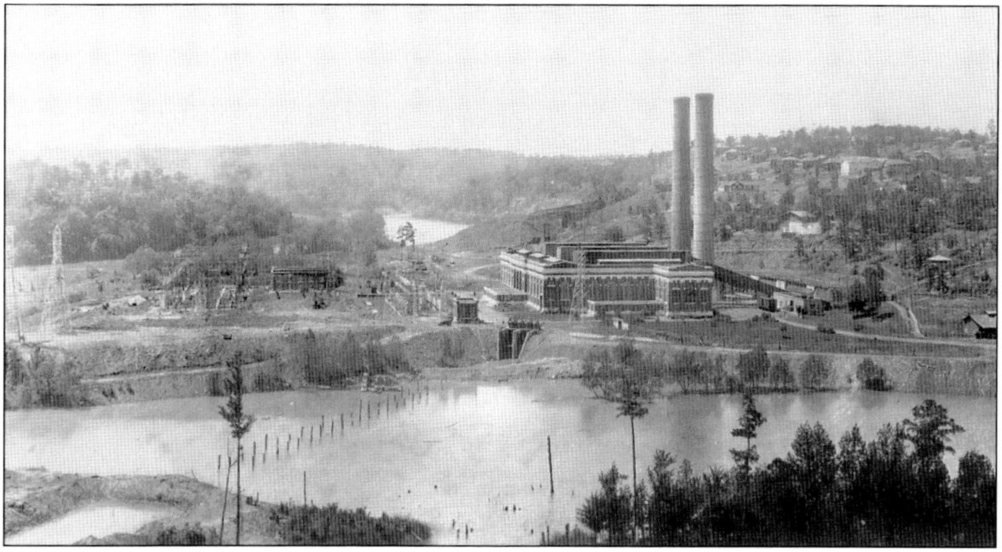

Gorgas Steam Plant and Village School. In response to increased electricity needs for wartime manufacturing, the Warrior Reserve Steam Plant (above) was built on the Black Warrior River in Walker County, Alabama, in 1917. In 1944, the steam plant was dedicated to William Crawford Gorgas in appreciation for his distinguished career in medicine and public health. In the early years, the steam plant operated continuously, so a village was constructed for the families of the coal mine and steam plant workers. On the hillsides surrounding the plant, the company built hundreds of houses for the workers, as well as churches, a ball field, a post office, and a hospital. The company also constructed a school within the Gorgas village (below), where children attended elementary and middle school. (Above, APC; below, APC, Charles E. Jowers Collection.)

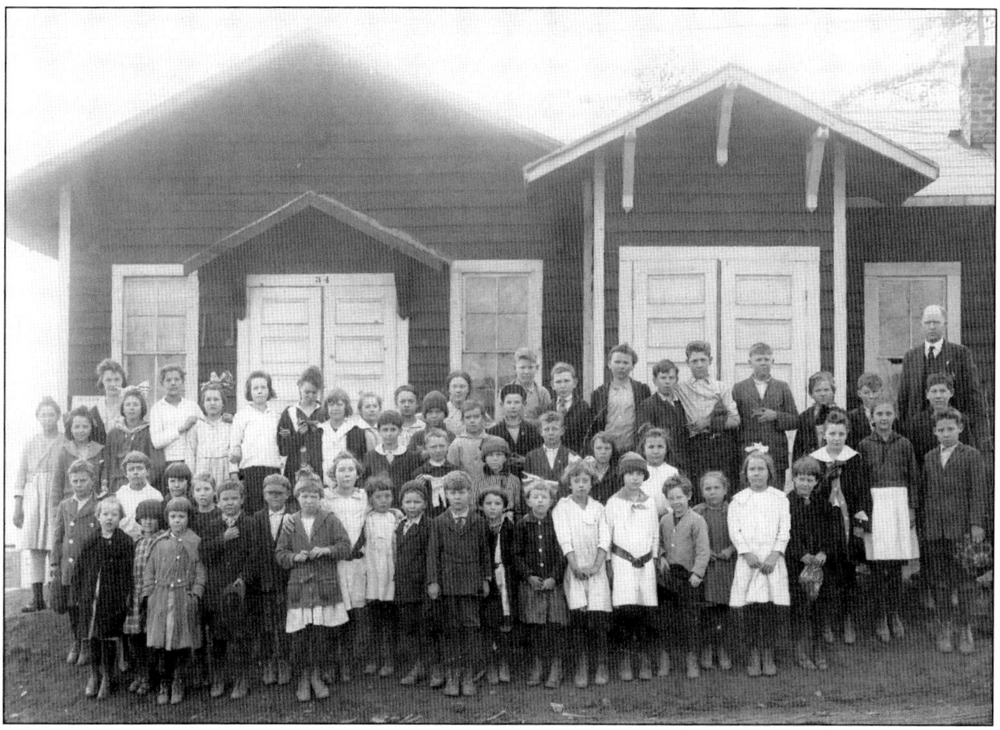

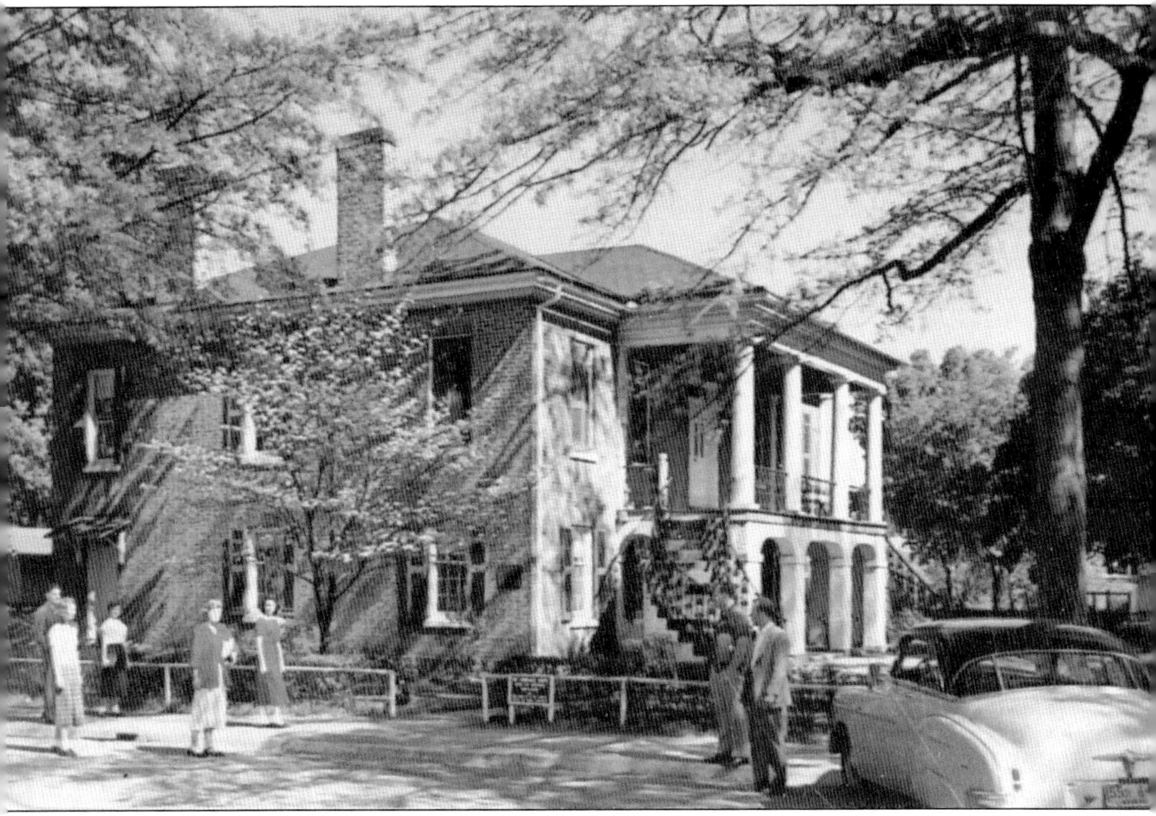

GORGAS HOUSE AS A MUSEUM. In 1954, the university designated the Gorgas family residence as a museum. The succession from private residence to a museum happened quickly with the support of Gorgas family members. The rapid progression allowed many artifacts and mementos of the family to be preserved in the museum's collection. (GHM.)

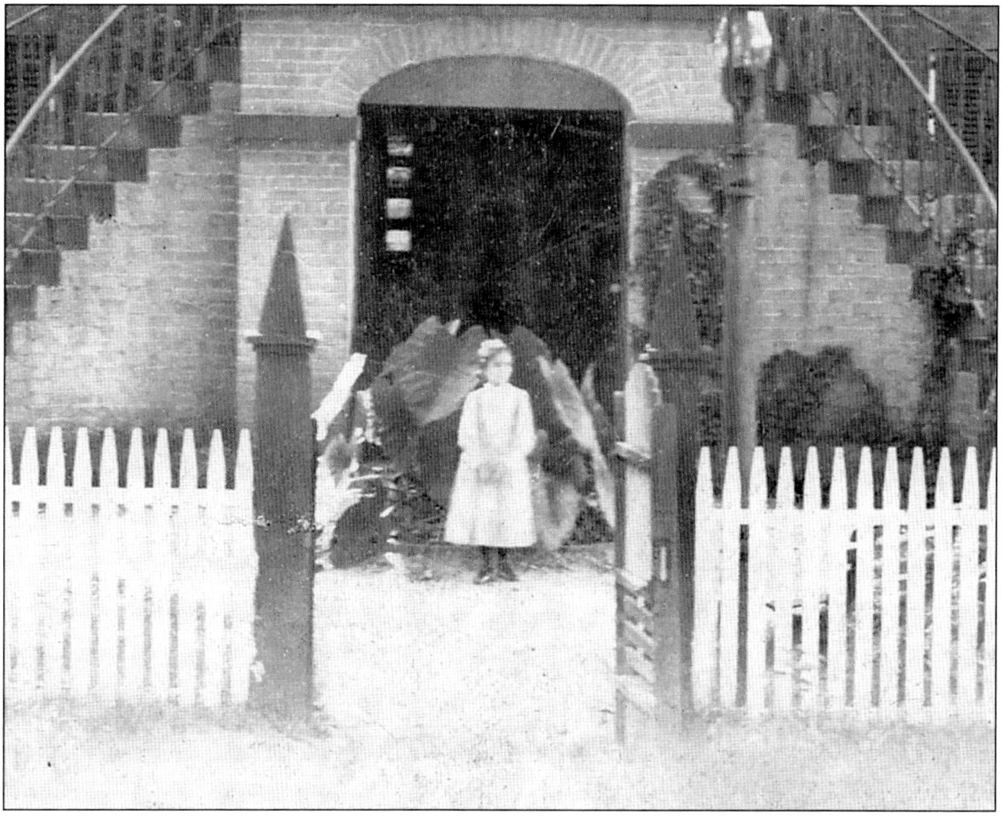

Jessie Palfrey Leake. Born in 1883, Jessie Leake was the granddaughter of Josiah and Amelia Gorgas. The photograph above shows her as a young girl visiting her grandmother. Later in life, Jessie lived in the home with her mother, Minnie (Gorgas) Palfrey, and her aunt Ria Gorgas. She served as custodian of the home until her mother and aunt passed away, after which she supported the conversion of the building into a museum. The photograph at right is on display at the Gorgas House Museum. (Above, ULDSC; right, GHM.)

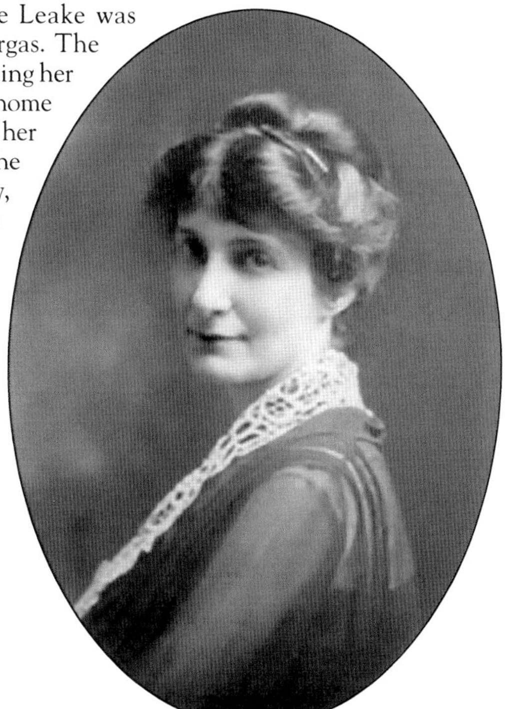

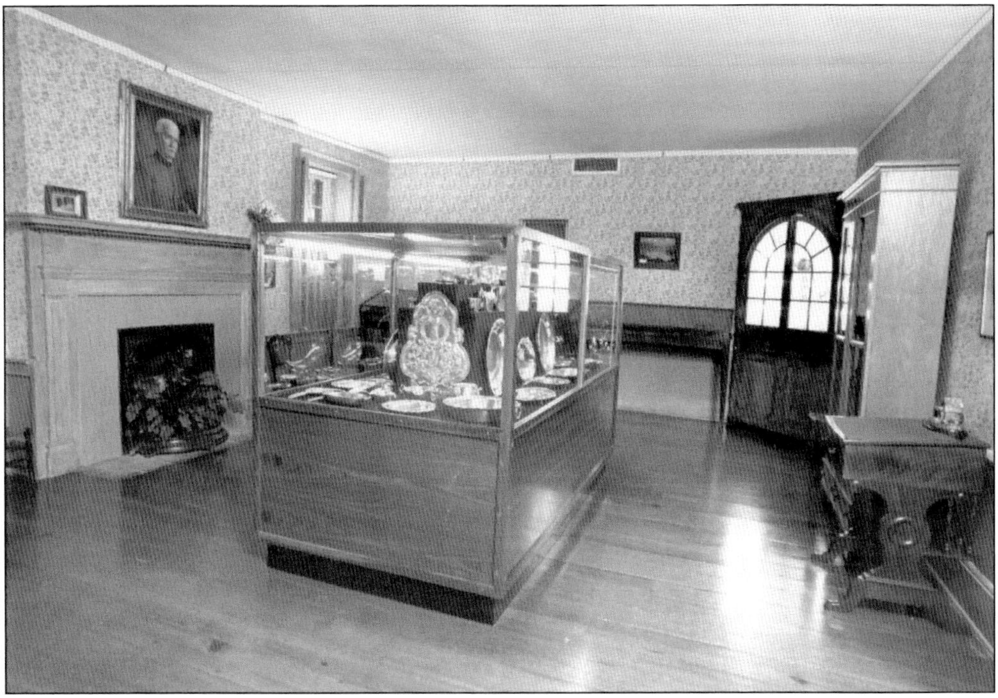

Gorgas House, Museum Room, 1950s. During the process of establishing the museum, one of the lower-level rooms was designated as the Museum Room. Exhibition cases were donated to showcase a collection of Spanish Colonial silver that belonged to William Crawford Gorgas and his wife, Marie. The silver (below) was collected during William Crawford's work in Central and South America. The collection includes pieces that date to the early 1680s. (Above, GHM; below, ULDSC.)

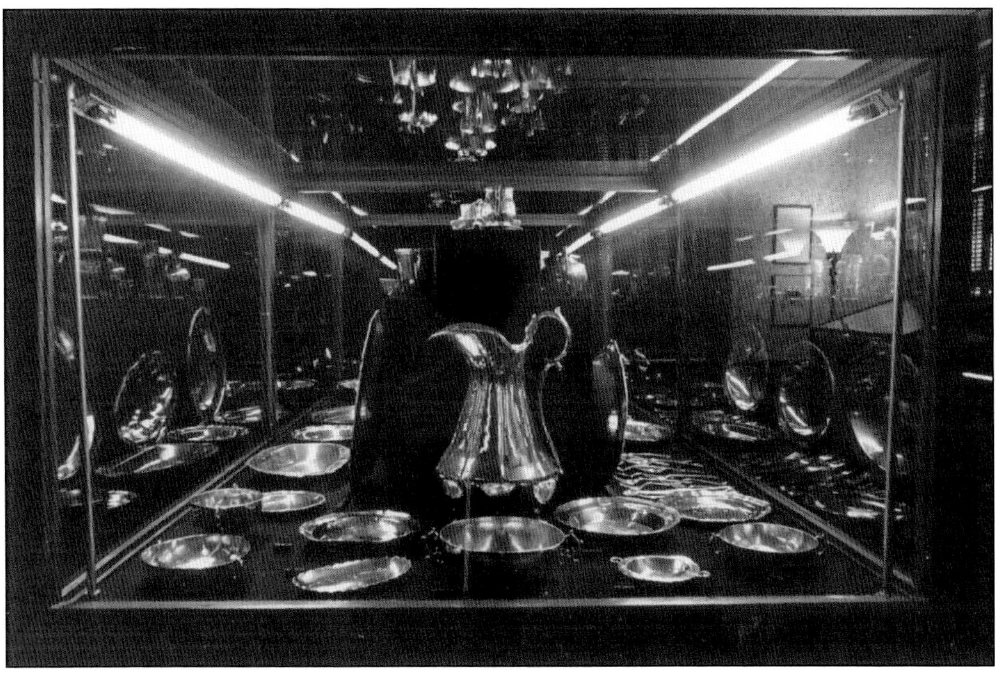

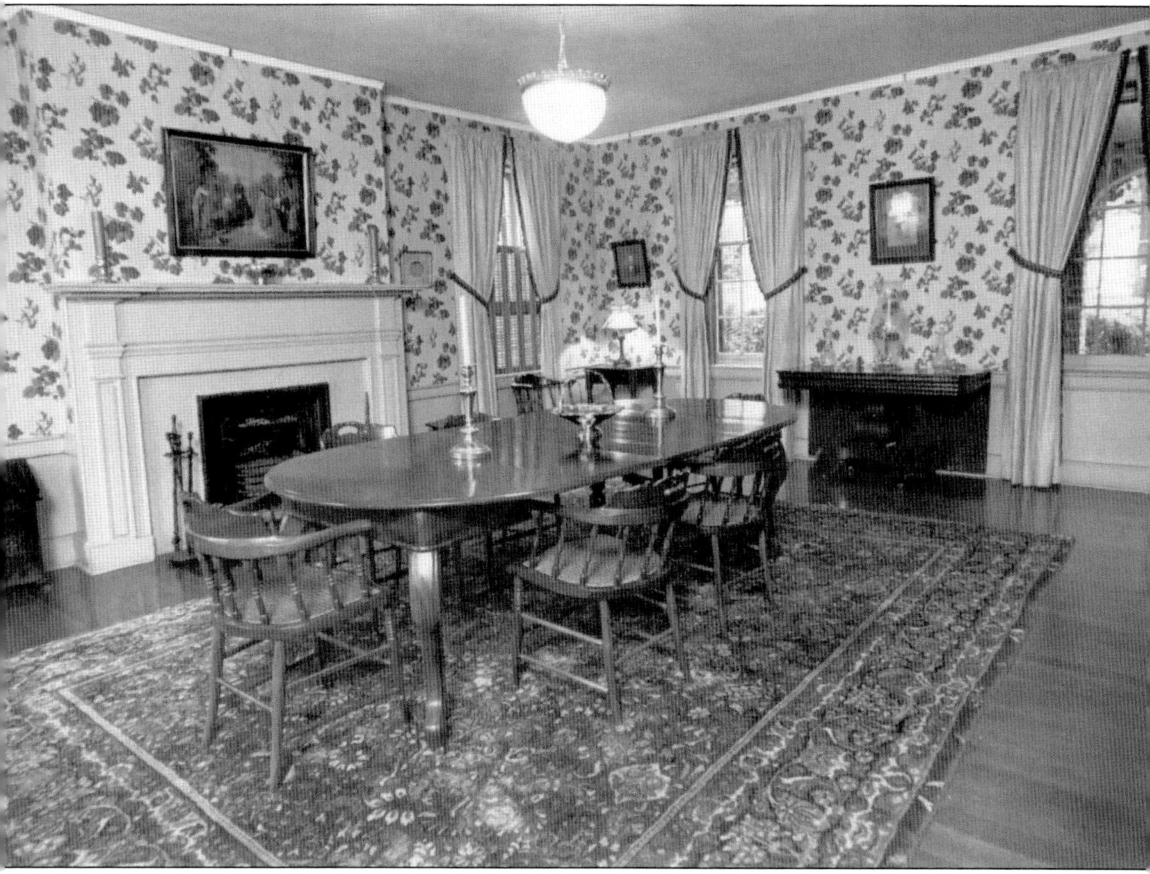

Dining Room, 1955. The home's furnishings and artifacts reflect the lives of the Gorgas family, with pieces collected throughout their military appointments and travels, gifts from friends and family, and cherished family keepsakes. In this photograph, the dining table was donated to the Gorgas family by Prof. Robert Hardaway in the 1890s, the drop-leaf table came from the Mobile home of Gov. John Gayle (Amelia Gorgas's father), and the chairs likely belonged to Amelia's sister Sarah Gayle Crawford and were given to Amelia around 1895. (GHM.)

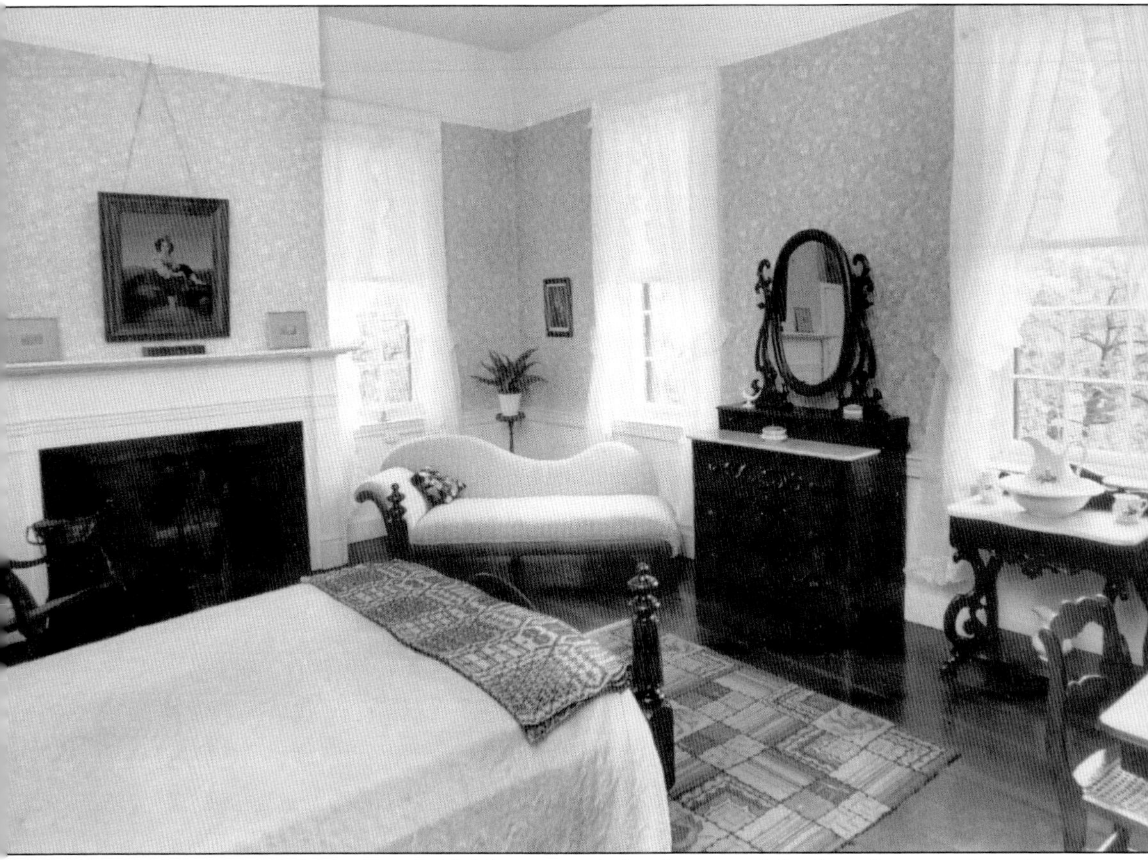

AMELIA GORGAS BEDROOM, 1955. The stories behind many of the furnishings and artifacts on exhibit in the museum allow visitors to learn the personal character and life stories of Gorgas family members and experience life in the 19th century. This photograph shows Amelia Gorgas's bedroom. According to museum records, the bedroom set was first used by the Gorgases early in their married life. The small Limoges powder box on the dresser was given to Amelia by the wife of Charles Barnwell, a university professor of English around 1899. The painting above the fireplace (left) was given to Amelia by her brother-in-law Dr. William Crawford, who received it in lieu of payment for medical services rendered to a family. (GHM.)

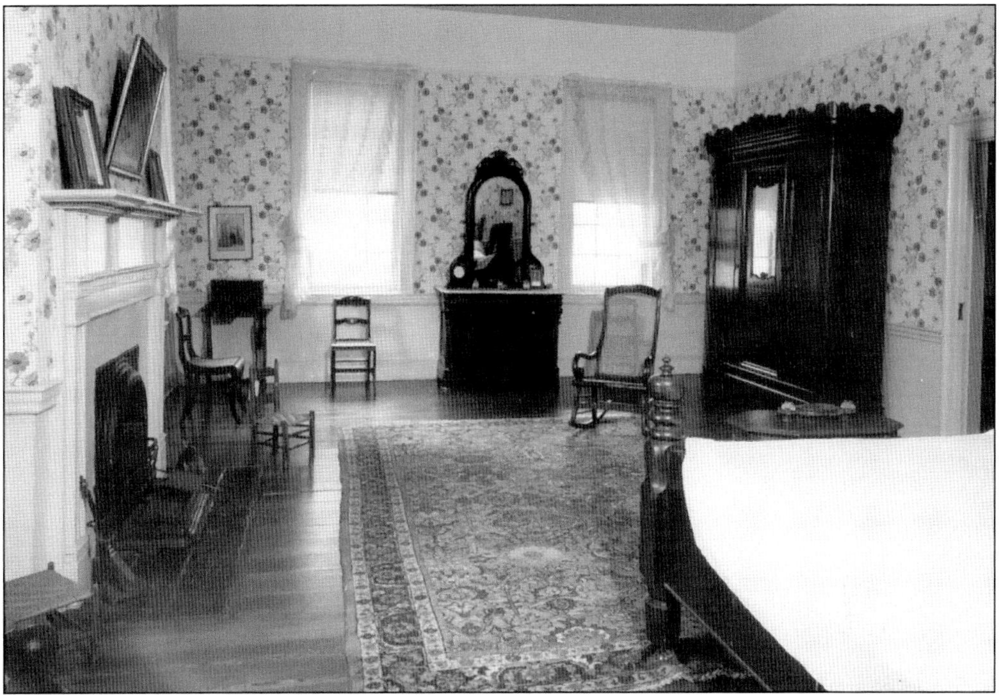

Gorgas House, Master Bedroom. During the 1950s, members of local women's associations who frequently gathered at the museum sought to modernize the building (above) by adding wallpaper, chandeliers, and many of the large rugs visible in these photographs. From 2001 to 2005, the university supported extensive interior restorations, which included removal of the wallpaper and a paint analysis by Artifex, Ltd., of Baltimore, Maryland, to determine the original wall colors. The upper level was restored to its 1890s appearance (below), including a variety of wall colors, with the wood trim "painted to imitate mahogany," as noted in a written account by Jessie Palfrey Leake. The lower level was painted to match the 1840s appearance of a dining hall, with whitewashed walls and dark bluish-gray trim. (Above, ULDSC; below, courtesy of Jaron Berman.)

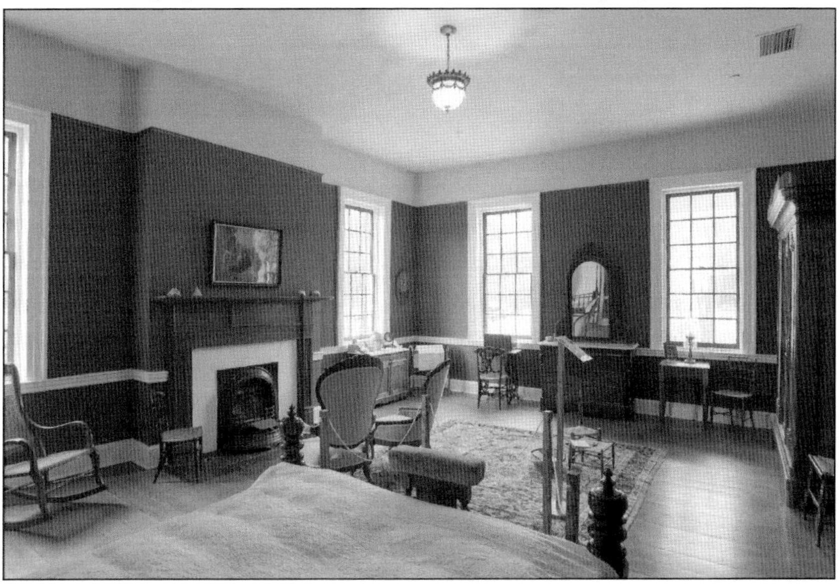

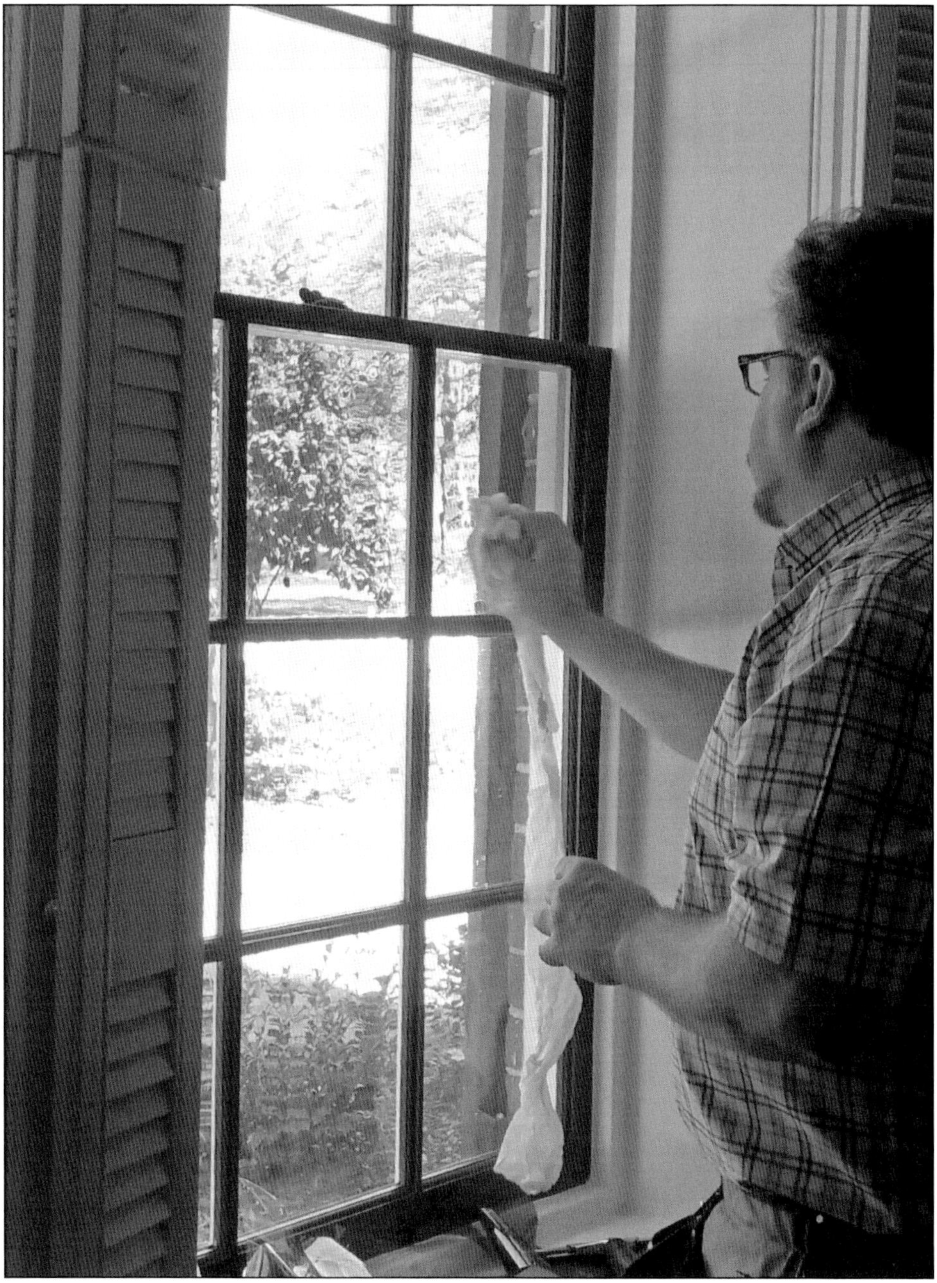

Preservation at the Gorgas House. As part of the original 1831 campus, the Gorgas House's preservation is a significant component of the mission of the Gorgas House Museum. In this photograph, UV-filtering film is being installed on the windows of the museum to prevent fading of the artifacts and floors. In 2011, the museum was selected to participate in Heritage Preservation's Conservation Assessment Program, a national program funded by the Institute of Museums and Library Services. The program evaluated the building's structure, prior restorations, and the care of the art and artifacts on display at the museum. The assessors provided strategic planning recommendations for the immediate and long-term stewardship of the museum. (Authors' collection.)

Student-Centered Historical Site. The Gorgas House Museum serves the campus and Tuscaloosa communities as an active historical site that seeks to involve students with opportunities for hands-on learning in history and museum studies. At right, a student from the university's School of Music performs a concert on an 1875 square grand piano in the formal parlor of the Gorgas House Museum. Dr Edward Uehling, retired physician and museum docent, supported the restoration of the piano in 2011. Below, University of Alabama Museums staff member Bill Allen works with student Jocelyn Brabrahm to install a temporary exhibition at the museum. (Right, authors' collection; below, GHM.)

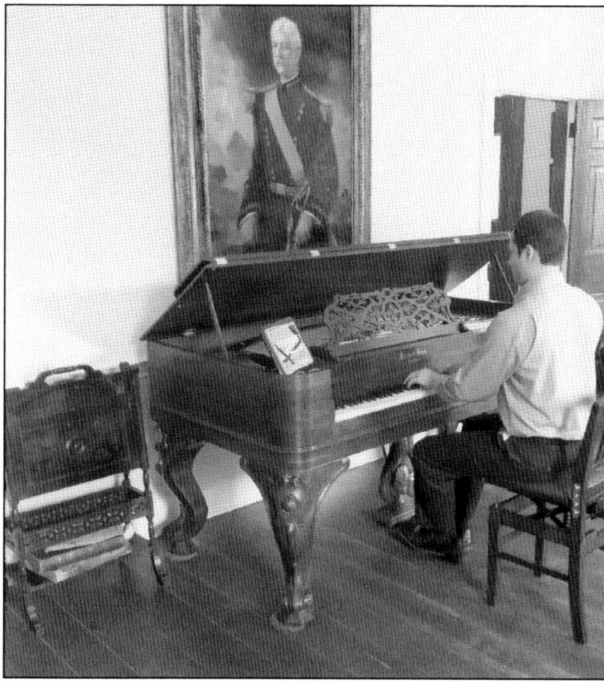

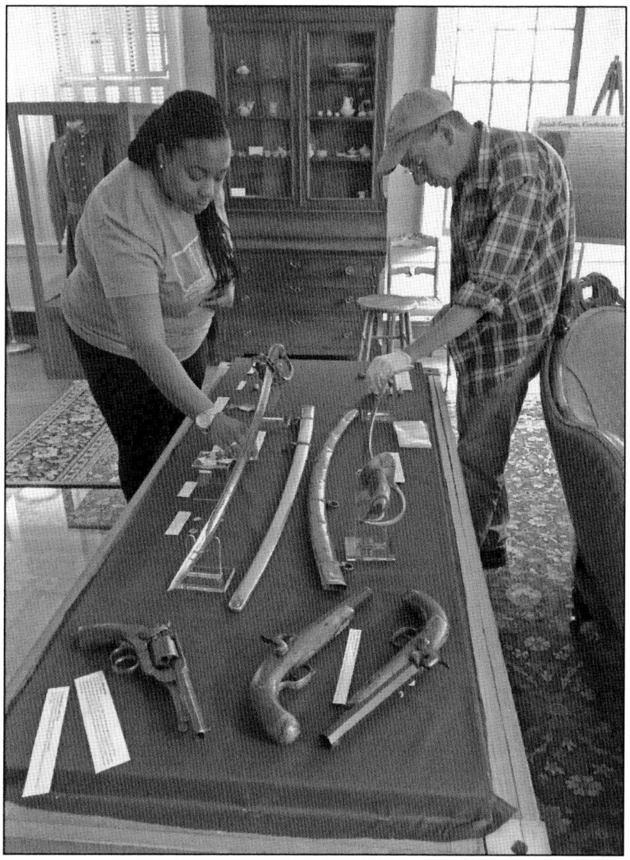

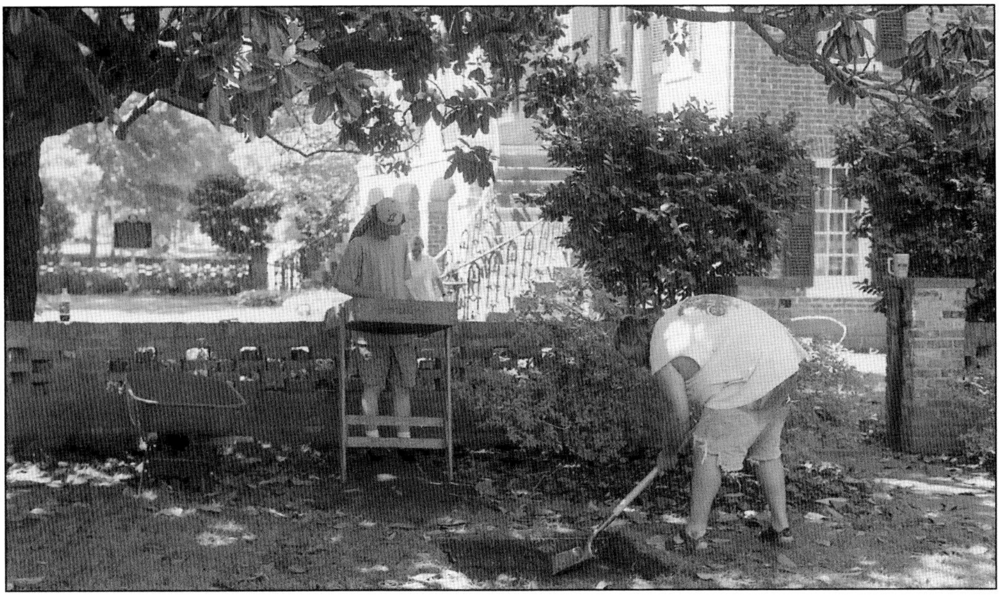

Archaeological Investigation at Gorgas House. In 1999, the University of Alabama's Office of Archaeological Research used ground-penetrating radar and archaeological excavation in an effort to verify historic oral and written accounts of the Gorgas House, as well as to locate sites of garden plots and long-demolished outbuildings around the structure. The actual findings confirmed the location of the separate kitchen building, as well as the location of a privy and two refuse pits. Through the material culture, which included an ink well, pharmaceutical bottle, animal bones, and buttons, the archaeologists were able to add rich, personal details to the ongoing narrative of the Gorgas House legacy. (Both, OAR.)

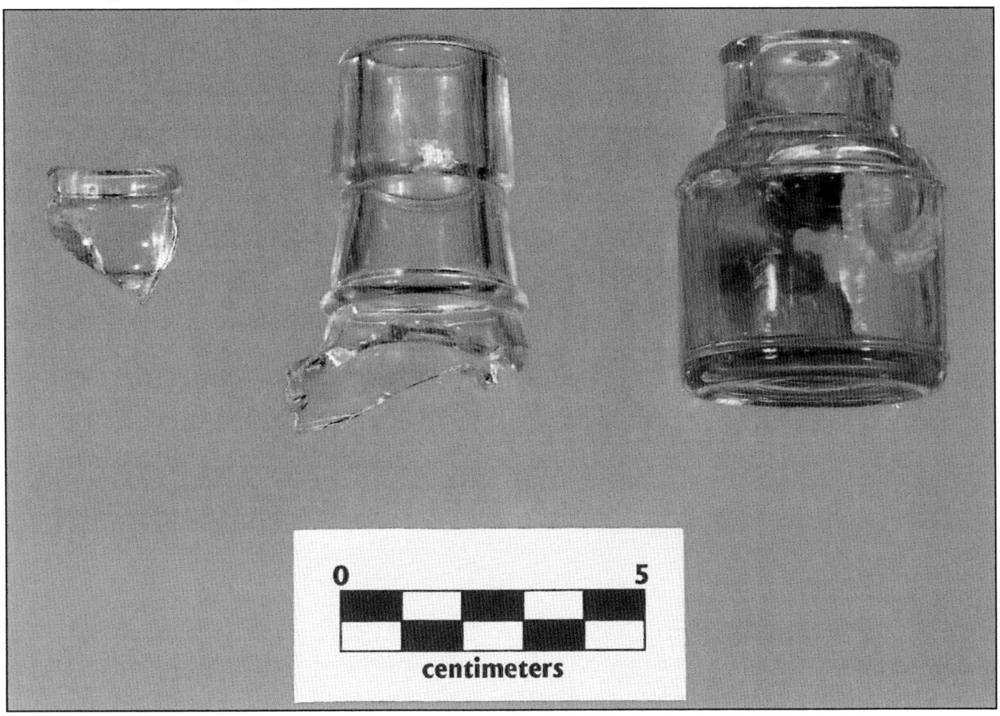

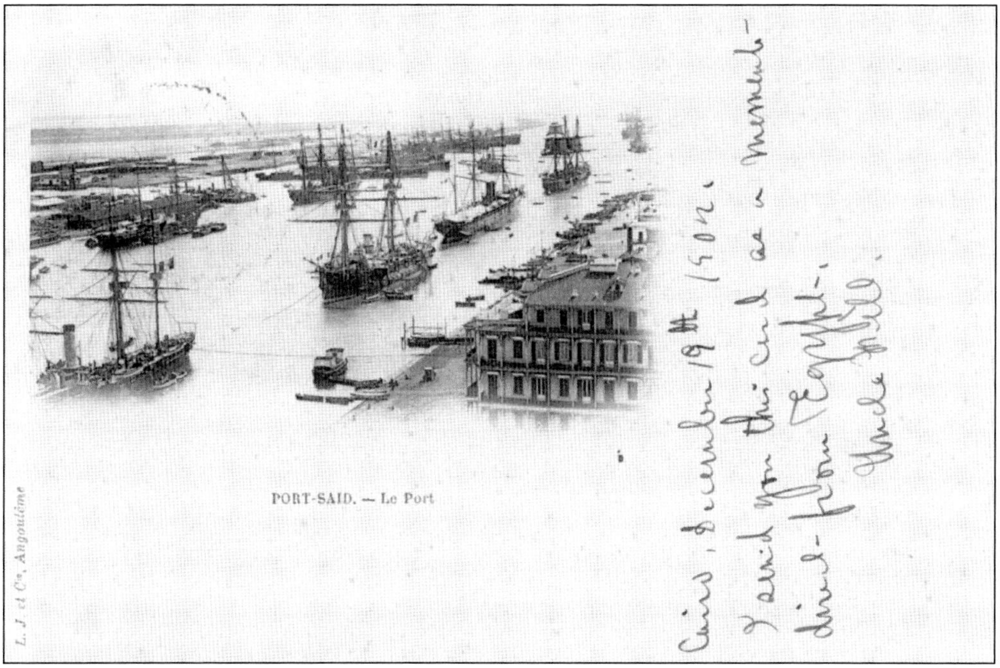

GORGAS FAMILY PAPERS. In addition to the artifacts preserved at the Gorgas House Museum and the University of Alabama Museums, 48 linear feet of archival records and photographs have been donated to the W.S. Hoole Special Collections Library, housed in the Mary Harmon Bryant Building on campus. Included in the holdings are the correspondence and diaries belonging to William Crawford Gorgas, such as the postcard from Egypt (above) that he mailed to his niece. Scrapbooks belonging to Amelia and Josiah Gorgas are also maintained in the archive. The telegram (below) informs Josiah of his election as president of the University of Alabama in 1878.

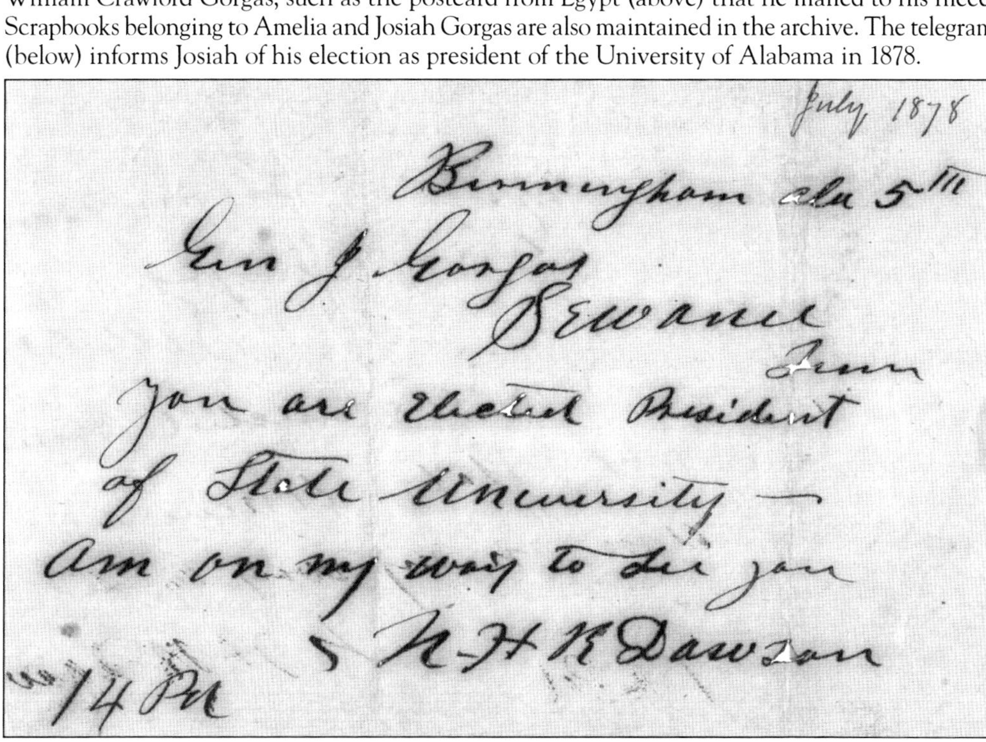

July 1878

Birmingham Ala 5th

Gen J Gorgas
Sewanee
Tenn

You are Elected President
of State University —
Am on my way to see you
N H R Dawson

14 Pd

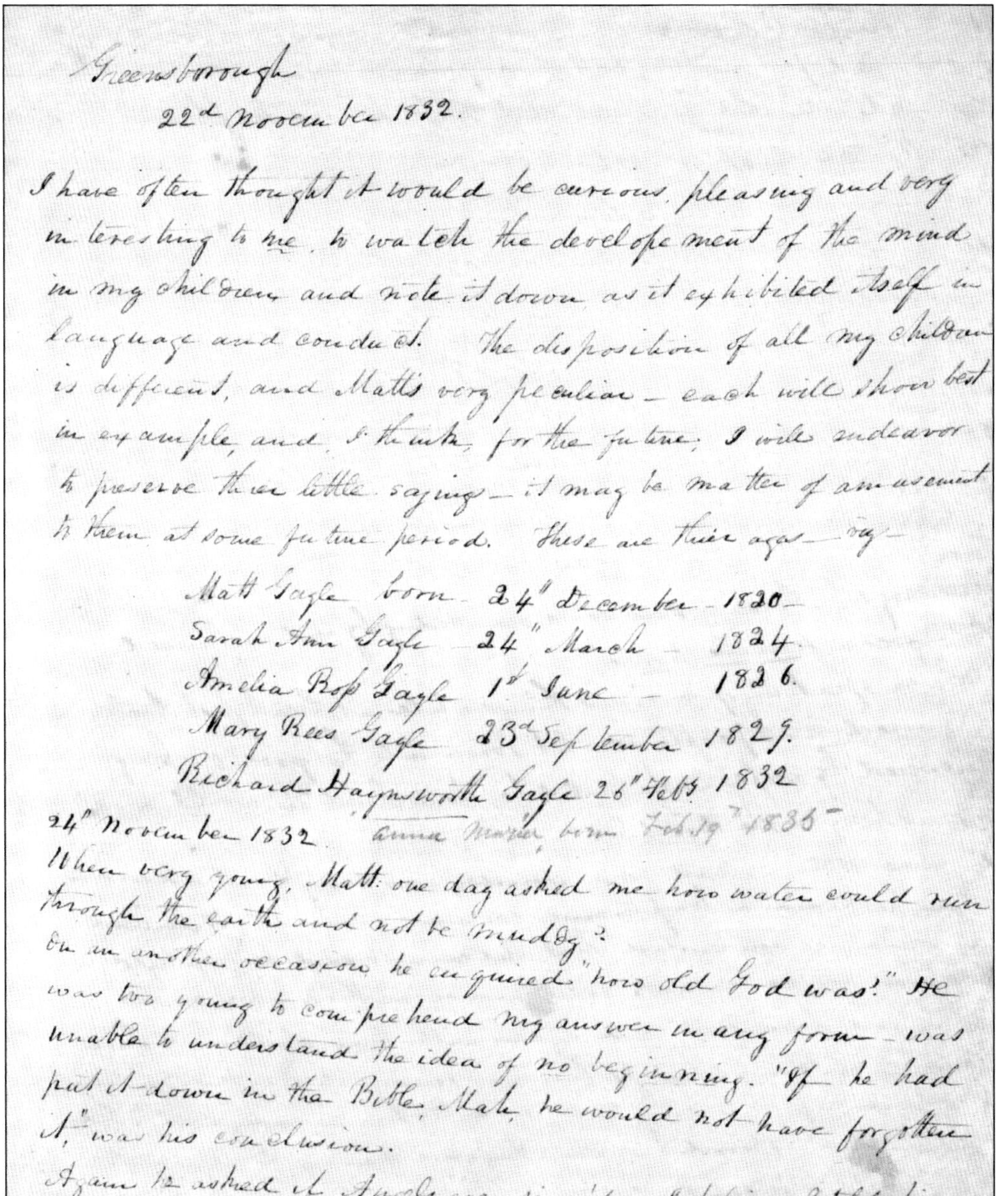

Greensborough
22d November 1832.

I have often thought it would be curious, pleasing and very interesting to me, to watch the developement of the mind in my children and note it down as it exhibited itself in language and conduct. The disposition of all my children is different, and Matt's very peculiar – each will show best in example, and I think, for the future, I will endeavor to preserve their little sayings – it may be matter of amusement to them at some future period. These are their ages – viz –

Matt Gayle born 24th December 1820
Sarah Ann Gayle 24th March 1824.
Amelia Ross Gayle 1st June 1826.
Mary Rees Gayle 23d September 1829.
Richard Haynsworth Gayle 26th Feby 1832
24th November 1832 Anna Maria born Feb 19th 1835

When very young, Matt one day asked me how water could run through the earth and not be muddy? On another occasion he enquired "how old God was?" He was too young to comprehend my answer in any form – was unable to understand the idea of no beginning. "If he had put it down in the Bible, Ma, he would not have forgotten it," was his conclusion.
Again he asked if Angels ever sinn'd – I believe I told him no, but he puzzled me, by enquiring if Satan was not an Angel

38

Journal of Sarah Haynsworth Gayle. Sarah Gayle, the first wife of Alabama governor John Gayle and mother of Amelia Gorgas, was inducted into the Alabama Women's Hall of Fame in 2016. From 1827 to 1835, Gayle recorded daily life in Alabama during the early 19th century in her journal. Hall of Fame officials credit Gayle's journal as one of "the most widely studied and seminal accounts of antebellum life in the American South." The journal is housed at the W.S. Hoole Special Collections Library.

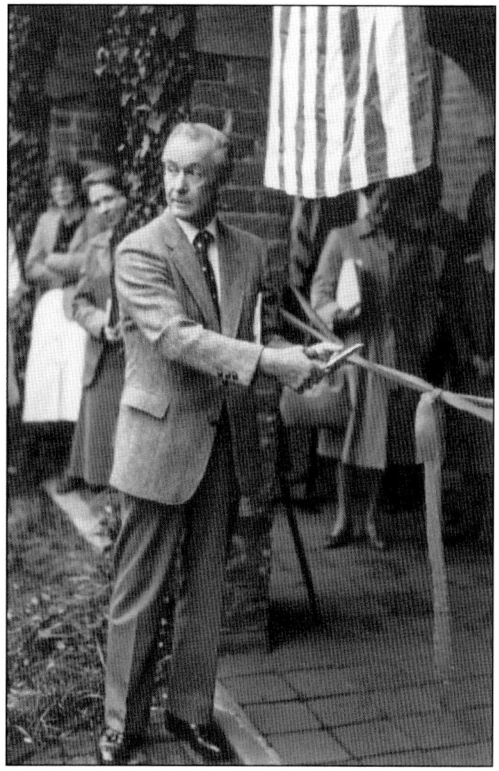

Gorgas House Events. The Gorgas House Museum has been a focal point of the University of Alabama campus since it was established, hosting campus events, concerts, meetings, historical reenactments, and weddings. At right, interim university president Howard Gundy is shown cutting the inaugural ribbon at the university's sesquicentennial celebration held at the Gorgas House in 1981. The photograph below was taken at the University of Alabama's annual Haunting at the Museum in 2015. (Right, ULDSC; below, GHM.)

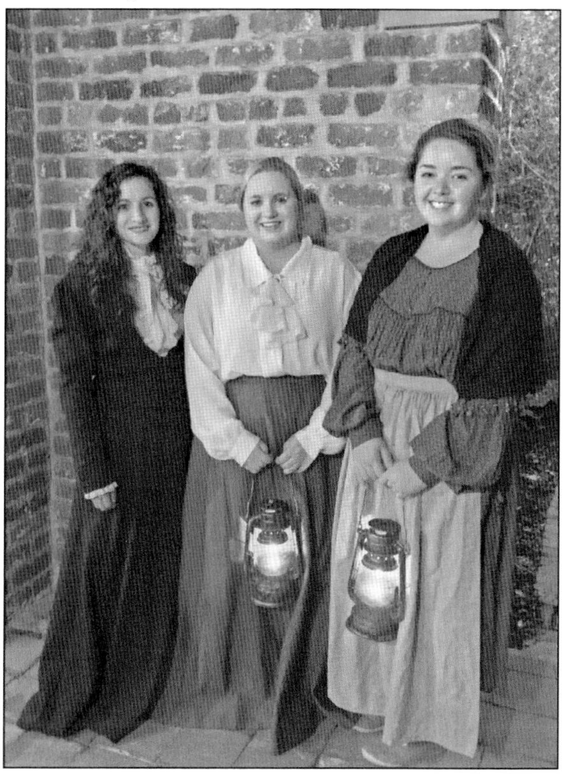

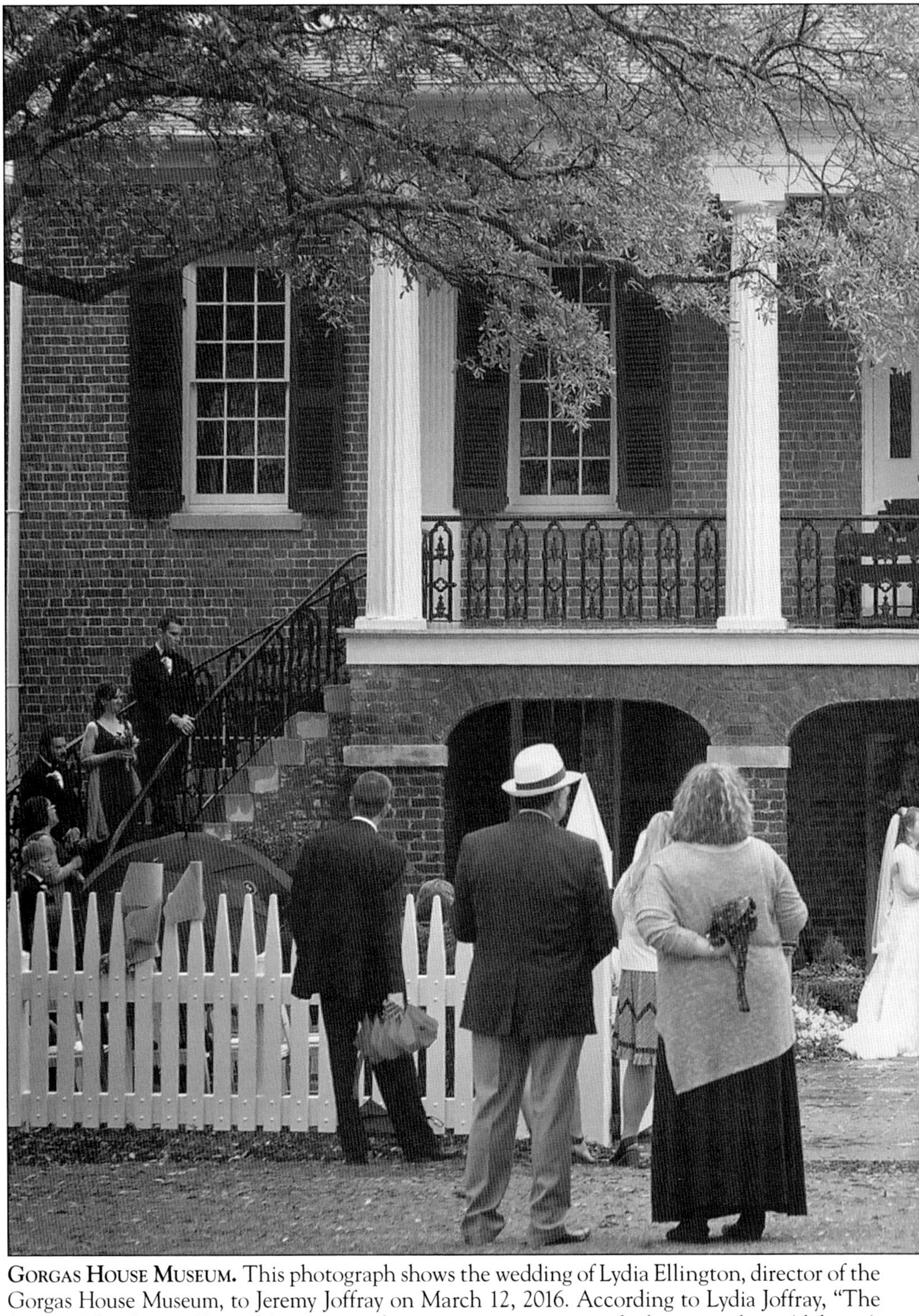

GORGAS HOUSE MUSEUM. This photograph shows the wedding of Lydia Ellington, director of the Gorgas House Museum, to Jeremy Joffray on March 12, 2016. According to Lydia Joffray, "The future of the Gorgas House Museum is to be a community resource for learning about Alabama's diverse history and a place where the story of our shared past can be explained through the building

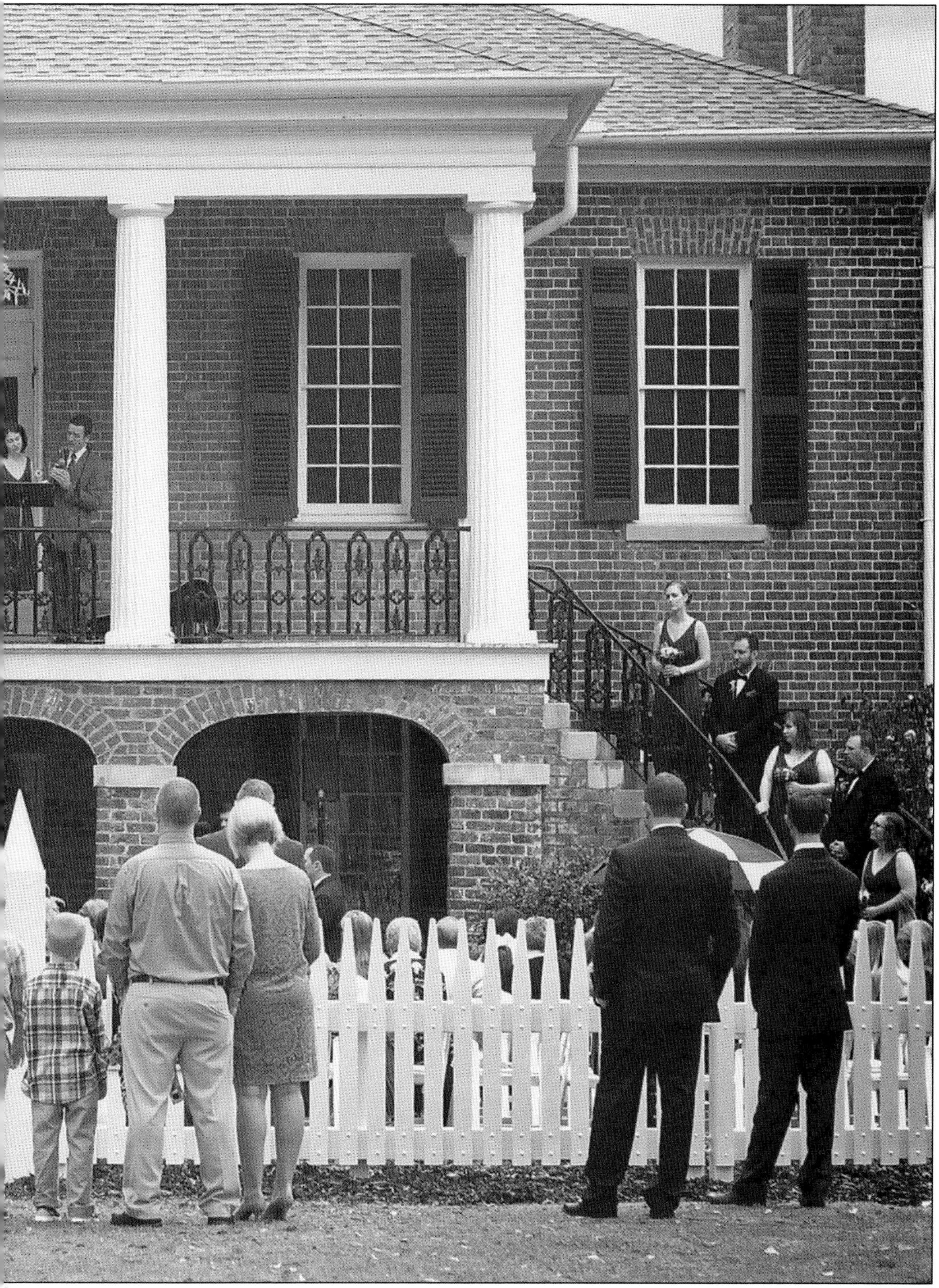

of a university. The house also is a hands-on learning opportunity for University of Alabama students interested in pursuing a career in the museum field. I hope that anyone who comes into the house takes away a better understanding of the past as well as a sense of appreciation for the future." (Courtesy of Ashley Hester Photography.)

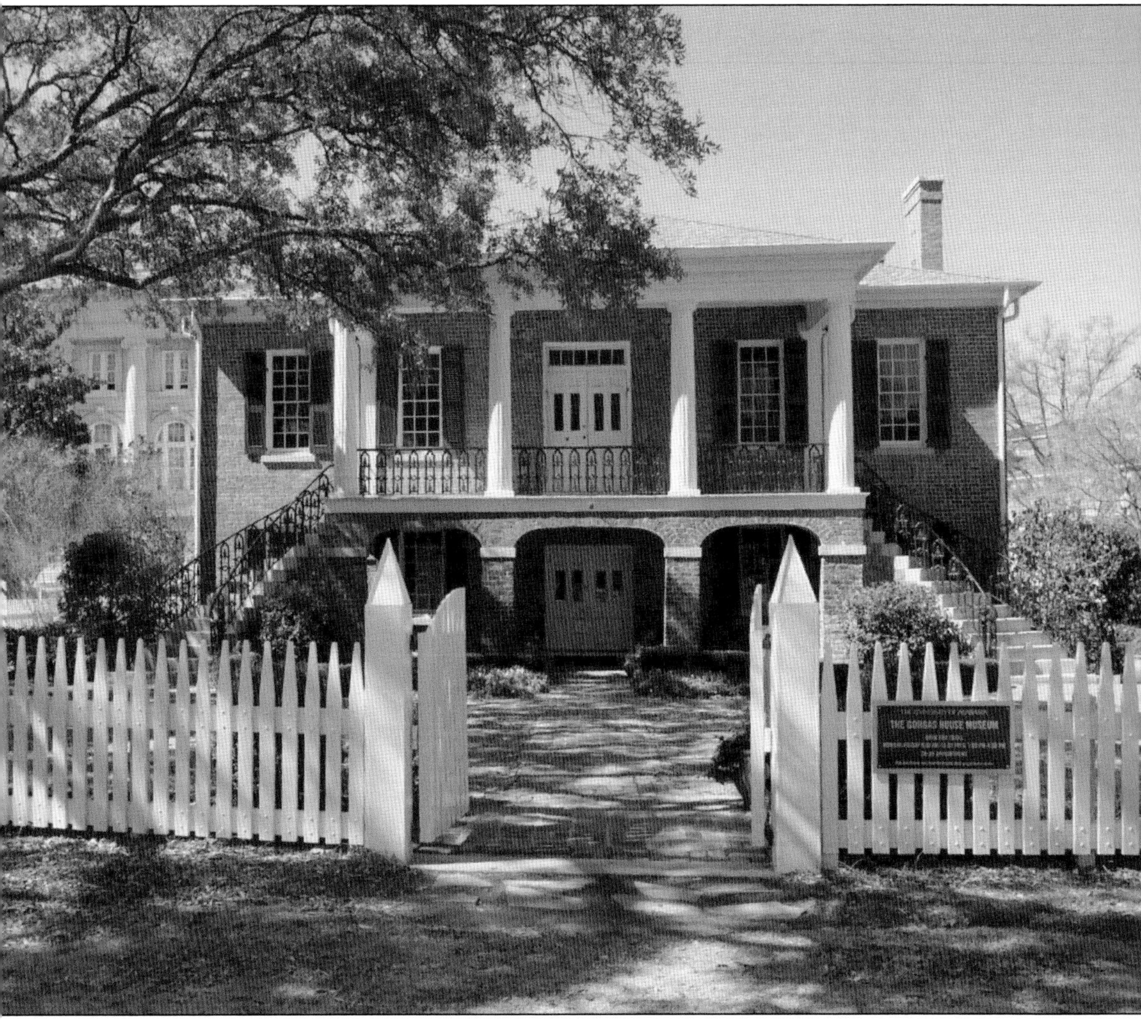

GORGAS HOUSE MUSEUM. The Gorgas House has witnessed the entire history of the University of Alabama, from first opening its doors in 1831 as a seminary of learning to its establishment as a top-ranking research university. Today, the Gorgas House Museum preserves and interprets the Gorgas family legacy and stands as a historical record of the heritage of the University of Alabama. (Authors' collection.)

Bibliography

Clark, Willis G. *History of Education in Alabama: 1702–1889*, vol. 370. Washington, DC: US Government Printing Office, 1889.

Gamble, Robert S. *Historic Architecture in Alabama: A Guide to Styles and Types, 1810–1930*. Tuscaloosa: University of Alabama Press, 2001.

Gayle, Sarah Haynsworth. *The Journal of Sarah Haynsworth Gayle: 1827–1835*. Edited by Sarah Woolfolk Wiggins and Ruth Smith Truss. Tuscaloosa: University of Alabama Press, 2013.

Gibson, John M. *Physician to the World: The Life of General William C. Gorgas*. Tuscaloosa: University of Alabama Press, 1989.

Gorgas, Josiah. *The Journals of Josiah Gorgas: 1857–1878*. Edited by Sarah Woolfolk Wiggins. Tuscaloosa: University of Alabama Press, 1995.

Johnston, Mary Tabb, and Elizabeth Johnston Lipscomb. *Amelia Gayle Gorgas*. Tuscaloosa: University of Alabama Press, 1978.

Kapp, Paul Hardin. *The Architecture of William Nichols: Building the Antebellum South in North Carolina, Alabama, and Mississippi*. Jackson: University Press of Mississippi, 2015.

Lewis, Herbert James. *Lost Capitals of Alabama*. Charleston, SC: History Press, 2014.

Mellown, Robert Oliver. *The University of Alabama: A Guide to the Campus*. Tuscaloosa: University of Alabama Press, 1988.

———. *The University of Alabama: A Guide to the Campus and Its Architecture*. Tuscaloosa: University of Alabama Press, 2013.

Peatross, C. Ford, and Robert O. Mellown. *William Nichols, Architect*. Tuscaloosa: University of Alabama Art Gallery, 1979.

Sansing, David G. *The University of Mississippi: A Sesquicentennial History*. Jackson: University Press of Mississippi, 1999.

Sellers, James Benson. *History of the University of Alabama, Volume 1*. Tuscaloosa: University of Alabama Press, 1953.

Wiggins, Sarah Woolfolk. *Love & Duty, Amelia & Josiah & Their Family*. Tuscaloosa: University of Alabama Press, 2005.

Wolfe, Suzanne Rau. *The University of Alabama: A Pictorial History*. Tuscaloosa: University of Alabama Press, 1983.